The Cleveland Street Scandal

THE CLEVELAND STREET SCANDAL

HOW THE VICTORIAN ESTABLISHMENT WAS ALMOST BROUGHT TO ITS KNEES

NEIL ROOT

Cover Illustrations: A foggy Victorian street in the early evening (iStock/ John Shepherd); An extract from Cruchley's New Map of London, 1869 (Reproduced with the permission of the National Library of Scotland).

Quote from Henry Labouchère MP, Hansard HC vol 341, col 1541 (28 February 1890)

First published 2025

The History Press
97 St George's Place, Cheltenham,
Gloucestershire, GL50 3QB
www.thehistorypress.co.uk

© Neil Root, 2025

The right of Neil Root to be identified as the Author of this work has been asserted in accordance with the Copyright, Designs and Patents Act 1988.

All rights reserved. No part of this book may be reprinted or reproduced or utilised in any form or by any electronic, mechanical or other means, now known or hereafter invented, including photocopying and recording, or in any information storage or retrieval system, without the permission in writing from the Publishers.

British Library Cataloguing in Publication Data.
A catalogue record for this book is available from the British Library.

ISBN 978 1 80399 664 6

Typesetting and origination by The History Press
Printed and bound in Great Britain by TJ Books, Padstow, Cornwall

The History Press proudly supports

Trees for Life

www.treesforlife.org.uk

EU Authorised Representative: Easy Access System Europe
Mustamäe tee 50, 10621 Tallinn, Estonia
gpst.request@easproject.com

Contents

Prologue	7
Part I: No. 19 Cleveland Street	11
Part II: A Hush-up, Libel and Oaths on the Bible	63
Coda	229
Notes	241
Bibliography	245
Acknowledgements	250
Index	251

Prologue

At the turn of the twentieth century, as the Victorian era had just taken its final dying breaths, journalist John Philip Collins, originally from Birmingham, was a boarder in a house at No. 313 Clapham Road in Lambeth, south London. It was a well-appointed address for a professional man: leafy and suburban. After surveying that long road running from the Oval to Clapham High Street, the social researcher and reformer Charles Booth had judged it 'Middle-class. Well-to-do' in his 1898 *Map of London Poverty*.

As it still stands today, No. 313 was roomy, three storey and mid-Victorian, one of two sandwiching an identical terraced house. And Collins, aged 30 in March 1901, wasn't the only lodger. There was also Laurence Allen Jones, a 27-year-old consulting engineer, along with a 9-year-old 'visitor' named Harold Charles Gibbons. To keep the house in order, Mary Isabella Yates, aged 18, was a general domestic servant supplied by the Hanover Square Workhouse. Mary was undoubtedly a great help to the lady of the house: 54-year-old Emma Abberline. Her husband, the head of the house, was 58-year-old Frederick George Abberline.

Fred Abberline, a former policeman, who had served with the Metropolitan Police over a lengthy career, had done very well for himself. He'd ended up with the senior rank of chief inspector and was stationed at Scotland Yard. However, his two most interesting cases, both internationally infamous in quite different ways, had occurred when he was one rung below his final rank and known as Inspector Abberline. He'd been retired from the police force for almost a decade as Britain moved into the Edwardian era.

Having a famous ex-detective as his landlord was a professional godsend for John Philip Collins. Abberline had tales that any up-and-coming journalist would have been desperate to tell. At the time he was Abberline's tenant, Collins was employed by the *Pall Mall Gazette*, a London evening newspaper which had been a crusading social-reforming publication under its legendary editor, W.T. Stead, but was now under the much more conservative editorship of Sir Douglas Straight. Collins' career would flourish, with him becoming the literary editor and the assistant editor on the *Pall Mall Gazette* and later moving to the *Daily Telegraph*.

Collins managed a real coup in persuading the professionally reticent Abberline to talk about the hunt for Jack the Ripper back in 1888, a massive, exhausting and ultimately fruitless investigation, which Abberline had led on the ground in London's East End. The failure to find and capture the brutal killer of five women, the most notorious 'serial killer' in history almost nine decades before that term was coined, deeply rankled every policeman and detective who worked on that case, especially Abberline. It had happened on his patch, which he knew so well, having been stationed in the East End for much of his service. And Abberline was professionally proud, highly industrious and used to getting results.

Walter Dew, who worked under Abberline on the Jack the Ripper case in Whitechapel and later, as a chief inspector, captured the wife killer Dr Crippen in 1910, recalled Abberline as being 'portly and gentle speaking ... who might easily have been mistaken for the manager of a bank or a solicitor. He also was a man who had proved himself in many previous big cases ... No question at all of Inspector Abberline's abilities as a criminal hunter.'

In two issues of the *Pall Mall Gazette*, published on 24 and 31 March 1903, Abberline gave Collins his thoughts on Jack the Ripper, almost fifteen years after the horrific murders. The spur for Abberline to finally speak out was the imminent execution by hanging of Polish-born

'George Chapman' for the poisoning of three women in London. But Abberline knew him under his real name, Seweryn Klosowski, in 1888, when Klosowski was working as a barber in the East End.

Abberline relayed to Collins that Klosowski had been a strong suspect for the Jack the Ripper killings. This was despite the detached and sadistic modus operandi of the poisoner, which was so vastly different from the up-close, but also sadistic, barbaric mutilations carried out in the 1888 serial murders. Abberline explained this fundamental discrepancy by saying, 'There is much to be said for Chapman's consistency. You see, incentive changes; but the fiendishness is not eradicated.'

Abberline was still frustrated, and pointing the finger at Klosowski was merely professional speculation on his part, with no firm evidence attached. In the second article, Abberline starkly said to Collins, who relayed his words directly to readers, 'You can state most emphatically that Scotland Yard is really no wiser on the subject than it was fifteen years ago.'

Conversely, no speculation would have been needed as to the perpetrators in the other major case of Abberline's career, which he took charge of in the year following his Jack the Ripper investigative defeat. The culprits were known, and some of them had been publicly named, but Collins never managed to get Abberline to divulge anything about that case, which, like the Jack the Ripper inquiry, had triggered headlines all over the world.

It was an inside story that Collins, like any self-respecting journalist, would have loved to publish, but he would have been aware of the very real and dangerous sensitivities of that affair, which implicated the highest echelons of the aristocracy, government and even the royal family itself – and led to a shameless Establishment cover-up.

It's unknown whether Collins ever questioned Abberline about that case, which had swiftly become known in the UK as the Cleveland Street Scandal and abroad as the London Scandal. Collins was most probably resigned to that affair being off-limits, especially as a prime mover in that cover-up, the Prince of Wales, was now King Edward VII. Consequently, it's also little wonder that Abberline never spoke about it, even though it was a case that frustrated him deeply and made him feel very disillusioned about his policing career; it was a key factor in his retirement soon afterwards.

It all began in the summer of 1889, with a routine investigation by a policeman several ranks below Abberline. But the gravity of what was uncovered and the seismic implications for the fabric of Victorian society would mean that Abberline, still considered one of Scotland Yard's finest, even after the Jack the Ripper debacle, was soon brought in to oversee it.

PART I

NO. 19 CLEVELAND STREET

One

4 July 1889

Fifteen-year-old Charles Swinscow knew that he was in very real trouble. Dark-haired, with a full mouth and jug ears, he habitually wore a serious expression, ready-made for his circumstances that morning.

Smartly dressed in his messenger uniform for the London Central Telegraph Office, his place of work, Charles felt a deep sense of foreboding when Police Constable Luke Hanks singled him out for attention and took him into a vacant room alone. There was no formal caution given to suspects at that time by the Metropolitan Police, so PC Hanks simply told Charles that he was being questioned in relation to the theft of some money. 'I believe that you have been in possession of a large sum of money – 18/-. What can you tell me about that?'

Charles, now red-faced and afraid, denied having had so much money, but did admit to having had 14/- 'on his person' a few days earlier.

'From where did you obtain that money?' asked PC Hanks.

'I got it for doing some private work away from the office.'

'For whom?'

'For a gentleman named Hammond,' said Charles, quietly.

'Where does he live?'

'At 19 Cleveland Street, near the Middlesex Hospital.'

'What kind of work did you do for him?'

'Will I get into trouble if I tell you?' asked Charles.

'I cannot say,' said PC Hanks, solemnly.

'Must I tell you?'

'Certainly.'[1]

Charles looked down at the ground in front of him and then slowly raised his head to face PC Hanks. Shaking with trepidation, he knew that what he was about to say would be deeply shameful for him and his family – and would almost certainly lose him his coveted position at the General Post Office (GPO). Finally, Charles stilled himself enough to speak in a wavering voice.

'I will tell you the truth. I got the money from Mr Hammond for going to bed with gentlemen at his house.'

Inwardly shocked at Charles' statement and its implications, PC Hanks ended the interview and went to report to his superior, Chief Constable John Phillips. Phillips was, in fact, a police constable like Hanks, but as the highest-ranking officer attached to the GPO at that time, he had the title 'Chief'. This was unique to the police unit attached to the Victorian and Edwardian GPO and is not to be confused with the modern role of chief constable, which now heads the forty-three police constabularies of England and Wales and oversees hundreds or thousands of police officers.

On being appraised of the disturbing revelation made by Charles, Phillips ordered Hanks to resume Swinscow's questioning and to gain as much further information about this serious matter as possible. Seated, Swinscow was cowed when PC Hanks re-entered the room, but stood up at once.

'Please sit down and tell me everything you know,' said PC Hanks, with the natural authority earned by an experienced policeman. That was enough. It took no more for Swinscow to begin to open up and offer the sordid details of what he'd done, the implications for him and his family being more than sufficient to make the boy come clean.

Charles Swinscow started by saying how he had met Henry Newlove, an 18-year-old messenger in the Secretary's Office at the London Central Telegraph Office, around the previous Christmas of 1888, although Newlove had since been promoted to the role of 'tracer' in the Receiver and Accounts Department, giving him the higher ranking of third-class clerk. Henry Newlove had asked Charles to 'go into the lavatory in the basement of the Post Office building'. And as Charles' recollection continued, with PC Hanks maintaining his professional demeanour and outwardly showing no outrage, it seemed that he had followed Newlove into that basement.

'We went into the water closet and shut the door, and we behaved indecently together. We did this on other occasions afterwards.'

It took only gentle prompting from PC Hanks for Charles to continue:

In about a week's time, Newlove said – as near as I can recollect – 'Will you come to a house where I will go to bed with a gentleman, you'll get four shillings each time?' I said at first, I wouldn't do, but he persuaded me at last and I went with him to 19 Cleveland Street, a road near Tottenham Court Road, near the Middlesex Hospital. Newlove rang the bell, and the door was opened by a boy about my own age. We went into a parlour on the ground floor, and I saw a gentleman there who I learnt since is the proprietor. His name is Hamlin.[2]

In fact, it would soon be shown that the man Swinscow was referring to was Charles Hammond, the proprietor of No. 19 Cleveland Street.

Strangely, at the beginning of Hanks' questioning, Charles had named him as Hammond, but the official statement then had him referring to him as Hamlin. Whether this was an attempt by Swinscow to not name the man who had paid him to carry out illegal acts out of fear or whether it was a simple police transcription error is unknown. Although, due to the gravity of what Charles said, the former is most likely, as Charles Hammond would immediately have been the focus of the investigation. And as Charles Swinscow told PC Hanks, Mr Hamlin/Hammond soon introduced himself on that first visit to No. 19 Cleveland Street:

He said, 'Good evening, I'm very glad you've come.' I waited a little while, and another gentleman came in. Mr. Hamlin introduced me, saying 'that was the gentleman I was to go with that evening.' I went into the back parlour, a room on the same floor with the gentleman.

> There was a bed there. We both undressed and being quite naked, got into bed. He put his person between my legs and an invasion took place.
>
> I was with him about half-an-hour and then we got up. He gave me a Sovereign [20*s* or £1], which I gave to Mr. Hamlin [Hammond], who gave me four shillings. I have never seen this gentleman again. I went once more to the same house, and only once. It was about a month ago. Newlove showed me a letter which I understood was from Mr. Hamlin [Hammond], asking him to ask me to go up. It was signed Charley. I went and saw another gentleman with whom I also went to bed. I think that Newlove went with me to the house, but I'm not sure. This gentleman gave me half a Sovereign, which I gave to Mr. Hamlin [Hammond] who gave me twelve shillings.

Interestingly, the 12*s* Hammond paid Swinscow on this second occasion was 2*s* more than the man had paid Swinscow – half a sovereign being worth 10*s* – and three times more than he received on his first visit, even though, on that occasion, the man parted with a whole sovereign. This certainly would not have escaped PC Hanks, but at that stage he just wanted the full story to unfold.

Hammond may have wanted to entice Swinscow into returning to No. 19 Cleveland Street regularly by offering more payment as a calculated incentive. But it seemed that the man whom Swinscow went to bed with on his second visit warned him off going back there:

> This gentleman after we got out of bed told me I ought not to return to the house again. He did nothing more to me than the other gentleman had done. I have never been to the house again, though Newlove on one occasion only has asked me to go. I was not in uniform on either occasion when I went to the house. I did not give Newlove any portion of the money which I received.

The fact that Swinscow made a point of emphasising that he wasn't wearing his messenger boy uniform when he visited No. 19 Cleveland Street reveals just how ashamed he was at having to divulge what he had been doing and how fearful he was of losing his position with the GPO. But that was just the start of his troubles – penetrative homosexual intercourse (then known as 'buggery' or 'sodomy') – was highly illegal, socially taboo and potentially ruinous for his family as well as himself. Charles was a tough working-class boy, but he was crying inside, his panic mounting within him as PC Hanks sat opposite him, listening and making notes, yet betraying no emotion or the shock he felt at the revelations he was hearing.

Now that it was a police matter, Charles knew that he had no choice but to tell everything, as the creaking door to the unpalatable truth had been opened. At PC Hanks' pressing, in addition to his recruiter Henry Newlove, Charles named two other telegraph messenger boys who had also visited No. 19 Cleveland Street – Charles Ernest Thickbroom and George Alma Wright, both aged 17. It had now become a network of debauchery, uncovered as part of a routine investigation of a case of theft.

The imposing, Grecian-influenced London Central Telegraph Office, on the corner of Newgate Street and St Martin's le Grand in the financial City district, was a hive of activity that day. For over twenty years, it had become the hub of communications for Britain and the Empire, constantly receiving and dispatching telegrams all over the United Kingdom and the world.

Business was booming. Ever since the first telegraphic despatches had been sent in the early 1840s, public demand for them had increased. The GPO's London Central Telegraph Office was at the centre of the telegram phenomenon, which continued to gain momentum through the 1870s–90s. By the end of the century, the London Central Telegraph Office employed 4,500 clerks and 150,000 telegrams were going through there every day. By 1907, the GPO would be Britain's biggest civilian employer.

At the bottom of the hierarchy of employees, but looking upwards, were the young messenger boys. They wore smart small-checked woollen suits with a dark display handkerchief protruding from the jacket pocket, white starched-down-collar shirt and checked folded-down cravat, matching waistcoat and a hard flat cap with a band with 'Telegram' emblazoned on it in capital letters between horizontal white stripes. The boys would deliver telegrams by bicycle to businesses and private clients all over the city. Speed was all important, as they weaved in and out of streets filled with hansom cabs and horses and carriages.

Charles Swinscow was just one of hundreds of boys and young men between the ages of 14 and 18 who were employed in the late 1880s delivering telegrams. It was a regimented job, disciplined and rigorous, and they were expected to exhibit the highest standards of personal conduct. It was regarded as a prestigious start to a career in the civil service and an exceptionally good opportunity for working-class boys, offering job security with scope for promotion in time, if they were taken on full time as 'established' employees. They were considered lucky to have the job by their parents, who undoubtedly felt pride in their sons as they bicycled off to work, representing the GPO, a pillar of Victorian life.

By 1860, the prestige that the GPO and its headquarters at St Martin's le Grand held had already become ingrained in society. In that year, the Victorian painter George Elgar Hicks, well known for his studies of everyday London scenes depicting groups of people, painted *The General Post Office, One Minute to Six*, which immortalised a crowd of socially diverse characters queuing to make the last post of the day. The art historian Mark Bills has described how the painting makes 'a striking statement about the pace of activity in the city, about the behaviour of the crowd, and the role of the centralised post and press system at the heart of a vast empire'.[3] The fact that it was featured by a popular painter such as Hicks, who also painted other national landmarks including the Bank of England, shows what an important institution the GPO was in Victorian Britain.

As part of their duties, the messenger boys had to collect payment from those who had telegrams delivered and hand it over to their supervisor immediately on their return to the office from 'a run'. The boys weren't allowed to carry any personal money while on duty to avoid the danger of getting it mixed up with the collected revenue. They were expected to be punctual, polite, applied, always well turned out, and to have integrity. Honesty was intrinsic to the role's requirements, due to the sums of cash being transported.

The morning of Thursday, 4 July 1889 started no different from any other day when PC Luke Hanks of the Metropolitan Police, specially attached to the GPO, arrived at the London Central Telegraph Office. Hanks was 35, having been born in Southsea, near Portsmouth, Hampshire, in June 1854. His father, Isaac, was from Malmesbury in Wiltshire, and his mother, Catherine Agnes (née Daley) hailed from County Cork in Ireland. Isaac was a gunner in the Royal Marine Artillery and then became a policeman in the Metropolitan Police, which, although its jurisdiction was London, also oversaw the Royal Dockyards. By 1861, when Luke was 7, Isaac was a police sergeant at the Royal Naval Hospital in Haslar, near Gosport.

In 1871, aged 16, Luke was finding his own way and living in lodgings in Portland, Dorset, working as a ship's steward boy on HMS *Achilles*. It was an armoured frigate, and at that time was in use as a guard ship to the Royal Navy's Fleet Reserve around Portland, having been launched at the end of 1863.

By 1879, aged 24, Hanks had emulated his father, who had died three years previously, and become a police constable in the Metropolitan Police, which then had more than 10,000 officers. Luke was assigned to the policing of Her Majesty's Dockyard in Portsmouth. In 1881, Hanks was in the capital, a police constable attached to Commercial Street Police Station in East London and lodging with other bachelor officers at No. 230 Fleur de Lis Street in Spitalfields, which would later be at the centre of Jack the Ripper's hunting ground in 1888. But PC Hanks always dealt with theft, not murder, and by March 1885, he was attached to the GPO.

In the December of that year, Hanks married Ellen Shaw, known as Helen, and they lived at No. 405 Bethnal Green Road, Bethnal Green, in east London. On 11 January 1886, Luke and Helen had a son, Luke

Cornelius, and on 2 September 1887, a daughter, Mary. By the following year, the Hanks family were living at No. 164 Finnis Street, Bethnal Green.

The Metropolitan Police unit attached to the GPO where PC Hanks served had originally been called the Missing Letter Branch but was retitled the Confidential Enquiry Branch in 1883. This unit grew quickly, largely due to the Fenian bombings of the 1880s, orchestrated by a group of Irish Americans wanting independence for Ireland from the UK, which was contemporarily known as the 'Dynamite War' and resulted in a series of explosions on the young London Underground. By 1889, the Confidential Enquiry Branch was a substantial force, with fifteen plainclothes detectives and many police constables, PC Luke Hanks being one of them.

In June 1885, Hanks had served as a witness at the Old Bailey in the trial of the thief and embezzler Henry Gamble; in October 1887, he had to testify in a case of simple larceny brought against the thieves Henry Sumner and Frank Beckett; and in January 1889, he'd appeared there again as a witness in the trial of the postal order thief, Charles Osborn Dunn. At all three trials, the defendants, whom Hanks had arrested, were convicted and imprisoned.

By early July 1889 Hanks had been a policeman for a decade and was seasoned in dealing with myriad types of thievery and gathering evidence. Now he was investigating reported thefts from the London Central Telegraph Office, and the messenger boy, Swinscow, had been, as Hanks later reported in his police report, 'seen to leave a room from which money had been stolen, and he had also been seen with a sum of money, 18/- [18s] in his possession'. It was an exceptionally large sum of cash for a boy of Swinscow's age and station to be carrying.

Swinscow was just over two months short of his sixteenth birthday when PC Luke Hanks interrogated him, having turned 15 on 14 September 1888. He had been appointed to the position of telegraph messenger on 2 January 1888, so he'd been in the role for eighteen months by early July 1889. His official job title was 'Boy Messenger in the Receiver and Accountant General's Office, General Post Office'.[4]

Charles Thomas Swinscow was born on 14 September 1873, in Islington, north-east London, to Thomas, a 35-year-old newsagent, and Emily Ann (née Wright), aged 22. In 1881, they lived in Stoke Newington, at No. 3 Little Cross Street (now Angle Street). They had four lodgers, in their fifties, sixties and seventies. Charles was 7 then and at school, and his sisters Emily and Hannah were aged 5 and 3 respectively. Charles almost certainly wouldn't have known then that a career at the GPO awaited him, although a family connection would undoubtedly gain him his place there. Charles Swinscow and his family had everything to lose.

5 July 1889

The following morning, PC Hanks went back to Chief Constable Phillips and briefed him on the further details he had gleaned. Phillips saw the gravity of the situation and reported what he had learned to the top, the Postmaster General, Henry Cecil Raikes, who, in turn, informed James Monro, the Commissioner of the Metropolitan Police. Some of the highest levers of late-Victorian British domestic power were now turning swiftly, and Swinscow, the other boys and their families would soon be caught up in the grinding machinations of the state.

And this wasn't the first homosexual sex scandal that had rocked the GPO, a fact of which Phillips, Raikes, Monro and probably PC Hanks were well aware. Twelve years earlier, in 1877, during Disraeli's second Conservative government, an internal GPO investigation had uncovered the fact that three telegraph messenger boys had prostituted themselves to a man of much higher social standing for 5s a go. He was a 37-year-old, well-connected secretary in the City of London named James Smith. According to the *Morning Post* newspaper, Smith would meet the boys in the street and then take them to his home in Park Street, Islington, north-east London.

After his conviction, Smith petitioned the Home Secretary Richard Assheton Cross directly, claiming that he was being made a scapegoat and writing, 'The crime for which I am sentenced has been very prevalent amongst the Telegraph lads', and the state wanted to prosecute him 'as a warning to others'. But Smith's appeal failed and he was sentenced to penal servitude for life at London's Central Criminal Court.

Just one of the telegraph messenger boys, 17-year-old George Wright, faced prosecution in the end, and he was given a ten-year sentence, although the judge said that Wright should receive a much lighter sentence on appeal as he had 'unhappily fallen in' with Smith. They were serious punishments, but publicly, it had been a small affair, not one that was allowed too much press publicity.

But a dozen years later, in July 1889, the situation would soon reveal itself to be quite different. Neither PC Hanks, Chief Constable Phillips, Postmaster-General Raikes nor Commissioner Monro had any idea of the true wider implications of what they had learned, that there was far more to come or quite how high up the strata of society the snowballing scandal would eventually reach.

Yet, the case was already of such import that Commissioner Monro would turn to one of his leading detectives to oversee the investigation into the murky goings-on at No. 19 Cleveland Street. Enter Detective Inspector Frederick Abberline of Scotland Yard.

Two

6 July 1889

Inspector Abberline wasted no time, and just after dawn he applied for arrest warrants for Charles Hammond and Henry Horace Newlove, which were quickly granted at Marlborough Street Police Court. The charge against Hammond and Newlove was 'that they did unlawfully, wickedly and corruptly conspire, combine, confederate and agree to incite and procure George Alma Wright and divers other persons to commit the abominable crime of buggery against the peace of Her Majesty the Queen'.[1]

Abberline's next destination was the alleged house of ill repute at No. 19 Cleveland Street, where he aimed to enforce the warrants. With six storeys, including an attic and basement, No. 19 was a tall and narrow townhouse with two windows on each floor, including on the ground floor, with windows to the right of the heavy wooden front door. Running parallel to the major thoroughfare of Tottenham Court Road in the West End, Abberline's destination was indeed, as Swinscow had said, almost directly opposite the Middlesex Hospital.

The hospital had previously been a workhouse before becoming a workhouse infirmary, and this large, imposing building had, over fifty years earlier, almost certainly been a key inspiration for the workhouse in *Oliver Twist*, as Charles Dickens had lived at No. 22 on two separate occasions as a child and in his late teenage years, when that stretch of Cleveland Street was called Norfolk Street.

In his bowler hat and suit, which, by late morning, would be too heavy for the summer's day, and hobbling slightly on his left leg – the result of a varicose vein that he'd had at the beginning of his police service but had worsened because of years of incessant walking and standing – Abberline made his way onto Cleveland Street with two constables beside him. It was six o'clock in the morning.

All was quiet as Abberline rapped on the door loudly. There was no response. So Abberline knocked again, and then again. There was still no sign of life from within, which was ominous to Abberline.

The telegraph messenger boys who had frequented the house had described it as a hive of activity in their statements to PC Hanks, and a large house would surely have had occupants, even at that hour. At the very least, the proprietor Hammond should have been there in bed, just as Abberline had planned, to take him by surprise.

But Abberline wasn't leaving without gaining entry. He used his rank and policing experience to instruct the constables to storm the door, even though he didn't have official permission to do so by warrant. If there was any evidence inside, it had to be found before it could be disposed of after a tip-off, and Abberline was already suspicious that somebody may have already warned the guilty parties.

After a few burly shoulder shoves, Abberline and the constables were inside No. 19, and Abberline's suspicion was soon confirmed. Not only was nobody there but the house, which had obviously once been expensively furbished, was stripped of any sign of personal effects, with just the furniture remaining. Hammond and his associates had absconded from the scene of the crimes.

Abberline ordered two constables, changing in shifts, to be put on duty to keep a watch on No. 19 Cleveland Street around the clock. One of them, PC Richard Sladden, will feature later in this story. Nobody entered the premises, but several well-heeled men walked up to the front door over the coming days and knocked, seeming disappointed when there was no answer.

In his police report dated 18 July, Abberline relayed that 'a number of men of superior bearing and apparently of good position have been seen to call ... accompanied by boys in some instances, and on two occasions by a soldier, but after waiting in a suspicious manner left without gaining admission'. Discreet tails were put on the callers.

The high status of individuals in social and military circles would soon begin to be revealed. One of them especially, a man from within the royal family's inner circle, would become the focus of the ensuing scandal.

Later that same day, 'the sworn informations' of the telegraph messenger boys, Charles Thomas Swinscow, Charles Ernest Thickbroom and George Alma Wright, were heard at Marlborough Street Police Court. Adding to Swinscow's revelations, Wright and Thickbroom, both aged 17, said that Henry Newlove had recruited them for Hammond. And while Thickbroom hadn't gone to the basement lavatory at the London Central Telegraph Office with Newlove like Swinscow, Wright had done so, confessing that on one or two occasions Newlove had 'put his person into me, that is to say behind, only a little way, and something came from him. I never did this to him.' It was also revealed that Thickbroom, who said that he was motivated into attending No. 19 Cleveland Street for money, had worn his GPO telegraph messenger uniform when going there, unlike the others.

But in the meantime, Abberline knew that he would have to chase his prey and run down Hammond and Newlove, and arresting one of them could lead to the apprehension of the other. That's just how things worked. And after making inquiries, the detective discovered where he might find Newlove.

7 July 1889

It was a Sunday, but that made no difference to progressing the investigation. North of Cleveland Street and just over half a mile north of Euston Station was where Inspector Abberline headed with two constables, one of them being PC Luke Hanks.

Down-at-heel Bayham Place, which runs through the much larger Bayham Street in Camden Town, where Charles Dickens had lived at No. 16 in 1823 as a boy, was their destination. Henry Newlove was known to live at No. 18 Bayham Place, with his mother, Margaret, and two of his three older brothers, his eldest brother and two elder sisters having left and made their own way. Henry had never known his father, John, a stonemason, who had died shortly before he was born.

It was just before 1.30 p.m. when Abberline knocked and Newlove's mother came to the front door. After some disingenuous denials from Margaret that her son was there, Abberline and the constables made entry and soon found 18-year-old Henry Newlove cowering in one of the two upstairs rooms. When Abberline read out the arrest warrant, which also named Hammond, Newlove's reply went halfway to explaining why No. 19 Cleveland Street had been vacated: 'Mr Hammond, after I told him about the affair Friday morning, told me to deny everything.' Newlove had tipped off Hammond, who had fled.

But it was what Newlove said to PC Luke Hanks, who was assigned to take him in, that was truly enlightening. Unprovoked by Hanks, and obviously feeling very aggrieved by his treatment, the handcuffed Newlove started talking as they made their way to Scotland Yard in a hansom cab.

'I think it very hard that I should get into trouble while men in high position are allowed to walk free,' said Newlove.

'What do you mean?' asked PC Hanks.

'Why, Lord Arthur Somerset goes regularly to the house at Cleveland Street. So does the Earl of Euston and Colonel Jervois,' said Newlove.

'Who is Colonel Jervois?'

'He lives at Winchester Barracks, Winchester,' said Newlove.

His name was, in fact, Colonel Robert Jervoise, of the Hampshire Regiment's 3rd Battalion.

There was no need for Hanks to ask who Lord Arthur Somerset and the Earl of Euston were. They were very well-known men, members of the aristocracy, and Somerset was a close confidant of the heir to the throne.

The gravity of the case and its profound implications, with such highly placed men mixed up in a homosexual prostitution scandal, was not lost on Hanks, and back at Scotland Yard, he at once told Abberline what he had learned. Abberline was stunned but he knew that he immediately had to discreetly inform Commissioner Monro about the troubling and potentially explosive development.

9 July 1889

Once in custody at Scotland Yard, Newlove was questioned at length by Abberline and confirmed all the details given by his fellow arrestees – Swinscow, Wright and Thickbroom – in their statements.

Abberline now focused on Hammond, the proprietor of what was really a male brothel at No. 19 Cleveland Street. But as Hammond had been warned off by Newlove on 5 July, and with the seriousness of the charges against him, Abberline knew that Hammond could be anywhere.

Meanwhile, PC Hanks made a courtesy call back to Newlove's mother's house in Bayham Place, where Henry had been arrested just the previous day. One of Henry's elder brothers had asked Hanks to return to talk to their mother, Margaret, to explain the truth of Henry's situation. It was while Hanks was doing this that he was to get another break in the case.

There was a knock on the door, and Hanks heard Margaret say to her son that it was 'George Veck', a name Hanks recognised professionally. Going outside the house, Newlove's mother and brother made sure to leave Hanks inside the house while they spoke to Veck, who was wearing a dog collar and appeared to be a vicar. But Hanks had long learned to use his ears in such situations and soon realised that Veck was connected to the Cleveland Street case, and what he was saying was much more criminal than godly.

'I saw Hammond at Gravesend yesterday, and I have been down there today, but he has flown. I cannot say where he is,' said Veck. 'I will see Henry is right and I will see you all right as well. Do you want any money? If so, let me know. I will instruct a solicitor to defend Henry in the morning.'

It was obvious that Veck was heavily involved in the affair, and he was trying to keep the Newloves, especially Henry, onside: as a procurer of boys for Charles Hammond, Henry Newlove knew a great deal. It would later be discovered that Veck, aged 48, had been living with Hammond at No. 19 Cleveland Street until very recently and they were close associates, perhaps even business partners. Veck by then lived in Gravesend, Kent, south-east of London, and Hammond had undoubtedly gone there when he left No. 19 Cleveland Street, with Veck harbouring him before he escaped somewhere else – quite possibly abroad, if Hammond had any sense.

And George Veck was not a priest at all. He had studied theology years earlier but had never been ordained. It was a good, respectable cover for criminality, especially in an era when the Church of England reigned supreme. Veck himself had been a telegraph clerk almost twenty years earlier, in Gosport, Hampshire. In 1877, he was fired by the Midland Railway Company for improper conduct with boys.

George Daniel Veck was born in a pub, The Battle of Trafalgar, on 5 October 1840 in Forton, Hampshire. His father, George, was then a labourer, but later became the 'licensed victualler' or publican, of that same establishment. Both Veck's father and mother Elizabeth had died in the late 1870s, and his two younger brothers had passed away two decades before that.

Veck was still living in the same pub in 1871, when he was a telegraph clerk, but ten years later, after being fired from that position, he was living in Brixton, then in Surrey, and working as a beer retailer. Eight years later, he was firmly embroiled in the coming Cleveland Street Scandal.

PC Hanks didn't arrest George Veck – or the Reverend G.D. Veck, as he styled himself – that day, but he would be put under surveillance in the hope that he might lead the police to Hammond or others involved in the case, which was now looking much more complicated.

Abberline was aware of the growing complexity of his new case, which was fast becoming a major inquiry, if not on the huge scale of the Jack the Ripper investigation the previous year. He wanted Hammond, who was at the centre of it all and the guiltiest party, in his eyes.

Intelligence would soon come in that Hammond had escaped to Paris, and Abberline wrote in his report of 18 July that Hammond was staying, care of a Madame de Foissard, at 8 Passage des Abbesses in the Montmartre area of the French capital. After consulting his police superiors and getting approval, Abberline asked the British government's Home Office, which then, as now, had overall responsibility for policing, to request that the French government 'assist in surrendering' Hammond.[2]

When the Foreign Office replied to the Home Office's request on 24 July, it can hardly have been the response that Abberline was expecting. Addressed to the Undersecretary of State at the Home Office, it revealed that the matter had gone to the very highest level – to the British Prime Minister Lord Salisbury, head of the incumbent Conservative government, who was also the Foreign Secretary and in charge of the Foreign Office:

> The Marquis of Salisbury has given his careful consideration to your letter of the 22nd instant, relative to the case of Charles Hammond, charged with conspiracy to incite certain persons to commit unnatural offences, who is believed to have escaped to Paris. I am now directed to request you to inform Mr Secretary Matthews [Sir Henry Matthews, the Home Secretary] that His Lordship does not consider this to be a case in which any official application could justifiably be made to the French Government for assistance in surrendering the fugitive to this country.[3]

This decision would have been passed from the Home Secretary to the Metropolitan Police Commissioner James Monro and then down to Inspector Abberline on the ground. It was an inexplicable decision. There was so much evidence against Hammond, and from multiple witnesses. Both Monro and Abberline would feel very frustrated but very aware that hidden and far more powerful forces than them were in play. Hammond knew many unsavoury and shocking facts about some very prominent people and it was obvious that special treatment was being applied to prevent him divulging what he knew.

But Abberline just wanted to uphold the law. He didn't give up and by the beginning of August would find himself on a steamship to France to try to bring Hammond back.

Three

No verified photograph of Fred Abberline has ever been found, there are only newspaper sketches illustrating reports of his investigations. He wasn't a Londoner. Although he spent much of his life policing and roaming the dark back alleys of the East End, as well as the upmarket thoroughfares of the West End, Abberline was born on 8 January 1843 in Blandford Forum in the county of Dorset, in the south-west of England, just over 100 miles (163km) from the capital.

Blandford Forum had been known for lacemaking, brewing and malting (turning grain into malt) in the Georgian period. Most of the town's buildings that Fred knew in the mid-nineteenth century were built in this era, after a major fire flamed through the town in 1731, destroying the earlier premises. The Abberline family lived at No. 116 East Street in the town – a very long road.

Fred's father Edward was a saddler by trade, and was latterly a local government official, while his mother Hannah (née Chin) was kept busy looking after Fred and his two older siblings, Harriett and Edward. His eldest sibling Eliza died in 1846, aged 12, when Fred was 3 years old. Edward senior died in 1850, aged 49, three days after Fred's seventh birthday, and from then on, Hannah also ran a shop to support her family.

Fred's entry into the world of work saw him apprenticed to a clocksmith, learning how to make and mend clocks, but this was very poorly paid and rendered him so impecunious it afforded him no life after he had contributed to the family upkeep. Having peaked in the late eighteenth century, the clockmaking industry was on the wane in Britain by the time Fred began his apprenticeship, and by the late 1850s Switzerland had become the hub of the artisan trade. For immediately financial and aspirational reasons, feeling the need to break away and build a career, penny dreadful fan Fred didn't see his future in timepieces. His future was going to be in London.

In 1860, Blandford Forum took the first small step in leaving the coaching era behind when it connected to the burgeoning rail network, becoming part of the Somerset & Dorset Joint Railway, two years later. The following year, Fred may well have made the first leg of his journey to the capital, when he left his family home. His sister Harriett had already left, so he said goodbye to his mother and brother Edward, aged 23 and a cabinetmaker, and moved there, three days short of his twentieth birthday. He joined the Metropolitan Police ('the Met'), then just over three decades old, as a police constable, warrant number 43519, attached to 'N' Division in Islington, north-east London.

It was a stable career, with real opportunities for advancement, but it must have been a very adventurous step for Fred and a challenging change of environment, from a small provincial town (even almost a decade later in 1871, the population of Blandford Forum was just 3,900) to the sprawling, crime-ridden metropolis, where around 3.2 million resided when he began his policing career on 5 January 1863.

In 1866, three years after Fred Abberline joined, the Met had 6,839 police officers, and it was a force that was growing fast, more than doubling to 14,191 officers by 1887. He would soon prove to be temperamentally suited to policing and would develop a rare rapport in the areas he patrolled, forging links with locals and cultivating useful informants (known as 'auxiliaries' then), a Victorian 'community' policeman, identifying 'hooks' (pickpockets) and ensuring that all kinds of miscreants were 'piped off' (put under surveillance).

In the *Islington Gazette* of 1 October 1864, a report mentions Fred, along with another constable, catching three young men who had thrown a cracker (firework) into a local church, frightening the congregation. Fred would regularly appear in local – and increasingly, national and international – newspapers throughout his career for catching thieves, those accused of illegal card and billiard-playing, fraud and embezzlement, wounding and assault, through to the serial murders of the Jack the Ripper inquiry and the great scandal of the Cleveland Street case.

On 19 August 1865, Fred was promoted to the rank of sergeant. It was a swift rise, and a few months later he was transferred to 'Y' Division in Highgate, north-west London. For much of 1867 he was undercover in plainclothes, investigating the Fenians, members of the Irish Nationalist Brotherhood, who in that year attempted a revolt against the British in their native Ireland, which became known as the Fenian Rising. The group had already begun building a presence on the British mainland, based in Lancashire in the north-west of the country, but also had members in London, the home of the British Parliament and the nucleus of political and economic power.

Fred was exposed to real danger, working undercover to gather intelligence about the Fenians. In November 1867, three Fenians, known as the Manchester Martyrs, were executed in Salford, near Manchester, for attacking a police vehicle holding fellow Fenians to try to spring them. And in the following month, the Fenians exploded a bomb at Clerkenwell Prison, near Islington, London, to free a comrade awaiting trial there. Twelve people were killed and 120 injured, with widespread damage to nearby housing, although the prisoner wasn't freed. The Fenians were seen as a real threat to national security and the public.

Fred started to collect police commendations, and he would amass scores of them by the end of his career. In his personal life, he married Martha Mackness, the daughter of a labourer, on 1 March 1868 in Holloway, north-east London, when he was 25, but she tragically died of consumption in Northamptonshire just two months later. She was only 20 years old. It must have been heartbreaking for Abberline, who wasn't a natural romancer, being shy and a little socially awkward, according to his biographer, Peter Thurgood.[1]

Professionally, Fred kept progressing quickly, and now living in police quarters in St Pancras, near King's Cross, London, he was promoted to inspector on 10 March 1873, at the early age of 30. Within a few days, he transferred to 'H' Division in Whitechapel, east London. There, he would make his good reputation among his policing peers and superiors as a solid, painstaking and persistent detective, who knew his area and its inhabitants intimately. Just over five years later, on 8 April 1878, aged 35, Fred was made local inspector, in charge of the whole of 'H' Division's CID.

Meanwhile, Fred had married Emma Beament, the daughter of a merchant, at St John the Evangelist Church in Wembley, north London, on 17 December 1876. Emma was 32, just a year younger than Fred, and she was from Shoreditch, east London, where they would soon set up home. They would remain happily married until Fred's death, decades later. There would be no children.

After almost nine years in charge of 'H' Division CID, Fred was transferred to 'A' Division in Whitehall, central London on 26 February 1887, and then on to 'CO' Division (Central Office) at Scotland Yard, on 19 November that year. On 9 February 1888, Fred Abberline was promoted to inspector (first class) at Scotland Yard, but the terrible events in London's East End in the late summer of 1888 would see him seconded back to his old territory of Whitechapel.

1888

It had been a colder than usual summer, with heavy rain and flooding in many parts of England. On Friday, 31 August, the *Northern Whig* newspaper reported that the weather remained erratic and on the previous day, 'after a magnificently fine morning, the weather completely changed, and a heavy thunderstorm broke over London at half-past two o'clock ... The lightning was extremely vivid, and the thunder loud.'

Just over thirteen hours later, at 3.40 a.m. on Friday, 31 August, the mutilated body of Mary Ann Nichols, known as 'Polly', was found on Bucks Row in the Whitechapel area of London's East End. Among other lesser stabs and slashes, her throat had been cut twice, once very deeply, her genital area suffered two hard, thrusting stabs and the lower area of her abdomen was torn open by a very profound wound, causing her bowels to be fully exposed. Her terrible plight was discovered by Emily Holland, a woman with whom Polly had previously shared a meagre lodging house room.

The severity of the injuries caused the local Whitechapel police to ask Scotland Yard for assistance, and three police inspectors, Abberline, Moore and Andrews, were sent to oversee investigations. Over the next weeks, due to his vast knowledge of the East End and its criminality gained through years of policing the area, as well as his organisational efficiency, Detective Inspector Abberline would come to the fore of the inquiry, in charge of the investigation on the ground. He reported to Detective Chief Inspector Donald Swanson, while Dr Robert Anderson, the Assistant Commissioner of CID, was in overall control.

It would soon become known as the Jack the Ripper inquiry, due to the ripping injuries the perpetrator inflicted on his victims, and this name was adopted by the newspapers, especially after it was signed in letters to the authorities and the media, purporting to be from the killer.

Disease hung in the thick and musty air in the East End, the only brightness coming in the sky on a fine spring or summer's day, but even that was unable to improve the environs of the insipidly hazardous streets. The tenement slums, flea-ridden dosshouses and workhouses were dens where murderous cutthroats and thieves lived sunken cheek by bloody jowl aside those unfortunates whose lives had fallen into such a desperate state. In the following year of 1889, the social reformer and philanthropist Charles Booth would publish the first volume of his study of the city's poverty, *Life and Labour of the People of London*. It contained the first of his now famous 'poverty maps'. Whitechapel's map was shown to have numerous pockets marked as being inhabited by people he labelled the 'lowest class/vicious/semi-criminal', and among them lived many shades of criminal, as Inspector Abberline knew only too well.

But Booth's survey also showed how other classes of people lived razor-close to such dangerous areas, including those termed 'very poor' and 'middle-class/well-to-do'. This area of immigration, from all over Britain, Ireland and abroad, was tightly packed and densely populated.

Abberline also understood this, and his hard-earned policing instincts and East End nous meant he could identify where to look for suspected culprits and potential witnesses swiftly and stealthily.

It was the toughest area of London for policing. Many of the inhabitants of the worst areas were transient and difficult to locate, with their movements hard to track. And as the historian Hallie Rubenhold has powerfully ascertained, the women who lived by prostitution, some every day and others sporadically, were human beings too.

Nobody would put themselves in harm's way of often-violent clients by choice. They did so out of dire need: to get a few pennies to share a bed in a stinking hovel, buy bread or other basic sustenance, or feed their alcoholism, the 'demon drink' used as medication from the pain of existence. Like many others, the Ripper's first victim, Mary Ann Nichols, had been born into a solid working-class family but descended to where she had her last breaths stolen from her because of a broken marriage after her husband's infidelity, a series of family tragedies and her increasing addiction to alcohol. Police officers on the East End patch in 1888 needed an understanding of the people who lived there, a keen eye, wily cunning, strong nerves and a hard stomach.

Fourteen years later, the American writer Jack London spent a few weeks living in Whitechapel to assemble the material for his book, *The People of the Abyss*. Living conditions in the East End had marginally improved by 1902, but London, a beady-eyed journalist and realistic chronicler, saw no hope there. Although London was also somebody who felt great empathy with the poverty-stricken and their lot, how he described the milieu in which the East Enders lived is nihilistic, and he advocated a form of eugenics driven by mercy:

> And day by day I became convinced that not only is it unwise, but it is criminal for the people of the Abyss to marry. They are the stones by the builder rejected. There is no place for them in the social fabric, while all the forces of society drive them downward till they perish … So one is forced to conclude that the Abyss is literally a huge man-killing machine.

This was the part of London that 45-year-old Inspector Abberline knew like the back of his ungloved hand. Side-whiskered and balding, he was methodical, hard-working and driven to the point of obsession – a man who lived by the then much slimmer Metropolitan Police officer's rulebook, and who was well liked and respected by those who worked with him. And Abberline would need every ounce and inch of his investigative and management skills and knowledge of London's East End over the coming months.

There would be four more horrific murders following his arrival back in Whitechapel on 1 September, within twelve hours of the murder of Mary Ann Nichols, with the last that could be attributed with certainty to Jack the Ripper on 9 November. That final victim would suffer some of the most horrific mutilations ever inflicted upon anyone, anywhere.

Abberline would be off the case by Christmas 1888, having failed to arrest the killer. But the case would continue to obsess and haunt him for the remainder of his career, which inexplicably had less than four years to run, and the rest of his life, a further four decades. However, back in 1889, within seven months of coming off the Jack the Ripper inquiry, and by now away from the East End and ensconced at Scotland Yard again, Inspector Abberline was thrust into the most politically and socially sensitive case of his career, the Cleveland Street scandal – his last big case.

Four

Under Abberline's orders, PC Richard Sladden had kept watch on No. 19 Cleveland Street for ten days between 9 and 18 July 1889, assisted from 10–12 July by PC Plowman. It was on the first day of surveillance that Sladden saw a tall but rotund man, with rich ginger whiskers, knock on the door. The man waited for some twenty minutes, and finally, after receiving no response from inside, went away. He would also return on 13 July, accompanied by a corporal from the Life Guards regiment, leaving more swiftly after receiving no answer again.

Other 'gentlemen' visitors also called that day, but it was the return caller, with the ginger facial hair and aristocratic bearing, who was most significant. Known as 'Podge' to his friends, the man was Lord Henry Arthur George Somerset, whom Hammond's recruiter, telegraph messenger rent boy Henry Newlove, had named as a frequenter of the brothel to PC Hanks back on 7 July.

Publicly known as Lord Arthur Somerset, he was the third son of the Duke of Beaufort. He was also a major in the Blues (the Royal Horse Guards, an elite regiment) and the assistant equerry to and keeper of the stables of Edward, Prince of Wales, known as 'Bertie', Queen Victoria's second child and eldest son and heir. The possible connection of Somerset to the scandalous goings-on at No. 19 Cleveland Street was therefore potentially incendiary, as he was a member of the Prince of Wales' inner circle.

Somerset, who was aged 38 in the summer of 1889, had always been highly placed in the British aristocracy. His father, Henry Somerset, the 8th Duke of Beaufort, had served as an MP and held various honorary titles. And, less grandly, as the authors Colin Simpson, Lewis Chester and David Leitch highlighted,[1] Somerset's father had a penchant for very young girls, and 'subsidized a procuress called Madame Marie in Conduit Street [in Mayfair] in order to ensure a regular supply' of them.

The family owned more than 50,000 acres of land in Monmouthshire and Gloucestershire, the approximate equivalent area of the royal family's Balmoral Estate in Scotland and double the size of Manhattan in New York City. The ancestral home in which Lord Arthur Somerset grew up was the palatial Badminton House in Gloucestershire, which is where some say the game of the same name began in the eighteenth century with the invention of the shuttlecock, but most likely, it became popular after being played there.

Somerset attended Eton, where he was close friends with Reginald Brett, the son of Lord Esher, a lawyer and judge who served as Solicitor General in the Conservative government of Benjamin Disraeli in the 1860s, and was Master of the Rolls in Lord Salisbury's administration at the time of the Cleveland Street scandal. Reginald Brett would figure in the scandal, as his correspondence with his old school friend Somerset would much later reveal a great deal.

Somerset served with the Royal House Guards in Egypt (1882), which saw Britain occupy the country after defeating the Egyptian Army, and Sudan (1884) as part of the force sent to rescue General Gordon in Khartoum, although they arrived two days after Gordon was killed. William Gladstone's Liberal government (Gladstone's second administration) delayed action as it hadn't wanted Gordon to become besieged there, and only immense pressure from the public had seen Gordon, a hero for his leading role in quelling the Taiping Rebellion in China in the 1860s, sent to Sudan in the first place.

It was an interview with the famous crusading journalist W.T. Stead, published in the *Pall Mall Gazette* in January 1884, entitled 'Chinese Gordon for the Sudan', which created a public clamour for Gordon to lead an army to Sudan. In the interview, Gordon attacked the government's lack of intervention in Sudan to suppress the Mahdists. Stead, the editor of the *Pall Mall Gazette*, who would resign from that position in late 1889, would on the surface seem a peripheral figure in how the Cleveland Street scandal unravelled, but had in fact been indirectly influential on the passing of the law that enabled the arrests and prosecution of the men and boys involved in it.

Somerset was injured and his commanding officer was killed in the unsuccessful Battle of Abu Klea in the bend of the River Nile north of Khartoum on 17 January 1885, where the British force (1,400 strong) was overwhelmed by the Mahdist force (14,000 strong, but only around 3,000 took part), and he was awarded the Egypt Medal with bars. On his return home, Somerset wasted little time, standing as MP for Chippenham in Wiltshire, but failed to be elected and returned to the army. Soon after, he was appointed as the Prince of Wales' private equerry and the keeper of Bertie's stables.

The issue of *Vanity Fair* of 19 November 1887 carried a characteristically playfully exaggerated caricature of the bachelor Somerset by the famous 'Spy' (Sir Leslie Ward), which is now in the National Portrait Gallery's collection. He was respectably described in the magazine as:

> Extra Equerry to the Prince of Wales and as such has the control of the Marlborough House stables, for which his knowledge of and affection for horses well fits him. He hunts much with his father's hounds, he is the best of sons, a true Somerset, a gentleman, a good sportsman, good natured, and of much solid sense. He is favourably regarded by the fair sex, and his irreverent brother officers long ago nicknamed him Podge.

The following year, although he did a lot of travelling for his role with Bertie and was frequently at the prince's London home of Marlborough House, where he was given an office, Somerset was based at Hyde Park Barracks in Knightsbridge, London, when he came to the police's attention in relation to the goings-on at No. 19 Cleveland Street. And the police were soon on Somerset's trail.

It was on 25 July that PC Sladden, under Abberline's instruction, arranged to meet the telegraph messenger rent boys Charles Swinscow and Charles Thickbroom in Piccadilly, then London's gentlemen's clubland, in the very heart of the West End. Sladden needed the boys, especially Swinscow, to identify Somerset (Swinscow said that Somerset had been at No. 19 Cleveland Street), and to confirm that it was the same man Sladden had seen calling twice at the house, along with a young army corporal, during police surveillance.

Somerset had been a member of the most exclusive private members' club in London, the Marlborough, since at least 1873, as he appears in the 'Marlborough Club Members & Rules – A List of the Committees and Members' for that year. The Prince of Wales himself had formed the club, which was in Pall Mall, St James's, near Trafalgar Square, in 1869.

Men of Somerset's standing often had membership of several elite clubs, but there is no official record of which one Somerset was seen leaving in Piccadilly that day, so enabling Swinscow and Thickbroom to confirm his identification as a client of No. 19 Cleveland Street to Sladden. As James Monro, Commissioner of the Metropolitan Police, would later write in a memo to the Home Office on 3 February 1890, Swinscow also told Sladden that Somerset had 'acted indecently' with him at the brothel. But it was Thickbroom who was first to make the identification that day.

PC Sladden and the boys followed Somerset back to his barracks in Knightsbridge, near where he was seen being saluted by another officer, and Somerset's identity was corroborated by other officers at the barracks. There was little doubt now that Somerset was directly implicated, and a course of action had to be decided. But due to the peer's prominent position and his closeness to the Prince of Wales, this was an unprecedented situation in connection to such socially taboo criminality, and more of a migraine than a headache for the authorities.

The Director of Public Prosecutions (DPP) Sir Augustus Stephenson and the Assistant DPP, Hamilton Cuffe, had to make the extremely politically sensitive decision. Sixty-one-year-old Stephenson had been the DPP for five years and knighted for three when the scandal broke, and 40-year-old Cuffe, who was Irish but born in England, would later inherit the title of Earl of Desart. Cuffe would eventually lead the prosecution against Oscar Wilde for sodomy and gross indecency just six years after the events triggered by the Cleveland Street affair.

The DPP's Office instructed that the possible prosecution of Somerset should be the police's responsibility, due to the 'character' of the allegations and possible charges. But the Met Police Commissioner James Monro, who had made the plea to the Home Office on 19 July 1889 to get the French authorities to help apprehend Charles Hammond, was very aware that the prosecution of a man as highly placed as Somerset on such charges was of a different order and could be political poison for the police and himself, as well as potentially very costly.

Monro fought to have the DPP take control. To do this, he wrote directly to the Home Secretary, Sir Henry Matthews, his ultimate boss. His letter to Matthews of 22 July made his feelings very clear, 'I do not consider that his [Somerset's] prosecution is in any sense a Police prosecution'.

Fifty-one-year-old James Monro, a Scotsman, was shrewd and politically savvy and had served most of his career in the Indian Civil Service, rising high within its ranks. Back in Britain, as Assistant Commissioner (Crime) of the Met between 1884 and 1888, Monro had to deal with the ongoing 'Fenian problem', which Abberline had worked undercover gathering intelligence about two decades previously. Monro had used his political nous to navigate a very difficult relationship with the Met Commissioner Sir Charles Warren, but as he felt he was being sidelined and not listened to, he finally resigned as assistant commissioner at the beginning of the Jack the Ripper investigation in September 1888.

Sir Henry Matthews, a bachelor aged 63, had appointed Monro as the head of Special Branch and then Met Commissioner later, in 1888, when Warren resigned. Monro and Matthews had a good working relationship.

Matthews was the son of a judge and born in Sri Lanka, and after becoming a lawyer in 1850 became a Conservative Member of Parliament. After losing his first seat, he was elected MP for Birmingham

East in 1886. It was Matthews' prosecution of the Liberal politician Sir Charles Dilke in 1885 that made his name. Dilke had been accused of having an affair with 19-year-old Virginia Crawford for over two years from 1882, and he was cited in the divorce proceedings brought by Virginia's husband, Donald, a Scottish MP. The Crawford marriage would eventually be dissolved and Dilke was exonerated in court, the judge saying that he could 'find no case' against him.

But Dilke's link to the highly controversial divorce case meant that the damage was done in the minds of the late-Victorian public. His political career was looking to be in ruins, and as a member of Gladstone's Cabinet and President of the Local Government Board – and once thought of as a future prime minister – he had a long way to fall. This was exacerbated and whipped up by the campaign against Dilke by the crusading moralist journalist W.T. Stead in the *Pall Mall Gazette*.

Dilke responded by opposing the Crawford divorce and the granting of the decree absolute, but instead of clearing his name and salvaging his battered reputation, Dilke found himself facing the forensically probing and calmly effective questioning of Henry Matthews. It was disastrous for Dilke, and he lost his seat as MP for Chelsea in London at the 1886 election.

Matthews' performance against Dilke had gained the attention of none other than Queen Victoria herself, who disliked Dilke and had good reason to do so. When he entered Parliament in 1868, the Liberals were in power, and the radically left-wing Dilke began to give speeches that were extremely critical of the monarchy and even called for the institution to be abolished and a republic formed. But there had been a public backlash and, in 1871, he renounced that position. After the Liberals left power in 1874, in order to survive, he moved much closer to the accepted hierarchy, with the royal family firmly at the apex.

However, Queen Victoria had a long memory. For Matthews' work in ostensibly destroying Dilke, in late July 1886 she urged Lord Salisbury to give him a Cabinet position in his newly forming second Conservative administration, which followed Gladstone's five-month third Liberal administration. Salisbury duly obliged, and Matthews was made Home Secretary on 3 August 1886.

Generally considered a strong administrator and highly organised and efficient, Matthews' stint as Home Secretary was eventful. It saw both political and social protests, all requiring canny navigation, and Matthews came in for some criticism for his handling of them. There was 'Bloody Sunday', not to be confused with the 1972 massacre of twenty-six civilians by the British Army in Derry, Northern Ireland, also given that name.

On 13 November 1887, a crowd of around 10,000 gathered in London's Trafalgar Square, protesting about unemployment and the Irish Coercion Acts, which over many years had given the British authorities powers to quell public disquiet and protest. The gathering of supporters of both the Irish National League and the Social Democratic Federation, some of them armed with assorted coshes and knives, became heated and the Metropolitan Police arrested 400 protesters. Seventy-five people were seriously injured, including policemen.

The Matchgirls' Strike of July 1888, which saw more than 1,400 women and girls refuse to work at the Bryant & May match factory in the East End, was another key event. The protest was about poor pay, long hours and the sometimes fatal working conditions, as the white phosphorus used in production often led to 'phossy jaw', causing deformity and, in about one-fifth of cases, death. The strike led to the formation of a union for the female workers and set off other union organising among workers in other industries.

As Home Secretary, Matthews had to deal with this, as well as the Docker's Strike, which took place in mid-August 1889, just as the Cleveland Street scandal was beginning to build steam. This involved 100,000 dockers freezing the essential hub of the Port of London into inaction for a time; they won their claim for fairer pay and gained much public support.

There were also several criminal and policing controversies for Matthews. He was criticised for his glib handling of the wrongful arrest of the dress designer Elizabeth Cass in London's Regent Street in late June 1887, during Queen Victoria's Golden Jubilee week. The case resulted in a police officer going to court to face perjury charges, although he was exonerated.

On the very same day that Cass was falsely arrested in the West End, an entirely unconnected murder in the city's East End, that of Miriam Angel, would lead to further controversy for Matthews. The pregnant Angel, aged 22, who had only arrived in London with her husband from their native Poland the year before, was found dead in her bed in Spitalfields. She had been beaten around the head and face and forced to drink nitric acid. Somebody had also interfered with her nightdress.

Incredibly, a man was found, barely conscious, under Angel's bed while doctors were examining her in situ. Israel Lipski had also drunk some acid, although much less of it, suffering burns to his mouth and throat from which he would recover. Police officers from the local 'H' Division, coincidentally where Abberline had been Head of CID until four months earlier, arrived and arrested Lipski, who was an umbrella salesman. He claimed he was innocent and had been forced to drink the acid, and that two of his colleagues were responsible, the motive being robbery. But at his trial, Lipski was found guilty and sentenced to death.

The case caused a sensation that summer, with claims of antisemitism against the Jewish Lipski. Public interest and, in some quarters, protest was further aroused by W.T. Stead, who organised a press drive to get Lipski a reprieve because of the thin and circumstantial evidence thought by many to have been presented against him at trial. Matthews and the trial judge delayed Lipski's execution by a week while they considered it. Matthews was personally against capital punishment, but he didn't move to reprieve Lipski. In the end, this was rendered academic anyway, as Lipski broke down and confessed Angel's murder to a rabbi.

Lipski was finally hanged on 22 August 1887, but his name became an antisemitic slur in the East End following the case and was used generically for any murderer. It was infamously heard used during the Jack the Ripper investigation. That inquiry of the following year would be a heavy millstone around Matthew's neck, as it was for Abberline, dragging on as it did while women continued to be ferociously murdered throughout late 1888.

Fast-forwarding to 1889, Sir Henry Matthews tendered his resignation to Lord Salisbury early in that year because he disagreed with the administration's treatment of Ireland and the breaking of promises it had made in the 1886 election in that direction. But with the aid of Lord Halsbury, the Lord Chancellor, Matthews was talked into remaining in post, much to the prime minister's apparent relief.

And in late July 1889, James Monro got his way. After reading the Met commissioner's letter imploring him for his assistance in the matter of the potential prosecution of Lord Arthur Somerset, Matthews sided with Monro. The DPP, Sir Augustus Stephenson, was informed that he would have to take charge of any proposed prosecution against Somerset, a potentially exploding political hot potato.

Stephenson felt he needed another opinion and so he went to the Treasury, which oversaw the DPP's office. Horace Avory was a 37-year-old junior Treasury lawyer at the time, but he would later be knighted, having become a noted and, especially to the criminal fraternity, infamous judge. On his death in 1935, *Time* magazine reminded readers of his nicknames, 'the Hanging Judge' and 'Acid Drop', earned by his hard stance towards defendants and caustic wit in court over many years.

But that was still to come, and back on 3 August 1889, Avory replied to Stephenson, regarding the telegraph messenger rent boy and procurer Henry Newlove, who had been arrested almost a month prior, on 6 July, 'I am of opinion that it is not expedient to proceed with the evidence against the Prisoner Newlove until all means have been exhausted to compel the attendance of Hammond to answer the charge.'[2]

This was a delaying tactic to allow more time for consideration as to how to proceed. If Newlove wasn't put forward for prosecution, Somerset could hardly be arrested. And as detailed earlier, Prime Minister Lord Salisbury had blocked putting pressure on the French authorities to bring Hammond back to face the mordant music.

Abberline was also in Paris in the second week of August, trying to get the assistance of the police there in Hammond's apprehension, but he would make no headway. In fact, on 12 August, Abberline's 'Confidential Report' was sent to the DPP, Sir Augustus Stephenson, and the accompanying letter showed that the detective was still very much trying to get the British authorities to act on Hammond: 'Mr. Abberline thinks that unless great weight is brought to bear upon the French Police that they are not likely to put themselves to much trouble in the matter.'[3] No weight would be leveraged against Hammond for some time, and then only the minimum.

Meanwhile, before leaving for the Continent, on 8 August Abberline had interviewed John Saul, a veteran Irish rent boy, who had lived at No. 19 Cleveland Street and plied his trade there. In Abberline's absence, PC Luke Hanks interviewed Saul again on 10 August, with a further short statement being taken five days later. Saul was older than the other telegraph messenger rent boys, and far more hardened in character. James Monro would later say in a memo to the Home Office that Saul was 'evidently such a depraved and infamous character that the Public Prosecutor would have nothing to do with him as a witness'. But Saul would re-emerge as the scandal unfolded, giving evidence in a sensational civil case about events at the brothel.

On 10 August, Avory finally responded to Stephenson with a firm opinion about Somerset, whose name was at this stage blocked out in official correspondence (included in italics here), and the brothel-keeper Charles Hammond's partner-in-crime and fake priest George Veck, writing, 'proceedings should be taken against the man Veck alias Barber and also against *Lord Arthur Somerset*'.

On the same day, the Attorney General Sir Richard Webster added his thoughts: 'In my opinion some action must now be taken respecting *Lord Arthur Somerset*.'[4] However, also on that very day, Godfrey Lushington, the Permanent Undersecretary of State at the Home Office, who would be knighted three years later, sent a conflicting message to Stephenson on behalf of the Home Secretary: 'Mr. Matthews wishes you to stay your hand until he has seen Lord Salisbury on Monday morning.'[5] Special attention was obviously being taken by both Matthews and the prime minister over the highly sensitive situation.

By this time, Somerset had finally been interviewed by the police, three days earlier, on 7 August at Hyde Park Barracks. Although no record of it survives, he must have denied everything, brazening it out, although his private correspondence of the time would later reveal his true feelings and fears.

On 17 August, having read the 'further statements' taken from Thickbroom, Swinscow and PC Sladden over Somerset's identification in Piccadilly, the Attorney General Sir Richard[6] Webster reversed his opinion of two days earlier regarding action being taken against Somerset: 'These statements differ on important points from those previously before us and I am not satisfied with the evidence of identification of [Somerset]. I therefore give you directions that no proceedings be taken against him till further directions given. Directions against Veck in accordance with opinion of 10th [August].'[7]

A warrant for the arrest of George Veck was granted two days later, on the same charge as Henry Newlove, 'that they did unlawfully, wickedly, and corruptly conspire, combine, confederate and agree with one Charles Hammond to incite and procure George Alma Wright, Charles Thomas Swinscow and other persons to commit the abominable crime of buggery against the peace.' Hammond had been charged *in absentia*, along with Newlove, back on 6 July 1889.

With oily machinations going on behind the scenes, it would be almost another seven weeks before an arrest warrant was finally issued against Somerset.

Five

Although Lord Arthur Somerset at this time still had the full confidence of his boss and friend, Bertie, the Prince of Wales, he knew that he was potentially in real legal and social danger. And so, immediately after his first police interview, Somerset put himself in the hands of his solicitor, Arthur Newton, a colourful and unscrupulous man, who would later face his own legal travails resulting from his actions in the Cleveland Street scandal.

Arthur Newton was in his late twenties and he had been a practising solicitor for five years by 1889. He was born in 1860 in London, the son of Henrietta and Edward Newton – the manager of the Legal & General Assurance Society, the respected financial services and asset management company set up in 1836 in a coffee house in London's legal district of Chancery Lane. Edward's contacts undoubtedly helped his son Arthur build his solicitor's practice when the time came.

Newton went to Hawtreys School in Slough, Berkshire, where the future Prime Minister Stanley Baldwin and the arts-and-crafts architect Detmar Blow also attended a little later. He then attended Cheltenham College, with many notable alumni, especially from the military and sporting fields. Both were expensive and exclusive private schools.

In 1889, Newton's offices, accommodating Newton & Co. Solicitors, were at No. 24 Great Marlborough Street, just off Regent Street, in the heart of London's West End. He would later move to No. 32. It was one of the most successful solicitor's practices in London.

Newton chiefly worked in the police courts. According to Edward A. Bell, Newton 'always appeared in police court wearing kid gloves' and his private rooms displayed several cigar cabinets with various brands, the quality of which he would select and offer to suit his clients' level of 'legal adversity'.[1] Newton's hobbies were swimming and conjuring, and the sleight of hand required for the latter certainly suited his devious character.

A portrait by Spy, which appeared in *Vanity Fair* on 21 September 1893, four years after Newton acted for Somerset in the Cleveland Street scandal, is entitled 'The Marlborough Street Solicitor'. It shows Newton black-tied, wing-collared and dapper in his grey frock coat, gold waistcoat chain, his hair slicked back and parted in the middle, and sporting a coiffed and curled moustache. His expression is wily, knowing, respectable and personable, and gives only a hint of his opportunistic and near-criminal nature. The overall impression is of a well-heeled, silk-tongued and quick-thinking lawyer: a man whose actions were in truth morally questionable as well as ethically flexible – and sometimes illegal.

Another leading and crooked solicitor of the time, Bernard Abrahams, had his offices next door to Newton. As Laura Lee has pointed out in her article, *Strange Bedfellows*,[2] Newton and Abrahams had 'cosy relationships with the criminals in their orbit'. Both solicitors socialised together, and 'often worked on the same cases, with one appearing for the defence and the other for the prosecution'. They would be on opposing sides in the trial of Oscar Wilde in 1895, with Abrahams gathering and reportedly blackmailing witnesses for the Marquis of Queensberry and Newton arranging the counsel for Wilde's co-accused, Alfred Taylor.

Newton's managing clerk and right-hand man in the late 1880s was the tall and blonde-haired Frederick Taylerson, who was born in Faversham in Kent, the son of an engine driver. Taylerson was aged just 23 when the Cleveland Street scandal began. He was a bachelor at the time, but he would marry in late 1891. Taylerson would do anything that Newton asked of him, and that would throw him into legal jeopardy.

Arthur Newton was far more than Lord Arthur Somerset's solicitor in 1889. He was also his fixer. Knowing that Henry Newlove could do him great damage, as he could give evidence against him regarding his frequenting of No. 19 Cleveland Street at any upcoming trial, Somerset instructed Newton to arrange Newlove's defence. Newlove had named Somerset upon his arrest in early July, but the peer needed the rent boy and procurer to be onside and beholden to him. To this end, Newton began to prepare.

Then suddenly, on 19 August, the arrest warrant was issued for the Reverend G.D. Veck, the unordained sidekick of the pimp Charles Hammond and recruiter of rent boys to No. 19 Cleveland Street.

Abberline wasted no time. George Veck's London lodgings were now at No. 2 Howland Street in Fitzrovia, near to Tottenham Court Road, and not very far from where he had previously resided with Charles Hammond at No. 19 Cleveland Street. That was where Abberline and a constable rushed to on the morning of 19 August.

Veck wasn't there. But there was a 17-year-old boy in 48-year-old Veck's bed. He identified himself as George Barber, a name that Veck had used as an alias on occasion. Barber claimed to be Veck's private secretary.

When interrogated, Barber told Abberline that Veck had gone to Portsmouth, near to where he was born in Gosport. Barber then added that Veck was returning to London on the railway that very day. Then, as now, trains from Portsmouth came into Waterloo Station, so Abberline and his fellow officer went directly there, arresting Veck as he alighted onto the platform a little later. The cod clergyman came quietly.

Much incriminating material was found in Veck's pockets. There was a scrap of paper with his fellow accused, Henry Newlove's address in Camden Town, where Veck had visited in early July and been seen by PC Hanks. Written on that same paper were the words, 'Let me urge upon you the extreme necessity of utmost secrecy'. There was also a letter from Charles Hammond in which the pimp had written to Veck, 'Let me know when it is safe to come back'.

Finally, and most interestingly, there were some missives postmarked Suffolk from a young man called Algernon Allies, aged 20, requesting money from Veck, which also referred to 'Mr. Brown', who had seemingly been providing funds to Allies. Abberline would soon learn, after PC Hanks was sent to Suffolk to interrogate Allies, that 'Mr Brown' was an alias used at No. 19 Cleveland Street by none other than Lord Arthur Somerset.

Algernon Edward Allies was born on 14 April 1869 in the village of Wortham, Suffolk, close to the border with Norfolk. His father, Edward, was a coachman, and he was close to his mother, Elizabeth. Allies spent his early years in Suffolk, before moving to London in his late teens, where he got a job as a waiter at the Prince of Wales' Marlborough Club, of which Lord Arthur Somerset was a member. His mother would say that this was the 'one constant situation' that Algernon had ever had.[3]

In 1887, Allies was arrested for theft. On 12 September that year, 18-year-old Allies pleaded guilty at the Old Bailey, and the court records show that he went on trial for 'burglary in the dwelling-house of Charles John, Lord Colville of Culross, and stealing £16 and 8 shillings'. The judgement was respited and the sentence delayed. Allies was eventually given just one day without hard labour in Pentonville Prison on 24 October 1887.

Allies was fired from the Marlborough Club after having worked there for three years. His mother said it was for 'disobedience to a steward',[4] but it may well have been over the conviction for theft. But Allies had already become Somerset's 'friend'. They remained in touch, and Allies had lived at No. 19 Cleveland Street for around three months.

Somerset had been supporting Allies financially for some time. Allies lived in Sudbury, Suffolk, with his parents and brother Ernest, an unemployed groom, who was described as a 'confirmed invalid' in a police report, and when he was back in the countryside, he made multiple trips to London at Somerset's request.

On 23 August, Allies was taken back to London by Hanks, where he was held in police care as a witness. On 31 August, PC Hanks recorded in a police statement that he had spoken to the postmaster of Sudbury Post Office regarding Allies having cashed three postal orders on 21 August, to the value of 20*s* each. Hanks was able to confirm that Allies had been cashing in postal orders there for some time. It was also soon established that the postal orders had been purchased at South Kensington Post Office in London. The clerk there had no recollection of who had bought them, but they were soon traced back to Somerset.

Allies' mother Elizabeth also soon travelled to London, where she gave a statement to Abberline on 3 September. She said of her son, Algernon:

> He has been supported for the past two years by Lord Arthur Somerset, who has been in the habit of sending him postal orders, on the average about every fortnight. He allowed him 15/- per week. He frequently sent for the boy to go to 19 Cleveland Street, and from what the boy told me, I was under the impression that it was always for the purpose for waiting at table, as he said Mr. Charles [Hammond] used to give parties.

And there was more. A man had called at her home on Saturday, 24 August, the day after Algernon was taken to London: 'at 5pm a man called at my house and asked if Algernon Allies was within. I said "No." He said, "Where is he?" I said he had gone to London with a gentleman yesterday.'

Elizabeth Allies then said that the man asked who Algernon had gone with, but she told him she had forgotten his name. He said to her, 'Was it Abberline?' and she said it was (in fact, it was PC Hanks). Next, the man asked if there were any letters there belonging to Algernon and she said that there weren't. The man went on to enquire if Abberline had taken the letters, but Elizabeth said he hadn't, 'as there were none to take'.

He asked her twice if she was sure about this, and she replied that she was 'quite sure'. The man finally said, 'Oh, I didn't know that they had sent Abberline down.' The visitor then left.

Algernon's mother gave a description of the inquisitive caller. She described him as about 50 years old, about 5ft 8in tall, of stout build with a very dark complexion, a dark moustache and bushy beard, wearing a high hat and a long, thin, dark overcoat, very large, wide shoes – exceptionally wide – and he carried an umbrella. She said that he was of 'gentlemanly appearance' and 'superior education'. Finally, Elizabeth said, 'I should know him again.'

It was almost certain that the man who called at the Allies' family home was sent there by Arthur Newton, working on behalf of Somerset to find out the progress of the police investigation. The press had yet to report on events – that would begin in September the following month – but Newton would have learned of Abberline's involvement through gossip at the police courts. When the man reported back to Newton that the well-known Abberline had personally been up to Suffolk, the lawyer would have been concerned at how seriously it was being taken. But it was PC Hanks who had really made the trip and ferried Algernon Allies back to London.

The age and physical description of the visitor given by Elizabeth Allies does not remotely fit Newlove's managing clerk Frederick Taylerson, but it does fit one Adolphus de Gallo, who was around 50 at the time. Originally from Hanover in Germany, de Gallo often acted as an interpreter for Newton and undertook other work for him.

Six

On learning of George Veck's arrest, the horrified Lord Arthur Somerset swiftly instructed Arthur Newton to organise the fake priest's legal defence, along with the arrangements already in train for Newlove. Events were beginning to creep up and work against Somerset, who was interviewed again by the police at his barracks on 22 August.

With the prospect of the looming and potentially sensational trial of Veck and Newlove, both facing the same charges, and the persistent police interest in him, despite his high social standing and close links to the royal family, Somerset was now extremely concerned. After his second questioning by police, he asked his commanding officer in the Royal Horse Guards, Colonel Montagu, for immediate leave to travel abroad. A generous four months of leave was granted, and Somerset made his way in stormy weather via Dover to Bad Homburg in Germany, on the southern side of the Taunus Mountains, near Frankfurt, where Bertie, the Prince of Wales, was enjoying his summer holidays.

Although Somerset had admitted nothing to the police or anyone else, his correspondence with an old school friend and confidant from this time reveals his troubled thinking. Reginald Brett, who would become Lord Esher on his father's death, had been MP for Penryn and Falmouth in Cornwall between 1880 and 1885. He would later gather the letters between himself and Somerset and put them together for an unpublished book, *The Case of Lord Arthur Somerset*. But Brett wasn't just a correspondent of Somerset. He moved in the same circles and did his best to help his old friend. Brett may well have been a visitor to No. 19 Cleveland Street himself, but there is no firm evidence of this.

Somerset first made mention of the gathering scandal around him in a letter to Brett, just before his departure for Bad Homburg, thanking Brett, whom he called 'Redge', for seeing 'a fellow' on his behalf. As the writer H. Montgomery Hyde ascertained,[1] this was likely George Veck before his arrest, Brett presumably asking Veck for his silence, but whether any money changed hands is unknown. Somerset's worries about Veck are also revealed with his words, 'I expect others, very likely many others, will appear on the scene as this man did the correspondence and knows everything'. Veck had been Hammond's organiser and procurer, bringing both clients and rent boys to No. 19 Cleveland Street, with Newlove helping with the latter.

Somerset also wrote to Brett that he thought a further £1,000 would be needed to defend his name, added to the outlay he had already made for Newlove's, and now Veck's, defence. Ominously, Somerset made a statement which, when read in context with later correspondence with Brett through that autumn and winter, could be seen as the beginnings of a veiled threat disguised as a promise of discretion: 'I would not drag anyone into it for the world.'

Somerset knew that Brett would be in touch with others who feared exposure over their attendance at the brothel, and this could be extremely useful in raising funds to aid Somerset's defence fund. And Somerset's ultimate survival trump card would be when his lawyer, Newton, began to mention the name of a member of the royal family as an attendee, a final threat to ensure his client's escape from prosecution.

But for now, Somerset was safely away from the police in Germany with the Prince of Wales and his entourage.

Charles Hammond, the pimp and proprietor of No. 19 Cleveland Street, had been in Paris since he fled on 7 July, despite Abberline's efforts, including a trip to the French capital to bring him back, with Prime

Minister Lord Salisbury blocking efforts to compel the French authorities to help. Hammond was living in the Montmartre district of Paris with members of his French wife, Caroline's family.

Charles Richard Hammond was in his mid-30s in the summer of 1889, having been born in Gravesend, Kent in July 1853. His father, Edward, died aged 50 in October 1870, when Charles was 17, and his sister Mary Ann passed away, aged 21, in January 1875. After that, Charles left Gravesend for London.

In March 1876, when he was 22, Charles married Caroline Eugenie Cotte, known as 'Madame Caroline', a prostitute, in Westminster. Their son, Charles 'Manty' Hammond, was born on 2 March 1878 in Soho. 'Manty' would later become an actor in America, taking on some Shakespearean roles and appearing in films between 1916 and the early 1920s, including *Dr Jack*, starring the silent-film star Harold Lloyd, in 1922.

In 1881, Charles Hammond and his family were living at No. 14 Church Street in Soho and he was employed as a military braider, working on army uniforms. Hammond would have become acquainted with the prostitution underworld in the 1880s, probably through his wife, and saw an opportunity in providing male rent boys to wealthy clients. Moving into No. 19 Cleveland Street in late 1885, Hammond found the perfect premises; it was centrally located and just grand enough to attract the right clientele for that business.

Hammond wrote to Caroline from Paris before she joined him there on 17 July 1889. In the letter, he implored her to not 'fall out' with George Veck. Hammond was very aware that Veck knew everything and could incriminate him. He also told her that Veck wanted him to return to London, but assured Caroline that his self-preservation was paramount, 'that I shall not do until I can see that everything is all right'.[2]

Six days later, after Caroline had joined him in Paris, Hammond wrote to Manty, who was temporarily living with Hammond's brother, Ted, in Gravesend, Kent. Revealing how little he trusted Veck, Hammond instructed his son, 'Tell your uncle [Ted] not to tell Mr. Veck that your mother is over here with me. Tell him to write to him and ask him why he doesn't come over to see me or send me any money.'[3] Hammond would always be asking for money from anyone involved in the case and, in time, would reveal himself to be a blackmailer, using the substantial amount of damaging information he had on notable people with a great deal to lose to try to elicit funds.

In that same letter of 23 July, Hammond showed that he knew that Veck was now using the alias of 'George Barber' and asked Manty to ask his Uncle Ted to mail him any newspaper, 'if there is anything in it about Henry [Newlove]'. Hammond knew that Henry Newlove, like Veck, could reveal many damaging details about his brothel at No. 19 Cleveland Street.

In early September 1889, Hammond was finally expelled from France after pressure was put on the French authorities by two English detectives, one of them Inspector Lowe, who had succeeded Abberline on the Continent. It was both the very least they could do and the most that could be achieved.

Hammond arrived in the village of Halanzy, in Luxembourg, on 12 September. This became known to the police, and Abberline later forwarded to the Home Office a report about Hammond that he had received from the Belgian authorities.

But Hammond knew that he could never be definitively safe from apprehension in Europe, and on 5 October he sailed on the Red Star Line's SS *Pennland* from Antwerp, Belgium, to New York, arriving there on 19 October. Hammond's wife Caroline had remained in Paris for now, but he wasn't alone.

A small article in the *New York World* of 3 December that year, by which time the Cleveland Street scandal had been international news for some time, documented Hammond's arrival in America over six weeks earlier. It described him as 'Hammond, the man who kept the infamous house in Cleveland Street, London' and reported that he had checked into a hotel on Christopher Street, Buffalo, New York, registering as 'Charles Bolton of Paris'. He had then left for Philadelphia on 22 October 'accompanied by a boy who posed as his son'.

This wasn't Hammond's son Manty, who was still with his mother in Paris. In time, the identity of the boy would be revealed as Herbert Ames, Hammond's 'secretary'. Later, Ames would divulge a great deal about his time working for Hammond in Cleveland Street and in exile abroad.

But one line in that article, undoubtedly based on information passed to the reporter by the calculating Hammond, would send chills through Lord Arthur Somerset and some other well-heeled men back in England: 'Hammond is said to have in his possession evidence incriminating several prominent members of the English aristocracy.'

Hammond would remain in America, away from the clutches of the British authorities, who had ensured that little was done to apprehend him while still in Europe. Hammond's wife and son would join him, and Manty would later build his acting career there. But Charles Hammond would continue making headlines in America and back in England because of his central role in the Cleveland Street scandal as late as February 1892.

PART II

A HUSH-UP, LIBEL AND OATHS ON THE BIBLE

Seven

On 11 September 1889, George Veck and Henry Newlove were committed for trial at Marlborough Street Police Court in Soho in the West End, with Abberline in attendance. The significance of the event wasn't lost on the most attentive of the press, as Sir Augustus Stephenson, the DDP, was also in court. And there was the first warning whiff of a potential cover-up by the powers that be to protect themselves in the *Pall Mall Gazette* on 12 September 1889:

> The question [...] Stephenson will have to answer is whether two notable Lords [Somerset and Euston] and other notable persons in society who were accused by witnesses of having been principals in the crime for which the man Veck was committed to trial are to be allowed to escape scot free. There has been too much of that kind of thing in the past. The wretched agents are run in and sent to penal servitude; the lords and gentlemen who employ them swagger at large and are ever welcomed as valuable allies of the Administration of the day.

It was ever thus, seemed to opine W.T. Stead, the famous influential editor of the popular liberal evening newspaper, who wrote those words. But two days later, *The Man of the World* reported that Stead was soon vacating his position at the *Pall Mall Gazette*, so the crusading journalist would be leaving the helm just as the Cleveland Street scandal truly grew into a storm of national and international press coverage at the end of the year. Stead would go on to found and edit the monthly *Review of Reviews* in 1890.

Stead, who was born in Northumberland in north-east England, had just turned 40. He had married Emma Lucy in 1873, and they had gone on to have six children, two of their sons also becoming journalists: Alfred, who worked under his father on the *Review of Reviews* and then the *Daily Express*, and Henry, who worked in Fleet Street and later in Australia.

Stead was influential in the way the scandal played out, not by his reporting on it, but by how it was prosecuted by the authorities, although this was due to his sensational journalistic methods and actions four years earlier. It led to the revision of the Criminal Law Amendment Act of 1885. This was Section 11 of the Act, the architect of which was Stead's friend, Henry Labouchère MP, who would put himself at the very centre of the Cleveland Street scandal as it escalated and intensified.

Stead, who began his journalistic career in 1870 on the *Northern Echo* in Darlington in the north of England, had been editor of the *Pall Mall Gazette* since 1883. He was really leaving its editorship because he had fallen out with the newspaper's owner, Henry Thompson. Thompson had supported him through his hard-hitting series of articles in July 1885, a campaign against child prostitution entitled 'The Maiden Tribute of Modern Babylon', which caused a huge public furore. The aftermath saw Stead sent to Holloway Prison for three months for the methods he had used investigating, which exposed the iniquity he uncovered.

Stead's methods involved spiriting away 13-year-old Eliza Armstrong with the help of the Salvation Army to save her from prostitution. Stead was prosecuted and convicted on a technicality because he hadn't gained the permission of Eliza's father to buy her for £5. Incidentally, the case would much later go on to inspire Stead's friend, George Bernard Shaw, to use the name Eliza for the protagonist of his 1913 play *Pygmalion*.

Most significantly, 'The Maiden Tribute' dramatically changed the law, paving the way for the Criminal Law Amendment Act, passed in August 1885, which offered more protections against vice for young women and girls and raised the female age of consent from 13 to 16. But it was an indirect action taken privately by Stead that led Labouchère to lobbying heavily for Section 11, which would allow 'gross indecency' between males to be prosecuted, just as the men and boys were involved in the goings-on at No. 19 Cleveland Street.

By the early autumn of 1889, Stead's boss Henry Thompson at the *Pall Mall Gazette* had had enough. Thompson, who had been gifted the paper by his father-in-law and was not a vocational newspaperman, had no wish for further radical journalistic campaigns or social controversy. And Stead, who became known as 'the Muckraker', drew attention and dissension to himself and those around him as a moth to a bright light.

Newspapers were beginning to stir that mid-September of 1889, and news of the Cleveland Street scandal was beginning to ripple outwards to the public. The ripples would start to form into waves and then splash by the end of the month. That same issue of *The Man of the World* of 14 September carried the seemingly innocuous, though, to those in the know, insinuatingly juicy morsel that 'Lord Arthur Somerset has left England. He intends to remain abroad for an indefinite period.'

Somerset, who was now in Hanover, Germany, scouting for horses for the Prince of Wales' stables, was being kept well informed of events by his lawyer Arthur Newton and corresponding friends such as Reginald Brett. He must have been horrified but relieved to have removed himself from immediate danger and public and press scrutiny. But soon, Somerset would inexplicably return briefly to England.

On 16 September, *The Queen vs George Daniel Veck and Henry Horace Newlove* (indicted with Charles Hammond, who had evaded custody) took place at the Central Criminal Court of the Old Bailey. The sham vicar, Veck, was no longer dressed as a priest for the proceedings.

Under the instruction of Lord Arthur Somerset's lawyer Arthur Newton, and funded by Somerset, Veck was defended by Mr Charles Gill, a 58-year-old Irishman born in Dublin. Gill had been junior counsel to the General Post Office (GPO) from 1886 to 1887, and then senior counsel, but had recently become junior counsel to the Treasury. His legal experience with the GPO, where the scandal originated, was an excellent background for the trial. Gill was married, and belonged to the Conservative, Garrick and Beefsteak gentlemen's clubs in London. He would later go on to be the Recorder of Chichester.

Newlove's counsel was the theatrical Mr Charles Mathews, aged 38, known as 'Willie'. He had been junior counsel to the Treasury until 1886 and was senior counsel from 1888. A member of the Garrick, Turf and Beefsteak clubs, he would later become a good friend of King Edward VII, who was in 1889 still Bertie, the Prince of Wales. After failing to win a seat as an MP, Mathews would go on to be Recorder of Salisbury and was involved in Oscar Wilde's libel claim against the Marquess of Queensberry and several infamous murder cases.

Somerset's money had paid for two formidable briefs, and they were needed: Veck and Newlove were prosecuted by Mr Henry Bodkin Poland QC, known as 'Harry', who was senior counsel to the Treasury and an advisor to the Home Office. A bachelor, he was knighted in 1895 and later became Recorder of Dover. He was a lawyer for over seven decades. Poland was aided by Horace Avory from the Treasury, who had been giving his legal opinions to the DPP on the Cleveland Street affair for weeks.

The case was heard before the Recorder, the elderly Sir Thomas Chambers QC, who had previously been a Liberal MP. Newton and the defence briefs would have been pleased that Chambers was overseeing the case, because he was known to be much more progressive and less stern in sentencing than most other judges.

As undoubtedly approved by Newton, Newlove took Mathews' advice and pleaded guilty to a long list of counts of procuring the rent boys Charles Swinscow, William Meech Perkins, George Alma Wright, Charles Thickbroom, Algernon Allies and George Barber and conspiring to do so. Veck, following Gill's counsel, pleaded not guilty to all those charges – there wasn't strong enough evidence that he had done so. But Veck pleaded guilty to the sixteenth and seventeenth counts, which he alone had been indicted for: committing 'acts of gross indecency' with Somerset's 'friend' Algernon Allies and his own 'secretary', George

Barber. Newlove alone was charged with committing such acts with Swinscow and attempting to do so with Wright.

Newton (and Somerset) had no other choice. If the two defendants had pleaded not guilty to all charges in the face of the telegraph messenger/rent boys' statements as evidence, they would have faced dangerous and potentially scandalously revealing cross-examination by a counsel as adept as Poland. Veck and Newlove would have to take the fall. Hammond had only been added to the indictment because the French had finally expelled him at the last moment, after minimal and delayed pressure by the British government.

Hammond was found guilty *in absentia* of all the procuring and conspiracy charges. Veck was sentenced to nine months' imprisonment with hard labour, and Newlove to four months with hard labour, both to be carried out in London's Pentonville Prison. The charges were all misdemeanours and not felonies under the 1885 Criminal Law Amendment Act, but the sentences could have been harsher under the law.

As the journalist Ernest Parke would point out in late 1889, just a year earlier in 1888, a 'minister' in Hackney in London's East End had been sentenced to life imprisonment for gross indecency. The *Daily Telegraph* of 16 and 28 April 1888 identifies him as Charles Hart Burleigh, aged 28, and he had been charged the previous day, along with Francis George Widdows, aged 37, with 'improper conduct with three boys' at a Bluecoat school, a church charity school with many branches, in Newgate Street, Hackney. This school was known as Christ's Hospital and was originally set up in 1552.

Burleigh wasn't actually a priest but a priest's assistant and had been ordained as a deacon in holy orders by the Bishop of St Albans five years earlier, in 1883. Widdows was an ex-monk and pastor of the Martin Luther Chapel in Hackney. In early May that year, Burleigh would be sentenced to penal servitude for life and Widdows was given ten years in prison.

The fact that Burleigh and Widdows were representatives of the Church undoubtedly counted heavily against them in late-Victorian society, but life in prison, and even a ten-year sentence, were extremely harsh punishments for the offences. And they had been prosecuted by the senior treasury counsel, Charles Mathews, who would in the following year act in defence of Henry Newlove.

Conversely, the sentences handed out to Veck and Newlove were designed by backroom manoeuvrings not to be severe and engineered by a plea deal between the defence counsels and Avory, who did most of the prosecution's groundwork, supervised by his senior, Poland. It was all undoubtedly approved by Arthur Newton.

In a written statement that prosecutor Poland penned for the Attorney General Sir Richard Webster after the trial, it is revealed that either Veck's counsel (Gill) or Newlove's counsel (Mathews) had approached Avory and told him that the defendants would plead partially guilty, and 'the case would be disposed of in the course of the day'. Pleading partially guilty usually led to plea bargaining and this had become more common in criminal cases by the late-nineteenth century as capital punishment was used relatively less often.

The other telegraph messenger rent boys, Swinscow, Wright and Perkins, already suspended from the GPO, would be dismissed from their posts but not charged with gross indecency, so they were never prosecuted. They were allowed, after giving evidence at another trial related to the scandal, to slip back into obscurity.

Further legal proceedings against the other rent boys would have been seen by the authorities as opening the scandalous wound again, and the press and much of the public saw them as victims, not perpetrators, due to their age and class – prey for wolves of far higher social position. But the boys were socially disgraced and the loss of their jobs impacted them and their families greatly.

This swift winding up of Veck and Newlove's potentially damaging trial, with links to the aristocracy and, within weeks, potentially to those of even higher standing, was exactly what Avory and the authorities wanted. Gill, Mathews and Newton knew this very well. And that the offences were taboo is illustrated by the fact that an unnamed woman spectator had been asked to leave the court that day to spare her ears and embarrassment.

But as W.T. Stead had pointed out in his editorial six days before, what of the absent pimp-in-exile Hammond, the absent peer Somerset, and the other aristocrats and men of high station who had frequented No. 19 Cleveland Street?

On 20 September, *The Echo* carried a carefully worded and libel-cautious report under the sub headline, 'A Report on the West-End'. It offered more information, without naming Somerset or another aristocrat (almost definitely the Earl of Euston), who would soon be all over the front pages in connection with No. 19 Cleveland Street. It read:

> There is (says the London correspondent of the *Birmingham Post*) a report in the West-end that two well-known members of society – one a peer – are wanted by the police on the charge of having committed a very serious offence, which need not be specifically described. They are believed to have left the country, and Inspector Abberline, of Scotland Yard, is now in Paris, it is understood, in connection with the case. It is thought the alleged offenders may prefer voluntary exile to the risk of standing upon their trial.

Abberline had, in fact, returned from Paris weeks earlier, and the Earl of Euston never left the country. But regarding Somerset, it was wholly accurate.

Meanwhile, the others potentially implicated in the scandal were unsettled and fearful. A stockbroker named Hugh Weguelin, who knew Somerset and his friend Reginald Brett well, would be independently named as a frequenter of No. 19 Cleveland Street by Charles Hammond's 'secretary', Herbert Ames, in a sworn statement at the beginning of 1891. But by early September 1889, Weguelin was already disturbed by the course of events after Somerset's two police interviews in August.

In 1889, Weguelin, a bachelor in his early thirties, was renting 'rooms' in a house at No. 31 Sackville Street in Piccadilly, at a sizeable rent of £440 per annum. He had his stockbroking offices at Bartholomew House, Bartholomew Lane, in the heart of the financial district of the City of London, close to the Bank of England.

Hugh Weguelin was writing to Reginald Brett about Somerset, whom he calls 'AS' and 'our friend', and the brewing Cleveland Street scandal as early as 9 September. He, like Brett, was in close contact with Somerset's lawyer, Arthur Newton, at this time. Weguelin seems to be trying to reassure himself about his own possible legal and social jeopardy and attempting to distance himself from Somerset's plight. From his words, it can plausibly be inferred that Brett, who was gay, was also a visitor to No. 19 Cleveland Street. Brett was married with children, but later wrote that he'd had affairs with young men before his marriage:

> Frankly, Reggie, the only person seriously implicated is AS ... We cannot blind ourselves to the fact that he [Somerset] is primarily in this mess and that principally through his own act. We are only hangers-on and there is only a distant probability involving an immense stirring up of mud of our being injured. Therefore he must come back and do all he can to fight the battle. Telegraph him today and impress your strong opinion that this is his best method.[1]

On 10 September, Brett received a letter from Somerset in Bad Homburg in which he asked his friend to help him smooth matters over so that he could return to England by 19 September. Somerset wrote that his mother, the Duchess of Beaufort (Georgiana Charlotte, née Curzon), then in her mid-sixties, wanted him to visit her at the family home, Badminton House, as she was 'very ill'. He added that he would be inspecting some horses for the Prince of Wales in Hanover and Berlin on the way back to England, and the plan was to meet with the prince in London on 21 September, as Bertie was passing through there en route to Denmark.

It seemed that for his royal duties at least, Somerset was carrying on as usual. But in the London gentlemen's clubs, gossip and innuendo about Somerset and others in relation to No. 19 Cleveland Street was already rife and ripening, and the massive press interest in the case had yet to begin. His wish to return to England also showed that Somerset still thought that he could brazen things out. He did indeed still have Bertie, the Prince of Wales' backing at this time.

But Brett's letter to Arthur Newton that very same day of 10 September revealed how hard he was trying to fix things for Somerset regarding the impending trial of Veck and Newlove and the potential jeopardy of his old friend's situation. 'At present my strong suspicion is that efforts should be concentrated upon the two men in custody, i.e. to simplify and shorten the inquiry and arrange for their fate on the lines of least hardship.' This is exactly the course that Newton took in protecting his client, Somerset.

Brett also commented that Hammond being on the run may not have been the best scenario, because it was drawing more attention to the case, but he was undecided: 'I am not at all sure that in the long run it would not have been better had he been in a similar position to the other two [Veck and Newlove].'

It's likely that Brett wrote this letter to Newton immediately after reading Somerset's latest to him, because he mentions Somerset's mother, whom he knew well: 'Were you acquainted with the mother of our friend ... you would feel that no stone ought to be left unturned to spare her any blow.' Brett additionally made his feelings about the scandal clear to Newton, writing, 'I confess I shall be glad when this odious affair is disposed of, and I have no doubt that you share the sentiment.'

Newton was busy contacting those involved and friends of the peer to contribute to Somerset's defence fund, which had already funded Veck's and Newlove's defence. Later, it would also become clear that Newton had paid substantial amounts of money to Charles Hammond in exile with Newton travelling abroad to meet the on-the-run pimp on Somerset's behalf to buy his silence.

And on 14 September, Brett wrote to Newton informing him that Hugh Weguelin had contributed a cheque for £1,200 to Somerset's war chest. This wasn't the high price of loyalty – Weguelin had good reason to have an expensive iron in the fire in case he got dragged into the scandal, facing potential prosecution and social ruin himself.

Hugh Weguelin attended Veck's and Newlove's trials, and he wrote to Brett immediately after seeing them convicted. It seems highly likely that Weguelin was in contact with Arthur Newton around the Old Bailey that day, and the letter reveals that Weguelin was privy to Newton's machinations – which are soon to be detailed in this story – in trying to get others into safe exile. It also shows that the stockbroker was concerned about any incriminating paper trail naming names, especially Weguelin's own, that Somerset may have left behind him:

> The whole thing was hustled through in half an hour. The younger [Newlove] got only four months and the elder [Veck] nine. Newton considers this very light. He wishes to get one or two out of the country but this he will see to. It is most important that your friend [Somerset] should tell the truth and say whether he has written any letters, as now the enemy is defeated is the time to get him. I do not think he will have any more trouble.[2]

Weguelin had no idea at this point that the name of a member of the royal family would enter the scandalous Cleveland Street fray, or that Somerset would remain news for some time to come.

Hugh Weguelin would never be prosecuted for his involvement, but as the writer Peter Jordaan has detailed,[3] both Weguelin and Reginald Brett were implicated in another homosexual scandal thirteen years later, in 1902. At the dawn of the Edwardian age, the Liberal politician Lord Battersea (Cyril Flower), formerly the MP for Luton, was arrested for homosexual offences in the same month as Edward VII's coronation, and those involved around His Lordship also faced exposure. The new king would save Lord Battersea and other highly placed members of society, including Brett (who had become Lord Esher three years previously on his father's death) and Weguelin.

It was a smaller affair than Cleveland Street, and hardly mentioned in the press, as King Edward (Bertie) had intervened and applied pressure to the Conservative Prime Minister Arthur Balfour to prevent it exploding, just as Bertie had leant on Lord Salisbury over the Cleveland

Street scandal in late 1889 to limit the damage to the royal family and aristocracy when he was the Prince of Wales. Two men were convicted of procuring boys and received lengthy sentences, far longer than any given out in the Cleveland Street scandal. Lord Battersea, Lord Esher (Brett), Hugh Weguelin and all the other compromised notables in the 1902 affair would never be arrested.

Another very prominent person spoken of in the gossip rounds of the clubs and high society, and increasingly around the newspaper offices of Fleet Street and regional press outlets that autumn of 1889 in relation to No. 19 Cleveland Street was the Earl of Euston. By that winter, his name would be at the very centre of the scandal.

Henry FitzRoy was 40 years old and the eldest son of Anna, the daughter of the Scottish landowner, India trader and Conservative MP James Balfour, and Augustus FitzRoy, the 7th Duke of Grafton, who had acceded to that title in 1882. Henry, as Earl of Euston, was heir to the dukedom.

One of the grandest titles in the English aristocracy, the dukedom was created in 1675 by King Charles II for one of his illegitimate sons. It is fourth in the hierarchy, or 'order of precedence', after the dukedoms of Norfolk, Somerset (no connection to Lord Arthur Somerset) and Richmond. Until the end of the nineteenth century, the family owned the large area of Fitzrovia in central London – coincidentally, where Cleveland Street is located. Euston Station, Fitzroy Square, the well-known Fitzroy Tavern pub and many other features of the area are named after the FitzRoy family.

Henry was born in Grosvenor Square, London, but the dukes of Grafton family seat of Euston Hall is far from London, in the village of Euston, Suffolk, which originally dates to 1666. The grounds and park were first designed by the writer John Evelyn in the late-seventeenth century and redesigned by the noted landscape architect William Kent in 1738, and the famed landscaper Capability Brown worked on the grounds forty years later. However, Henry grew up at another estate, gifted to the family of Charles II in the village of Passenham on the Northamptonshire and Buckinghamshire border.

Henry attended the exclusive Harrow School to the north of London as a boy and would increasingly spend time in the capital as he grew older. He became an ensign, the lowest commissioned rank, in the Rifle Brigade in October 1867. On 29 May 1871, aged 22, Henry married Kate Walsh Smythe in Worcester, although Henry first knew her as 'Kate Cooke', as she had assumed that surname from an abusive man she had lived with, who worked in the circus. As a girl, Kate had been an equestrian performer, and this is presumably how she met Mr Cooke. In June 1863, after leaving Cooke, she married George Manby Smith, a commercial traveller, in Glasgow, but he ran off after only a matter of months.

In 1864, when she was in her early twenties, Kate moved to London and lived in a brothel in Sutherland Street, Pimlico, managed by a Mrs White. According to the writer Barry Anthony, just hours after her arrival, Kate became 'indebted to Mrs. Rosalie Bernstein, a widow who supplied the six women in the house with fashionable clothing to be paid for in instalments or by grateful customers' and 'there was soon no shortage of admirers to escort Kate to nightspots such as the Argyle Rooms, Cremorne and the Holborn Casino'.[4]

But the relationship between Kate and Mrs Bernstein, who married a Prussian milliner called Charles Ochse in 1866, became very strained. Mr Ochse went to court to recover the sum of £665, which Kate had accumulated in debt to his wife. Following the trial, the newspapers reported on Kate Cooke and her disreputable life, expensive accessories and underwear as her garments were listed, but the judge found for Kate, as the money had been knowingly lent to Kate 'for the purpose of enabling a woman to carry on her avocation of a prostitute', as the *Cork Examiner* relayed.

Kate went on to be a musical hall artiste, performing at the Variety Theatre, her stage name remaining Kate Cooke. It was in this period that Henry FitzRoy met her. She was at least six years older than Henry, who was not yet the Earl of Euston but still quite a catch for Kate when they wed in 1871. The ceremony's witnesses were a representative of the church and a solicitor called Mr Froggett. Henry placed £10,000 in trust for Kate, but Froggett, who administered it, subsequently absconded with the money.

And the marriage didn't go well either. Henry and Kate continued living together intermittently and unhappily until 1875 and had no children before separating and breaking contact.

Henry took a post as a government official in Australia and didn't return to Britain until 1881. Kate was still officially his wife and Lady Euston, but Henry learned somehow that their union was bigamous. He sued for divorce to have the marriage annulled, and this finally came to court in April 1884, with Kate claiming that her husband had perished when his ship sank en route to Australia. This was proved to be untrue, as it was a different man with a similar name.

However, at huge cost, Henry had hired a private investigator to track down George Manby Smith, whom Kate was still seemingly married to by law. Manby Smith had moved to New Zealand and he was brought back to give evidence. It transpired that as Manby Smith had married his first wife bigamously, his second marriage to Kate in 1863 was therefore invalid, ergo her 1871 marriage to Henry was actually legitimate. Kate remained Lady Euston, living in Chelsea and dying in Fulham in 1903.

Henry became the Earl of Euston in 1882. He was a Freemason and the Provincial Grand Master of Northamptonshire and Huntingdonshire from 1887 and held this position at the time he was pulled into the Cleveland Street scandal two years later.

Henry Newlove had also mentioned a man named 'Colonel Jervois' as a frequent attendee at No. 19 Cleveland Street 'parties' to PC Hanks when he was arrested back in July. His name was, in fact, Robert Ellis Jervoise, and he was a lower-ranked captain in the 3rd Hampshire (Hants) Regiment, having been promoted from the rank of lieutenant in 1883.

Born on 28 June 1857 in Herriard, a village near Basingstoke in Hampshire, Jervoise was a 32-year-old bachelor at the time of the scandal. His family were extensive landowners, owning estates in

Hampshire, Buckinghamshire, Wiltshire, Nottinghamshire, Shropshire and Worcestershire. His father, Francis Jervoise Ellis-Jervoise, was the High Sheriff of Southampton, and his mother Mary was kept busy running several family mansions, including that in Herriard.

When he was 13, in 1871, Jervoise was a pupil living in Worthing, Sussex, and in 1876, he was admitted to Cambridge University for several terms to study a BA in Theology, although not attached to a college, with his family connections likely gaining him his place. In 1881, he was a boarder at the Bishop's Hostel in Drury Lane, Lincoln, and was still describing himself as a student of theology.

Jervoise, who spoke French, then made a drastic change of direction and was commissioned into the army as a lieutenant. But he wasn't a cadet at the Royal Military College and didn't pass through Staff College. Like many of his class then, his promotion to captain was because of his good education, not for any aptitude for professional soldiering. He received no decorations or awards.

Jervoise was based at Wellington Barracks in London when he first entered the army, but in 1889 he was headquartered in Winchester Barracks, the home of his regiment. He seems to have made frequent trips to London, including to No. 19 Cleveland Street. As well as being named by Henry Newlove, Jervoise would be among the list of the brothel's clients revealed by Hammond's 'secretary', Herbert Ames, in early 1891. Robert Jervoise would never be arrested.

Another name put forward to police by Henry Newlove as a visitor to the brothel was a man called Captain Barber, and he would later be named as 'Captain Barbey' by Hammond's 'secretary', Herbert Ames. His name was Barber and, like Robert Jervoise, he had inflated his military rank to those at No. 19 Cleveland Street, and probably more widely. But Barber was no longer in the army in 1889 and had been dismissed from it nine years previously.

Charles Montague Barber was born in 1846 in Great Wigston, Leicestershire. His father was 'a clerk in Holy Orders', an unordained administrative assistant who carried out tasks for the clergy. At age 15, in 1861, Charles was living at St John's Vicarage in Leicester, which was undoubtedly accommodation connected to his father's job.

Just over a decade later, after living for a time in Nether Hall, a large house in Keyham, near Leicester, Barber was in London. There, in Westminster, he married Anne from Newcastle, who was ten years his senior, on 18 December 1872. On the marriage certificate, Charles' occupation was entered as 'Gentleman'.

Charles and Anne's daughter Isabel was born on 21 August 1874. By this time, Charles had begun to make appearances in the *London Gazette*, the oldest newspaper in Britain, established in 1665 as an official journal of the Crown, listing events, military promotions and resignations, appointments and other less wholesome news. On 26 May 1874, it was reported that the business of wine merchants Barber & Jervis had been dissolved, naming Charles as a partner and informing readers that his business partner, Augustus Whitehall Parker-Jervis, was to carry on and assume all debts.

Fast-forwarding to 1 September 1874, a bankruptcy petition was recorded as being filed against 'Charles Montagu Barber, of No. 46 Argyll Square, in the County of Middlesex', which is in the King's Cross area, north of Fitzrovia in London – incidentally, not very far from Cleveland Street. The petition was filed by Arthur Wright of Hobart House, Leicester. Just over four years later, on 9 July 1878, the *London Gazette* announced Charles' change of occupational direction. He had enrolled as a volunteer in the army that June and was made a lieutenant in the Forfar & Kincardine, a British artillery unit based in Scotland.

Then, on 23 August 1880, the *Police Gazette* reported the following item:

Absconded, charged with fraud by worthless cheques on Vivian Bank, Torquay – Charles Montague Barber, 35 years of age, 5ft 7ins high, fair complexion, sunburnt, dark brown hair and moustache (full), stout build; dressed generally in grey tweed suit, and a Lieutenant in the Forfar and Kincardine Militia, Montrose. Warrant issued. Information to the Director, CID, Great Scotland Yard SW, Metropolitan Police, August 18.

No record could be found of Charles' apprehension or prosecution, but on 15 October 1880, the *London Gazette* had, 'Forfar and Kincardine. The services of Lt. Charles Montague Barber are dispensed with'.

In a statement to police, the rent boy John Saul would say that a 'Captain Le Barber' used to visit No. 19 Cleveland Street and 'bring boys down with him ... He used to get the boys situations in the Post Office service.' Saul was almost certainly referring to Charles Montague Barber, but there is no other recorded police corroboration or confirmation of these allegations. Barber may have been a procurer, though, and could possibly have had connections in the GPO to put forward working-class boys for employment there, but this cannot be definitively verified. He was at the least, however, a client at the brothel.

Charles Montague Barber would never be arrested in connection with No. 19 Cleveland Street.

As well as Weguelin, Jervoise and Barber, George Veck's 'Private Secretary', George Barber (no relation to Charles Montague Barber), spoke of a man called Mr E.G. Ripley frequenting No. 19 Cleveland Street, claiming that Ripley had introduced him to the brothel, and presumably Veck, in the first place. At first, the DPP office certainly thought that this Mr Ripley should have been prosecuted alongside Veck and Charles Hammond.

In his 1976 book on the scandal, the writer H. Montgomery Hyde couldn't definitively identify Ripley, as there is no other documented mention of him, apart from passing ones in DPP reports showing that he was of interest. But Hyde briefly hazarded that it may have been George Ripley, one of the sons of Sir Henry Ripley, a Yorkshireman. This is likely to have been the case.

George Ripley was born on 31 March 1845 in Halifax, Yorkshire. His father Henry was the principal partner of Edward Ripley & Son, a highly successful dyeing and finishing business set up by Henry's grandfather in 1806, which thrived when Henry's father Edward invented a better system of dyeing than the ones in common use at that time. So profitable was this business that between 1866 and 1881, Henry Ripley built Ripley Ville, a model village in Broomfields, Bradford, which provided housing for the company's workers, along with a church and school.

Henry was also a politician: a Liberal MP between 1868 and 1869, and again from 1874 to 1880. But when he switched to the Conservative Party to fight the 1880 general election, he was defeated and was given the hereditary title of 1st Baronet Ripley in May of that year. Sir Henry died in 1882. Henry had engaged an architect to design a family mansion home, the fifty-two-roomed Bedstone Court in Shropshire. Construction began in the year Henry died and was completed in 1884.

George was Henry's second son, after Edward, who was born in 1840. Edward became a lawyer in 1870 and inherited the title of baronet, taking over the family business and later becoming a Justice of the Peace (JP) like his father, and then High Sheriff of Shropshire in 1891.

A year after George's birth, his younger brother Frederick arrived in 1846. Frederick was independently made a baronet in 1897, with no connection to his late father's title. His private correspondence reveals that Frederick was extremely well connected, exchanging letters with many of the leading political figures of the day, including Lord Salisbury, the Conservative prime minister.

George had three other brothers and two sisters. In 1851, George was living with his family in Hipperholme-cum-Brighouse, Yorkshire, and ten years later, aged 16, as a scholar in Cheltenham, Gloucestershire. According to the Cheltenham College Register, George entered the elite private school in 1857. His elder brother Edward and younger siblings Frederick and Henry (the 3rd baronet on Edward's death, as George predeceased him) also attended there.

Truly, little can be gleaned about George's life, except that he was a bachelor, had no children and doesn't seem to have distinguished himself in his career in the way his closest brothers Edward and Frederick did. No occupation can be found for him, which probably means that he was living on a private family income. In 1884, George was living in a furnished room at No. 65 Albany Street, off the Marylebone Road in central London, paying a rent of 14s weekly.

On 17 July 1889, less than two weeks after he had fled No. 19 Cleveland Street and England, Hammond wrote to his wife Caroline from Paris, mentioning that he had written to 'Mr. Ripley', asking him if he could find out anything for him about the progress of the investigation. Ripley's reply has never been located if he did answer Hammond, and this is the only other tantalising referral to Ripley anywhere in relation to the scandal, aside from those in several DPP reports.

In 1893, four years after the Cleveland Street scandal erupted, George was living in a late-Georgian terraced townhouse at No. 39 Paultons Square off the King's Road in Chelsea. He rented two furnished rooms on the first floor at 'over 21 shillings a week',[5] a much more modest rent than Hugh Weguelin was paying around this time. Aged 47, Ripley only had two more years to live and was by then living three doors down in the same square.

George Ripley was never arrested over the Cleveland Street case.

The late-Victorian London homosexual scene, which drew men such as Lord Arthur Somerset, the Earl of Euston, Hugh Weguelin, Captain Robert Jervoise, Charles Montague Barber, George Ripley and very likely Reginald Brett to No. 19 Cleveland Street, was a thriving subculture. A male prostitute was known as a 'Mary-Ann', and they used calling cards to introduce themselves. There were hundreds, possibly thousands, working in the capital at that time. And there was no shortage of clients, many of them outwardly respectable, married or of 'confirmed bachelor' status and highly placed in society, their homosexuality or bisexuality usually a necessarily taboo secret.

In the autumn of 1889, when Somerset's boss and close friend, the heterosexually serially adulterous Bertie, Prince of Wales, was told of the allegations against Somerset, the prince was incredulous, and it took him a good while to accept that it was true. It was socially shocking and untenable for a man such as Somerset, or in fact men of much lower public standing, to admit their true sexuality and the 1885 Criminal Law Amendment Act had created much greater jeopardy by introducing the crime of 'gross indecency' into law, which did not require proof of intercourse to secure a conviction.

John Saul, who had already been interviewed by Abberline in connection with No. 19 Cleveland Street and had lived there for a time providing services, would soon make a sensational appearance in court as the scandal unfolded further. Saul was a self-professed 'Mary-Ann' and a 'professional sodomite' of some years' standing. Saul would even say that Charles Hammond was a 'sodomite', the only time during the scandal that the evasive married pimp Hammond was accused of having sexual relations with other men – his clients.

Saul had, in fact, published a book anonymously about life as a male prostitute in 1881, titled *The Sins of the Cities of the Plain*. The late-Victorian pornography publisher William Lazenby produced 250 copies. Lazenby was prosecuted that year for his offerings, as he had been a decade earlier, and would later consequently operate mainly from Paris.

Since the passing of the Obscene Publications Act of 1857, many publishers of what was considered pornography had been taken to court, including those who had outraged Victorian morals with a progressive outlook. Most famously, Annie Besant and the atheist Charles Bradlaugh, later elected as a Liberal MP and founder of the National Secular Society, went on trial in 1877 for publishing *Fruits of Philosophy: or the Private Companion of Young Married People* through their new imprint, the Freethought Publishing Company. It was a book by an American doctor which encouraged sex education and promoted birth control. As the writer Michael Meyer has highlighted, Queen Victoria despised Bradlaugh, calling him 'immoral' and 'repulsive looking'.[6]

But it was Annie Besant, as a woman, noted social reformer and socialist, who attracted most of the morally outraged headlines. They were found guilty but released on appeal and eventually escaped punishment on a legal technicality.

Bradlaugh was later imprisoned, however, for trying to affirm his election as MP for Northampton in 1880 as an atheist, rather than taking the oath on the Bible. On his release he was heavily fined for voting illegally, finally taking the oath in 1886 but still risking further prosecution. Bradlaugh was instrumental in the passing of the Oaths Act of

1888, which allowed Members of Parliament to be affirmed rather than sworn to God. (Twenty-one-year-old Mohandas Ghandhi, the future Mahātmā Ghandi, then training to be a lawyer in London, would attend Bradlaugh's funeral in January 1891.)

But Saul's *The Sins of the Cities of the Plain*, four years later, was about as outrageous as it got in Victorian publishing and therefore very much underground. Oscar Wilde was reportedly an avid reader of it. According to H. Montgomery Hyde in his book *The History of Pornography*, Wilde was provided with his copy of it, along with other, in the terms of the time, 'Socratic' literature, in 1890 by the French bookseller Charles Hirsch. Hirsch, then aged 30, ran Librairie Parisienne, a bookshop of good repute, mainly selling French texts on the surface but also pricey porn by special appointment in Coventry Street, between Piccadilly Circus and Leicester Square in London's West End.

Saul's book, which is a novel, but obviously drawn from fact, described the male prostitution scene and how they operated – walking around the West End, peering into shop windows and then sneaking a look around them, trying to attract well-heeled clients with their youthful male beauty and well-dressed and often flamboyantly suited and buttonholed attire. Male prostitutes were usually working class, like Saul, who was born extremely poor in Dublin, but sometimes middle class.

Saul also focused on the activities of two men of a higher class named Thomas Boulton and Frederick Park, also known as 'Fanny and Stella', who went a stage further and dressed as women to procure their clientele. Saul called them 'Laura and Selina'. The real Boulton and Park took part in many theatrical performances dressed as women and had appeared on stage in the late 1860s with Lord Arthur Clinton, a Liberal Party MP (he represented Newark from 1865 until 1868). Boulton was also Clinton's lover and often referred to himself as 'Lady Arthur Clinton'.

But in 1870, Boulton and Park's indiscretions when picking up men had caught the attention of the Metropolitan Police, although they may not have asked for payment, so there is no proof that they were true male prostitutes. They were put under surveillance and both arrested in full feminine garb outside the Strand Theatre in Aldwych in the West End, in the company of two men. As the author Neil McKenna relayed, they were charged with 'feloniously committing and conspiring to commit the act of buggery' and by dressing as women and 'frequenting places of public resort, so disguised, and to thereby openly and scandalously outrage public decency and corrupt public morals'.[7]

The case was heavily reported in the press, but Bolton and Park were both acquitted in court in May 1871, partly due to the police having seized compromising letters written by the two men without a warrant. They had also been intimately searched without their consent, with the police surgeon who made the examinations concluding that he had found evidence of 'unnatural offences' not supported by two other medical witnesses.

But, as the writer and historian Donald Thomas wrote, 'The 1870s were the last decade of comparative innocence before the advent of psychopathology in the 1880s.'[8] The growing belief in psychopathology – the study of which focused on deviance, distress, dysfunction and danger – meant that many came to believe that homosexuality was deviant and then a mental disorder. A good illustration of this was the influential 'A Case of Sexual Perversion in a Man' by George Savage, published in the respected *Journal of Mental Science* in 1884.

Boulton and Park were charged under the Offences Against the Person Act of 1861, which updated the act of the same name passed in 1828, which had in turn replaced the Buggery Act of 1533, passed into legislature during the reign of King Henry VIII. The 1828 Act was used to obtain the death sentences for the crime of sodomy on James Pratt and John Smith, the last men to be hanged for the offence in 1835, fifty-four years before the Cleveland Street scandal.

The 1861 Act removed the threat of capital punishment in the prosecution of those accused of homosexual acts and this was the law that these acts were prosecuted under until the Criminal Law Amendment Act of 1885. And as the criminal legal historian Leon Radzinowicz underlined, conviction statistics for homosexual offences in 1856, fifteen years before Boulton and Park faced trial, thirty-three years before the Cleveland Street Scandal and prior to the passing of both the 1861 Offences Against the Person Act and the 1885 Criminal Law Amendment Act, were low.[9]

Just 28 per cent of those accused of these crimes in 1856 were successfully prosecuted, compared with a 77 per cent conviction rate when all other offences are taken together. By 1889, these actions deemed 'unnatural offences' or 'gross indecency' were still difficult to prosecute. But Section 11 of the 1885 Criminal Amendment Act had made it easier to do so, and professional rent boy services were thriving in the capital then.

The West End of London, which was largely created as an entity between the 1860s and the time of the Cleveland Street scandal in 1889–90, was where most male prostitutes worked and sought clientele. And male brothels sprang up to entertain clients with money, just as 'molly-houses' or 'molly-clubs' had once been used as rendezvous spots for homosexual men in the Georgian and early Victorian periods. But clients were often procured on major thoroughfares, as Jack Saul described.

And as the academic Matthew David Cook has highlighted,[10] the construction of Charing Cross Road, Shaftesbury Avenue and Piccadilly Circus in those thirty years before 1889 provided those thoroughfares and genteel central London shopping streets, restaurants and theatres. It was very possible for middle- and upper-class men to meet other men for sex clandestinely in the East End and in the city's parks, but the new brightly street-lamped West End was less intimidating and dangerous. And an elegantly furnished townhouse like that at No. 19 Cleveland Street, just to the north of Charing Cross Road, must have been very welcoming.

Eight

The first coverage of the scandal by the press in mid-September 1889 was a real blow to Somerset, and he wrote to Reginald Brett, exclaiming, 'What a curse the press is!' At this stage, brief pieces had only appeared in the *Pall Mall Gazette*, the *Times* and the *Star*, but there would soon be extensive media, and therefore public attention, to Somerset's deepening alarm.

Somerset had a very long way to fall from his place in Britain's social firmament, particularly due to his closeness to Bertie, the Prince of Wales, Queen Victoria's eldest son and the second eldest of her five children by Prince Albert, who had died almost three decades before, in 1861. Queen Victoria and her subjects had celebrated her Golden Jubilee just over two years earlier in June 1887, and that grand event symbolises just how ubiquitous the queen and royal family were in late-Victorian British society.

For her Golden Jubilee, on 20 June 1887, Queen Victoria hosted a lavish banquet at Buckingham Palace with over fifty kings and princes invited, as well as the governing politicians of many countries. The American writer Mark Twain, over in Europe on one of his many visits, described the main procession through central London on 21 June as 'stretched to the limit of sight in both directions'.

It was a huge, colourful and vastly expensive affair, the very best of Britain's pageantry and the very height of the small kingdom's globally tentacled domination on vivid ceremonial display. The following day, Queen Victoria hosted a party for almost 30,000 schoolchildren in Hyde Park. And there were many other balls and parties up and down Britain, as well as in British territories and colonies abroad. The celebrations in India, for example, had taken place months earlier in February, to avoid the oppressive summer heat there, with Lord Dufferin, the Viceroy of India, writing to Sir Henry Ponsonby, the Queen's Private Secretary, that all 'the ladies of Calcutta are ordering Jubilee bustles'.

It was an extravagant display of soft power on the face of it, but there was a great deal of hard power behind the scenes. Queen Victoria wielded enormous influence over her governments, and the events of late 1889 and early 1890 would show that her heir, the pleasure-loving and clubbable Edward 'Bertie', the Prince of Wales, was a formidably big wheel who could also pull levers in Lord Salisbury's Conservative government. As the monarch was truly the apex of power atop the rigid social class system (the very structure on which the British Empire was built), and with the royal family possessing enormous political and social influence, Somerset, through Bertie, was extremely well connected, being very much part of the royal inner circle.

In the autumn of 1889, Bertie was 47 years old, and by tradition for the eldest son had been the Prince of Wales since birth. He was home-tutored under his father, Prince Albert's guidance, studying for six hours daily at the age of 7. Bertie had an isolated childhood and was punished for underachievement in Albert's strict regimen. According to Prince Albert's biographer, Denis Judd, 'The Queen and Prince Albert had a low opinion of his [Bertie's] intelligence, and his mother openly preferred his elder sister, the precocious Vicky. It was not so much that Edward lacked intelligence, but rather that he lacked intellectual tastes.'[1]

Bertie went on a royal tour to Rome, and spent spells at Edinburgh, Oxford and Cambridge universities, but was never very academically adept. In fact, Bertie wanted a career in the army and to earn a commission, but was only allowed by Queen Victoria to take the honorary high rank of colonel. Bertie was never to see any active service, and this may well have been why he so admired soldiers such as Lord Arthur Somerset, who had fought in real battles.

In March 1863 when he was 21, Bertie married the 18-year-old Princess Alexandra of Denmark, a match arranged by his mother. Their ostentatious wedding was reported at length in the *New York Times* of 26 March of that year, opening with:

> Yesterday, the marriage ceremony in which the English nation feels so deep an interest was performed with fitting pomp and solemnity at Windsor. The fair Princess, who landed on Saturday morning a stranger to the people, their habits and modes of thought, is now a member of our State, the partner for life of the heir apparent to the throne.

The royal couple would go on to have three sons and two daughters. The eldest son, Prince Albert Victor, known as 'Eddy', would become enmeshed in the Cleveland Street scandal. The younger son would become the future George V.

By the late 1860s, Bertie's public image was that of a man of leisure – and soon that of a playboy prince. This was justified, as detailed by the noted genealogist and writer Anthony Camp, who estimated that Bertie had more than fifty-five extramarital affairs over the years. These included liaisons with many notable women, including Lady Brooke, Lady Susan Vane Tempest and Lady Mordaunt, as well as Lady Churchill, Winston's mother. And most famously, the heir to the throne had hook-ups with the widely known stage actresses Lillie Langtry and Sarah Bernhardt.[2]

Bertie's lifestyle displeased Queen Victoria a great deal. He was nothing like his disciplined father, whom Victoria, in lifelong mourning after his early death, idealised and worshipped. Writing to her eldest and favourite child, also named Victoria and known as Vicky, Queen Victoria wrote of Bertie, 'I never can, or shall, look at him without a shudder.'

This was at least partly because Prince Albert had reproached but forgiven Bertie about an affair with a young actress, Nellie Clifden, which took his virginity when Bertie was 19 and before he was married. Albert personally made a special trip to Cambridge University to do so. He died of typhoid fever after catching a chill just a fortnight later, aged 42. It is believed that Victoria blamed Bertie for contributing to Albert's death because he was so disappointed and disgusted with his son's behaviour and the trip had weakened his health. (Albert had, in fact, been showing signs of serious illness, possibly stomach cancer, for almost two and a half years.)

The meeting between Bertie and Nellie Clifden was engineered by Charles Carrington, later Lord Carrington, who would be Bertie's lifelong friend, and at the time of the Cleveland Street scandal was the Governor of New South Wales in Australia. On 2 January 1890, when the scandal was in full swing, Bertie would write to Carrington, revealing that he had washed his delicate hands of Lord Arthur Somerset (whom he refers to as 'AS'), who just a few months previously had been his trusted confidant and friend: 'I hardly like to allude any more to the subject of AS it is really a too painful one to write about, and his subsequent conduct makes me wish that he had never existed.'

In 1869, Bertie was called as a witness in the divorce of Sir Charles Mordaunt, a Conservative MP who had just stepped down, and Harriet (née Moncrieffe). Mordaunt even made a veiled threat to name Bertie as a co-respondent, although this was never carried through. But having her eldest son and heir's name attached to such scandal even as a witness must have horrified Queen Victoria, especially as the married Bertie had to admit in court to 'visiting' Lady Mordaunt. Harriet had taken a string of lovers, including Bertie, and had an illegitimate daughter with Viscount Cole, another Conservative MP. The divorce wasn't granted until 1875, at Mordaunt's second attempt, and Harriet spent the rest of her days in lunatic asylums.

In 1871, Bertie had a bout of typhoid fever, the same illness that had caused his father's early death, but recovered. He also began to show enlightened views about race for a man of his time and position in the British Empire, writing to his mother during his tour of India in 1875, 'Because a man has a black face and a different religion from our own, there is no reason why he should be treated as a brute'.

After their marriage in 1863, Bertie and Princess Alexandra lived at Marlborough House, next to St James's Palace, which had been specially enlarged and refurbished for them. By the time of the Cleveland Street scandal in 1889, the wide yet exclusive pleasure-seeking social circle around Bertie had been known as the 'Marlborough House Set' for over a decade. This moniker had been largely created by Bertie setting up the Marlborough Club, in response to his favourite club, White's, the oldest in London, having banned smoking on its premises.

The Marlborough Club's first membership of 400 men was personally chosen by Bertie. Caricatures drawn by Carlo Pellegrini accessed at the Royal Collection Trust show that they included his younger brother, Prince Alfred; Prince Victor, Count Gleichen, a naval officer and sculptor; Edward Bootle-Wilbraham, 1st Earl of Lathom, a Conservative politician, who was Lord Chamberlain of the Household, the most senior officer of the British Royal Household under Lord Salisbury in 1885–86; Lord William Godolphin Osborne, son of the 1st Baron Godolphin; Alexander Temple-Fitzmaurice, son of the 5th Earl of Orkney; Oliver George Paulet Montagu, later a colonel in the army, who served in the Egyptian campaign; Captain Batchelor, who served in the Indian Army; Percy William Doyle, a diplomat; Sir James Mackenzie, a noted Scottish doctor and cardiologist; Christopher Sykes, a Conservative MP; and Sir Hugh Charles Clifford, a British colonial official in Malaya and writer.

Other early members were Henry Petre, one of the founders in 1840 of the city of Christchurch in New Zealand; Alexander Duff, the 1st Duke of Fife, who would go on to marry Bertie and Princess Alexandra's daughter Louisa in 1889; Henry Chaplin, 1st Viscount Chaplin, a major British landowner and Conservative MP; John Delacour, formerly known as John de Burgh, a soldier; Algernon Bertram Freeman-Mitford, a diplomat and writer; Captain William Archer Amherst, the 3rd Earl Amherst, a British politician who had served in the Coldstream Guards in the Crimean War and a noted Freemason; and Edward Hyde-Villers, a British Liberal/Unionist politician, who would serve as Lord Chamberlain of the Household as Bertie acceded to the throne as King Edward VII.

Lord Arthur Somerset was also a member, and Somerset's 'friend' Algernon Allies was a waiter and was fired from the Marlborough Club in the late 1880s. The scene was all set for the further unfolding of the Cleveland Street scandal.

Meanwhile, Somerset's artful lawyer and fixer, Arthur Newton, was working hard on his behalf behind the scenes during that September of 1889. He placed a powder keg of revelatory rumour in society circles, lighting a fuse he knew would ripple out through clubland, spreading whispers through the cigar smoke.

The authorities soon discovered the hearsay, and a letter from the Assistant DPP, Hamilton Cuffe to the DPP, Sir Augustus Stephenson, written on 16 September, the same day Veck and Newlove were convicted, explained it all: 'I am told that Newton has boasted that if we go on a very distinguished person will be involved (PAV).' The initials referred to Prince Albert Victor, Bertie's eldest son, known as 'Eddy' and second in line to the throne after his father.

Somerset knew Eddy very well. Newton was obviously insinuating in a not-so-veiled threat that the prince was implicated in the Cleveland Street scandal, presumably that His Royal Highness had attended the brothel. In the same letter, Cuffe showed his wariness of the manipulative Newton and suggested that such a claim could be extremely damaging, whether true or not, writing, 'I don't mean to say that I for one instant credit it, but in such circumstances as this one never knows what may be said, be concocted, or be true'. Newton's ruse was having an effect.

Born two months prematurely on 8 January 1864, Eddy was named Prince Albert Victor at his grandmother Queen Victoria's insistence, in honour of her husband Prince Albert and herself. Eddy struggled with his studies under a private tutor, Reverend John Neale Dalton, an author who was also Queen Victoria's chaplain, and may have had learning difficulties. Eddy's health was also always fragile.

Eddy studied alongside his brother George (later King George V), who was born a year after him, and they did naval training together as cadets. Beginning in September 1879, this included three years serving as midshipmen on HMS *Bacchante*, an 'ironclad' or steam-propelled warship, which had been launched in 1876. Their tutor, Reverend Dalton, was on board with them and they travelled widely in the West

Indies, Mediterranean, Australia, China, Japan, South America and South Africa.

Eddy attended Cambridge University, but like any member of the royal family or aristocracy then, didn't have to take any examinations. Eddy was made an honorary Doctor of Law in 1888; this is usually awarded to those making a significant published contribution to the subject.

Eddy was also known in the military as 'Collar and Cuffs' after entering the 10th Hussars cavalry regiment as a gazette officer (announced in the *London Gazette*) in 1886. The nickname came from the fact that Eddy, who had an exceptionally long neck and arms, needed to have his collars and cuffs enlarged. Eddy passed his army exams and was promoted to the rank of captain in March 1887 and fulfilled some public engagements, including making two royal visits abroad.

Eddy was 25 in late 1889. The cunning Newton was also very aware that when the press got hold of this revelation there would be a frenzy, even if no publication dared to name Eddy. Gossip and innuendo of a sexually taboo nature alluding to a prominent member of the royal family would be enough to light the tinderbox. Newton's aim was to deflect attention from Somerset and prevent or delay his arrest by kindling the authorities' fear, under pressure from the royal family, that the prince would be publicly implicated.

None of the telegraph messenger rent boys named Eddy as a visitor to No. 19 Cleveland Street and there is no definitive proof that he ever went there. And as the writer H. Montgomery Hyde pointed out fifty years ago, 'There is no evidence that he was homosexual, or even bisexual'. Then, as now, Eddy's presence at the brothel cannot be proven.

Although, decades later in the 1950s, King George VI's biographer Harold Nicolson would privately tell Lord Chief Justice Rayner Goddard that Prince Albert Victor had been 'involved in a male brothel scene', whether Eddy was involved in that world or not is highly speculative, and largely immaterial with no direct evidence. But as Newton calculated, the mention of Eddy's name in relation to the scandal and his alleged involvement in it would stick in the minds of many at the time and elevate the scandal to an entirely new level.

Lord Arthur Somerset would certainly never come out publicly in Eddy's defence, as he would have to admit that he had been to No. 19 Cleveland Street himself. Somerset's own correspondence to Reginald Brett over the coming weeks, although not accusing Eddy of going to the brothel, would do little to privately quash the insipid rumour either. It was in Somerset's interest not to do so, as he knew that the speculation about Eddy spread by Newton would deeply unsettle senior members of the royal family and provide him with a trusty if perhaps only temporary protective shield.

On 28 September, the scandal made its first appearance in the radical and progressive newspaper, the *North London Press*, founded just months before by its editor Ernest Parke, who would go on to play an integral role in exposing the scandal publicly, and because of this, became a central figure in the drama himself. The headline in the fledgling paper was 'Shield the Principal Criminals'. In his editorial, Parke went on to outline his indignation, which, as an experienced journalist on other publications, he knew would be lapped up by his relatively small and largely working-class readership: 'We only want to know 1) why Hammond was permitted to escape 2) why his high-born patrons, who have been identified to police by witnesses in the case, were not in the dock with their wretched panders Veck and Newlove.' (The word 'pander' is today used as a verb meaning to gratify a distasteful or immoral desire, but at the time it was in use as a noun, meaning a pimp or procurer.)

Parke went on to issue a threat to name 'the heir of a duke [the Earl of Euston], the younger son of another duke [Somerset] and an officer holding command in the Southern district [Robert Jervoise?], who we may at once say, is not General Maitland'.

The latter could refer to General Charles Lennox Brownlow Maitland, then in his mid-60s, who had been promoted to the rank of full general in 1884, while commander of the Wiltshire Regiment, based in the south of England. He retired in 1886. As a younger man, he had played first-class cricket, been a mourner at the Duke of Wellington's funeral and been severely injured at the Battle of Inkerman in 1854, during the Crimean War. Maitland didn't have long to live in late 1889, dying in January 1891.

If a man as illustrious as Maitland was being gossiped about, it shows how the broiling rumour mill was already simmering to a high heat, even if General Maitland's involvement in the scandal was swiftly debunked by Parke. Hammond's 'secretary' Herbert Ames would later independently name a 'Dr Maitland' as a visitor to No. 19 Cleveland Street.

And the following day, the popular Sunday *Reynolds's News* was reporting on the story. It informed readers of 'Charges of Abominable Crimes against Peers and Officers', with the sub-headlines, 'Confessions of the Alleged Paramours', 'The Heir of a Duke Implicated' and 'The Inaction of the Police'. The 'paramours' were the telegraph messenger rent boys, the 'heir' was the Earl of Euston, the eldest son of the Duke of Grafton, and the criticism of the police, which would be repeated soon in other publications, would infuriate the Metropolitan Police Commissioner James Monro and undoubtedly, Inspector Abberline.

On 7 October, the Lord Chancellor Lord Halsbury, himself the son of the first editor of *The Standard* (later known as the *London Evening Standard*), gave his opinion on the Cleveland Street case, placing special emphasis on his reaction to the first press reports. He wrote:

> If, as alleged in these papers, the social position of some of the parties will make a great sensation, this will give very wide publicity and consequently will spread very extensively matter of the most revolting and mischievous kind, the spread of which I am satisfied will produce enormous evil.

Eddy's name had yet to be alluded to in the press, but Lord Halsbury would surely have heard the rumour connecting the prince to the scandal by that date. This would have been a key factor in the Lord Chancellor's fears, as the ultra-hierarchical fabric of Victorian society, from the royal family downwards, would be severely jolted by such a socially stigmatising revelation.

But there had been significant disagreement behind the scenes as those in power in the British government struggled with how to proceed against Lord Arthur Somerset. Back on 15 September, the day before Veck and Newlove went on trial, the DPP, Sir Augustus Stephenson wrote a long memo to the Attorney General, Sir Richard Webster. Stephenson, his tone almost desperate, referred to 'the responsibility from which you cannot relieve me, nor can I relieve myself', and was firm in his belief that Somerset, who he referred to as 'LAS', should be prosecuted. 'In my opinion there is at present direct legal and overwhelming moral evidence against LAS for conspiracy to procure [Algernon Allies]', and 'the moral effect leaves no reasonable doubt that LAS was a frequent visitor at 19 Cleveland Street for immoral purposes'.

Stephenson was fully aware of the ramifications of prosecuting Somerset, but this didn't deter him:

> The public scandal involved in a criminal charge against a man in his position in society is undoubted, but in my opinion the public scandal in declining to prefer such a charge and permitting such a man to hold Her Majesty's Commission and to remain in English Society is much greater.

Stephenson also took the opposite view to Lord Halsbury about the dangers of the press coverage in the scandal, writing, 'In my opinion, the attempt to avoid such publicity, even if such attempt was justifiable which in my opinion it is not, must absolutely fail, and the public scandal will then be infinitely aggravated.'

And Stephenson clearly highlighted that he felt a legal and moral duty to protect the working-class GPO telegraph messenger boys, who had fallen prey to Hammond, Veck and aristocratic men such as Somerset:

> The circumstances of this case demand the intervention of those whose duty it is to enforce the law and protect the children of respectable parents taken into the service of the public, as these unfortunate

boys have been, from being made the victims of the unnatural lusts of full-grown men, and no consideration of public scandal owing to the position in society or sympathy with the family of the offender should militate against this paramount duty.

Stephenson's memo was given to his deputy, Hamilton Cuffe, to pass to Webster.

Significantly, the day after Stephenson penned his memo to Webster and Cuffe received it to deliver, Cuffe warned Stephenson of the rumour of Eddy's involvement in the scandal being spread by Arthur Newton. To his credit, although startled, Stephenson didn't back off and again instructed Cuffe to send his memo to the Attorney General. In his reply to Cuffe, the DPP additionally outlined his thoughts about Arthur Newton, calling Somerset's lawyer 'a dangerous man', who 'may, or his clients may make, utterly false accusations against others'.

After receiving and reading Stephenson's strong opinion on the escalating matter, Sir Richard Webster agreed with him and put this argument forward to the Home Secretary, Sir Henry Matthews, who, having been against action being taken against Somerset previously, changed his position. Matthews replied to Webster that his thinking was now in line with his, but he had to 'communicate with Lord Salisbury' regarding the situation. And Matthews promptly did just this, but shrewdly qualified his about-turn of opinion, writing to the prime minister on 17 September:

> Fresh evidence has come to the hands of the Director of Public Prosecutions against Lord Arthur Somerset [...] Although I do not take quite so strong a view of the new evidence [the identification of Somerset by the telegraph messenger rent boys and Somerset's postal orders sent to Algernon Allies] I think it is sufficiently cogent to make it impossible to interfere with the ordinary course of the law [...] I have requested the Attorney General to delay if possible until I or he receive a reply from you. The first step would be to give notice of the charge to the military authorities. The next to apply for a summons or warrant. I am informed that Lord Arthur Somerset had gone abroad,

and, if so, proceedings will be suspended until his return. It is a hateful business; but upon the whole the risk of interference with this charge is greater than the mischief it will do.³

Lord Salisbury instructed that the case and new evidence should be passed to Lord Halsbury, the Lord Chancellor, who was then grouse shooting in Braemar, Scotland. Finally, on 7 October, Lord Halsbury, in line with his previous memo, would give his opinion that the prosecution of Somerset, and presumably other clients of the brothel, shouldn't proceed, due to the enormous damage the publicity would do.

Lord Salisbury, also known as the Marquis of Salisbury, was in the middle of his second administration at the time of the Cleveland Street scandal, having returned as prime minister in July 1886, after leading the country from June 1885 until January 1886 in his first term in office. In this second term, Lord Salisbury's government didn't have a Conservative majority, but shared power in an election-winning alliance with the Liberal Unionists. His Chancellor of the Exchequer from 1887 until 1892 was George Goschen, from that party.

As he was also the Foreign Secretary, Lord Salisbury had a heavy workload, especially in dealing with threats to trade routes going through the Suez Canal in 1887 and strengthening the Royal Navy by increasing its budget in 1889. His Home Secretary, Sir Henry Matthews, also had considerable domestic tasks in this period, which the prime minister had to oversee.

Born Robert Gascoyne-Cecil in 1830, Lord Salisbury was almost 60 in 1889 and was the 3rd Marquis of Salisbury. One of six children from his father James' first marriage, Cecil's sister, Lady Blanche, was the mother of Arthur Balfour, who would become Conservative Prime Minister in 1902, taking over from his Uncle Lord Salisbury, who stepped down from his third term in office due to ill health. Balfour had served in Lord Salisbury's government and it is said that the popular phrase 'Bob's your uncle' originally stems from this act of perceived nepotism.

Cecil went to Eton but left early after being tormented by bullies and attended Oxford University where, like Eddy at Cambridge University, as an aristocrat he wasn't required to take exams. He was awarded only a fourth-class degree in mathematics because of illness, although he was heavily involved in the Oxford Union, famous as a debating society, which pointed to his future as a statesman. He entered the House of Commons in 1853 as MP for Stamford in Lincolnshire, when still in his early twenties.

Cecil came from a major landowning family. The family home was the palatial Hatfield House in Hertfordshire, where the young Queen Elizabeth I had lived in the original palace on the site before it was partially pulled down and rebuilt by Robert Cecil, the 1st Earl of Salisbury. The earl, the future Victorian prime minister's namesake, served as Secretary of State under King James I, was instrumental in uncovering the gunpowder plot in 1605, and was a very powerful figure as England transitioned from the Tudor to the Stuart periods.

But two and a half centuries later, the 3rd Marquis Robert Cecil was largely cut off from his family's money in 1857 when he married Georgina Alderson against his father's wishes. They would go on to have a long marriage (Georgina died in 1903) and eight children. He became Lord Salisbury, 3rd Marquis of Salisbury, on his father's death in 1868.

Lord Salisbury was very tall at 6ft 4in (1.93m) and gained a great deal of weight to his heavy frame in later years. With his bushy beard, he was a commanding physical presence and had a quick and biting tongue, which could be stinging to those on the receiving end. Queen Victoria considered Lord Salisbury her favourite prime minister of her long reign, and he served her three times. He was a discreet operator, a conservative by nature with a small 'c' as well as the politically capital 'C', and a forthright protector of Britain's vested interests, of which as monarch she was the beacon and talisman of the empire. She offered to make him a duke in 1886, but he rejected the offer, reasoning that he preferred to remain a marquis, as dukes were expected to sustain a very expensive lifestyle.

Would Lord Salisbury allow an arrest warrant for Lord Arthur Somerset, the Prince of Wales' assistant equerry, to be issued, especially now that Eddy, Bertie's son and Queen Victoria's grandson, was potentially going to be dragged into the scandal publicly?

As the historian Andrew Roberts wrote in his authorised biography of Lord Salisbury:

> Protecting the Royal Family from embarrassment, whether it be political in Berlin, financial over the Royal Grants, sexual over disappointed mistresses, or even highly tangential, as over the Cleveland Street scandal, Salisbury simply saw as part of the duties of the premiership, and he carried them out impeccably.[4]

If an arrest warrant were granted, there would very soon be the perfect opportunity for Abberline to take Somerset into custody. Six days after Stephenson wrote his plea to Webster and five days after Veck and Newlove were convicted, Somerset reappeared on English soil.

Somerset had previously told Reginald Brett in a letter of his plan to meet Bertie back in London, and on 21 September, the peer and the prince came together at Marlborough House, Bertie's home in the capital. It's almost certain that Bertie knew nothing of the allegations against Somerset at this time and that he had no idea of the rumour doing the swift rounds of the clubs, nor among elements of his government about his eldest son, Eddy's potential involvement in the scandal.

After his meeting with Bertie, Somerset travelled to the equestrian centre of Newmarket in Suffolk intending to spend a week inspecting horses for possible purchase for the royal stables in the sales there. But Somerset abruptly cut his stay short after three days upon receiving a stark warning from Reginald Brett and Arthur Newton, likely by telegram. This was instigated by the well-connected Newton writing to Brett on 26 September:

> When I was at home in the country last night at 11 o'clock I received information of the most reliable nature that on Friday (tomorrow) a warrant will be applied for against your friend. I immediately came up

to town and was up till 3 this morning trying to find his [Somerset's] whereabouts [...] Kindly let me know where I can see you tomorrow.

Newton had, in fact, been informed of this by his managing clerk, Frederick Taylerson.

Newton and Brett must have met and they managed to locate Somerset and raise the alarm. After another arduous journey, which Somerset complained at length about in a letter to Brett, the disgraced peer fled British shores again, reaching Dieppe in France. But there would soon be another chance to arrest Somerset in his own country if there was official will to do so.

Meanwhile, Abberline, who on 24 September was reimbursed £2 6s for his expenses on the case so far, still had Somerset's 'friend' Algernon Allies in protective custody. The 20-year-old was considered a key witness in the case. Since PC Hanks had brought Allies back to London from Suffolk on 23 August, the rent boy and ex-employee of the Marlborough Club had been living at the Rose & Crown coffee house in Houndsditch in the City of London, not far from Abberline's old beat in the East End. Allies was under police supervision, but officers were not a constant presence and he could go out into the city as he pleased.

Somerset knew very well that Allies, who had already given a full statement to the Treasury, could give damaging, perhaps fatal evidence against him. He said as much in a coded letter to Reginald Brett, writing, 'Make N [Newton] look sharp and get AA [Algernon Allies] away.' Brett and Newton were in constant touch, and Somerset's wish would have been swiftly relayed.

The day before the peer escaped abroad again, his wily lawyer Arthur Newton acted. On 25 September, Newton sent his managing clerk, Frederick Taylerson, to the Rose & Crown, to speak to and lean on Allies. It's likely that Newton knew the location of Allies' accommodation through police contacts or gossip around the courts, but there is no record of this.

But at 4.30 p.m. that day, Newton's ruse was proven unsuccessful because Allies went to see Abberline, telling him that a man (Taylerson) had visited him. Abberline wrote in his memo of events that Taylerson had tried using all kinds of leverage. Referring to Allies' mother having come to London from Suffolk to give a statement, Taylerson said that 'the police haven't paid your mother's expenses yet' and 'they will tell you that you ought to be glad that you were not locked up and then you can go to the devil'.

Abberline immediately took Allies to the Treasury, where Hamilton Cuffe delegated a junior member of DPP staff to take a statement from him at 4.45 p.m. Allies said:

> I am now staying at 38 Houndsditch E.C. About a quarter past two this afternoon a man came to me at my lodgings. He was tall and fair and about 25, dressed like a gentleman with a thin light moustache and light trousers, light spats and a black jacket and waistcoat and high hat. He came upstairs by himself to the Dining Room where I was. There was another gentleman whom I don't know at dinner at the time. The person [Taylerson] said to me, 'Mr. Allies?' I said, 'Yes.' He then said he would like to speak to me for a minute. I took him into the Sitting Room where no one else was. He then said, 'I've come to persuade you to go away.' I said, 'Well, I must refer you to Mr. Abberline.' He said, 'If you go away to America, you will be found anything, clothing and everything you want, and I will give the Captain about £15 to give you when you get there to get on with.' I said I would go and told him I should want underlinen, two suits, a pair of boots and a hat. He said, 'All right,' and took a piece of paper out of his pocket and wrote down the articles I wanted. He said it would be all right. I asked him how I should get on when I got there. He said, 'Oh, unless you can get work you will be allowed about £1 a week.' I asked him where he came from and at first he would not tell me. Afterwards I remarked that Mr. Newton seemed to be very much against the witnesses and then he said, 'You must not take any notice of that – that is where I come from.' He then asked me to meet him this evening at 9 o'clock outside the A1 Public House in Tottenham Court Road to

go to Liverpool tonight and he would get my clothing here and see me off tomorrow for America. I agreed to meet him and I asked him to let me have the money to get a shirt, collar and tie and he gave me six shillings and then left. The man told me he had been down to my house in the country [Suffolk] the day before.

Later, giving evidence in court, Allies would add that Taylerson had also said, 'The reason why we want you to go abroad is because we don't want you to appear against you know who.'

After reading Allies' statement, Cuffe instructed Abberline to let Allies meet the man who had visited him and ascertain the man's identity. It was also decided that the Rose & Crown was no longer a sufficient haven for Allies and he temporarily moved in with PC Hanks, who was then living with his family at No. 164 Finnis Street in Bethnal Green in the East End.

The A1 pub where Taylerson had instructed Allies to rendezvous was at Nos 1–3 Bozier Court, just off Tottenham Court Road (neither the pub nor that street exist today, as they were demolished in 1900, when the junction with Oxford Street was widened). Allies was in place before 9 p.m. that night of 25 September, standing outside the door leading to the bar. Then Inspector Abberline and PC Hanks, keeping vantage nearby, saw Frederick Taylerson appear.

Newton's managing clerk approached Allies and said, 'Oh you have come then'. But Taylerson wasn't going to hang around and told Allies that he had left his bag at another pub and they should go there. Allies must have been nervous at this abrupt change of plan but could only hope that Abberline and Hanks were following as he and Taylerson crossed Oxford Street and stepped into a passing hansom cab. Allies would later say that in the cab, Taylerson had asked him if he had seen any policemen hanging about and Allies replied he hadn't.

The policemen were in swift pursuit, hailing a cab of their own, and they tailed the rent boy witness and Newton's right-hand man to the Marlborough Head pub at Nos 37–38 Great Marlborough Street (a tavern which also no longer exists). It was directly opposite the Marlborough Street Police Court and Arthur Newton's offices, where Taylerson was also based. Then under the stewardship of publican Charles Gwinnell, because of its location, the pub was popular with those in legal and police circles.

When they arrived, Abberline and Hanks saw Allies and Taylerson enter the pub and then noticed a man they recognised loitering outside. It was Adolphus de Gallo, another of Newton's aides, the very man whom Newton had sent to badger Allies' mother, Elizabeth, at their home in Suffolk back in August. But the policemen went straight into the pub – it was the man with Allies who they wanted. They approached them both inside, with PC Hanks taking Allies to one side and Abberline questioning Taylerson. When Abberline asked his name, he replied, 'My name is Frederick Taylerson. I am over the way at No. 24 [Newton's offices].'

'Are you Mr Newton's clerk?' said Abberline.

'Yes,' said Taylerson.

'What are you doing with this lad?' said Abberline.

'I will answer no questions,' said Taylerson. He then promptly departed the pub.

Abberline had no warrant to arrest him and the stakeout had been purely for identification purposes. But Abberline would push for Taylerson's arrest, and no lesser figure than the Met Commissioner James Monro wrote to the DPP, Sir Augustus Stephenson, requesting that a warrant be issued. The intimidation of police witnesses was taken very seriously.

It was Stephenson's deputy, Hamilton Cuffe, already well versed in the Allies affair, who dealt with it, as Stephenson was unwell. Cuffe personally wanted to proceed, but his hands were hardbound by the procrastinations of higher authorities – the case was still with the Lord Chancellor, Lord Halsbury, who was still on his shooting jaunt up in Scotland, and Cuffe couldn't act unilaterally. So Abberline and Monro's wishes for Taylerson's – and, perhaps by extension, if his supervision of Taylerson's actions could be proven, Newton's arrest – were stymied.

But that wasn't quite the end of the matter. Two days later, on 27 September, Arthur Newton fired off an indignant letter to the DPP, complaining about police conduct over Allies and claiming that he was innocent of ordering any wrongdoing, as he was acting for Allies' father to save his son:

> This boy had been kept by Inspector Abberline and PC Hanks in a small Coffee House in Hounsditch [sic] in a state of duress being threatened by these officers and commanded not to leave the place and they have even told him what to say in letters which he wrote to his own Father. Acting upon instructions (which we have in writing) received from his Father, with whom he was living prior to his giving evidence in the case (against Veck and Newlove), our Managing Clerk [Taylerson] called on Wednesday last at Hounsditch [sic] and saw this boy and told him that it was his Father's wish to remove him from the objectionable associations into which he had most unfortunately fallen and that his Father had given instructions to make arrangements for him to return home with a view to his being given a fresh start abroad. The boy stated that he [was] most anxious to get away from the objectionable surroundings but that he was in a state of terror and fright owing to the threats made by the Police. He accordingly on the evening of Wednesday last met our Managing Clerk, he was followed by Insp. Abberline and PC Hanks who took the boy into custody and actually had the audacity to threaten to detain our Managing Clerk. We can hardly imagine that this course has been carried out by your instructions, sanction, or authority, but with a view to avoiding the necessity of taking any unpleasant steps in the matter we ask you to be so good as to give us an appointment when Mr. Allies can in our company take possession of his son, as of course we are anxious to avoid any collision with the Police by going again to fetch him from where he now is without having communicated with you who had the conduct of the case. Mr. Allies is coming here tomorrow morning and we should be much obliged if you would kindly let us have an appointment in the course of today when our Client can fetch his son as he had written bitterly complaining of the way in which he is treated, not being supplied with clothes of his own, so as to render it absolutely impossible for him to go away. We may say that it is perfectly plain that when the Police were not present with their influence

upon him that he was perfectly anxious and willing to go away but that he was so overawed.

Hamilton Cuffe was having none of Newton's twisting of events, and the Assistant DPP replied to Somerset's lawyer on 1 October with a veiled yet stark warning about the intimidation of a witness: 'I am sure you will agree with me that anyone who [...] procures or attempts to procure Allies to leave the Country will incur serious responsibility.'

In fact, Allies didn't want to see his father, and he wrote a letter making this clear. Newton claimed that this was due to police coercion, but Cuffe was satisfied that this was Allies' true wish, that Abberline and Hanks had acted properly and Allies didn't want to be rescued. Allies didn't meet with his father and remained under police protection for the time being, so Newton's ploy on behalf of Somerset had failed and rebounded on the lawyer.

But there was still no movement on the arrest of Lord Arthur Somerset or other clients of No. 19 Cleveland Street, and the brothel-keeper Charles Hammond was now firmly ensconced abroad. Abberline wasn't giving up on Hammond, however. On 2 October, he served subpoenas on Allies and the telegraph messenger rent boys. He was still hopeful of getting Hammond back to Britain, and these witnesses would be needed if Hammond could be extradited and stand trial.

The next session of the Old Bailey was set for 21 October, but as detailed earlier, Arthur Newton, with Somerset's money, managed to spirit Hammond out of Europe to America on 19 October, where the pimp would prove out of reach.

Nine

Lord Arthur Somerset was eager to return to Britain to put out feelers to see if he could survive the scandal, especially as Newton's warning of the imminent issuing of a warrant for his arrest on 26 September (incidentally, the same day that Abberline made his police report on Algernon Allies) hadn't materialised. Somerset was also keen to keep his boss, Bertie, the Prince of Wales, onside, and sent Bertie a telegram apologising for not being in London to wish him *bon voyage* on his trip to Denmark and explaining that he had urgent private business to attend to in Dieppe.

Somerset was relieved when he received a telegram from Bertie himself in reply, accepting his apology. He wrote to Reginald Brett in a letter of 29 September, 'Of course that may mean that Matthews [the Home Secretary] has told him [Bertie] all, or it may mean that my reason was sufficient'.

With the Prince of Wales abroad until mid-November, Somerset felt more at ease, because Bertie would be out of earshot of all the London gossip about the scandal. Consequently, Somerset decided to take a risk and return to England against Arthur Newton's advice. On 30 September he had only been back in Europe for a very short time when he left Dieppe again, travelling overnight on a boat to the English port of Newhaven in East Sussex. Somerset, on both Newton and Brett's strong advice, went from there directly to his family home at Badminton

House in Gloucestershire, staying away from and avoiding refuelling the London clubland chin-wagging about him.

Somerset was growing in confidence and even considered accompanying Brett to Kempton Park Racecourse in Surrey, not very far from the capital. But then he learned that his grandmother, the Duchess of Beaufort, had died and her funeral was arranged for 8 October. A letter that Somerset wrote to Reginald Brett on 3 October revealed that the peer wasn't exactly grief-stricken, although the day at the races would have to be cancelled: 'Unfortunately my father's old mother aged 89 died in the night so here of course I must stay [at Badminton House, where the dowager duchess was to be buried on the estate] – very tiresome!'

News of Somerset's presence in England and his grandmother's death soon reached the authorities. Hamilton Cuffe of the DPP's office wrote with some sympathy in a memo to his boss Sir Augustus Stephenson on 4 October, 'One is almost glad that the old Duchess of Beaufort should have died before all this came to light. She was apparently devoted to Lord A.S. who lived at her house in London when not in barracks.' This also showed that Cuffe thought that Somerset's central role in the scandal was going to be publicly exposed.

And moves were being made to apprehend Somerset while he was back in England. Abberline and his superiors, including the Met Police Commissioner James Monro, were still pushing for his arrest. To this end, PC Hanks was sent down to Badminton the following day, to be in place for the funeral that coming Tuesday, in case a warrant was issued and Somerset detained. Police surveillance was also being carried out on Arthur Newton's offices in Great Marlborough Street in London, in case Somerset appeared there.

And before the funeral, Somerset suddenly decided to make a quick trip to London to speak to Colonel Oliver Montagu, his commanding officer, to assuage any unease Montagu might feel regarding the gossip about Somerset's involvement in the scandal. However, the very well-connected Montagu was already very much aware of it.

Montagu, the son of the 7th Earl of Sandwich, was almost 45 and had been made an equerry to the Prince of Wales twenty years earlier, in 1869, for Bertie's tour of Egypt in that year. Montagu's active military service career ended with that appointment, but he was later made honorary commanding officer of the Royal Horse Guards, so he was Somerset's boss in the army in 1889. Montagu had also accompanied Bertie and Princess Alexandra on their visit to Russia in 1874 for a royal wedding, and he collated a photographic album for Alexandra to mark that occasion. Oliver Montagu and Alexandra were particularly close friends and Bertie was also fond of him.

In addition to Colonel Montagu, Somerset saw Colonel Algernon Gordon-Lennox of the Grenadier Guards on his brief sojourn in London, where he stayed at Hyde Park Barracks. Lennox was an aide-de-camp to Prince George, Duke of Cambridge, Queen Victoria's cousin and long-standing Commander-in-Chief of the Forces. In another letter to Reginald Brett on 5 October, after meeting these two extremely influential military men whom he knew well, Somerset wrote:

> All went well today and Oliver Montagu and Algie Lennox have promised to help all they can in refuting the scandal. Oliver has kindly promised to go to Fredensborg [Denmark] and see the Prince so as he may hear the right story first, and Algie says he will delay everything at Newmarket [where Somerset had been inspecting horses]. Algie went to see Monro and he said he did not feel justified in saying anything one way or the other. He said these things are secrets of the office and cannot be divulged.

That James Monro was holding his cards close from one of Somerset's friends, even one as highly placed as Lennox, says a great deal about the professionalism of the Met Police Commissioner, not to mention the fact that Monro was desperate to have Somerset arrested to uphold the law. As a direct consequence of Lennox's visit, Monro reeled off a letter to Hamilton Cuffe:

> I learn on the best authority that Lord Arthur Somerset is in town. I cannot take any steps to arrest without a warrant. I must leave it to you to say whether I am to have that warrant that it may be executed while the accused is within my jurisdiction.[1]

Cuffe was sympathetic to Monro and urgently asked the Attorney General Sir Richard Webster what action was to be taken against Somerset. Webster told Cuffe to send a telegram to Lord Halsbury, the Lord Chancellor, who was still holidaying in Scotland, which Cuffe did, writing, 'Brown [Somerset] is in England. Can you send opinion to Attorney General or to me? I write by tonight's post. Time may be of importance.'

On 7 October, as previously mentioned, Lord Halsbury finally gave his opinion: 'I am unable on the present materials to advise further proceedings.'

In his 5 October letter to Brett, Somerset had also shown his deep concern about the Prince of Wales learning of his involvement in the goings-on at the brothel: 'I have asked Newton to draft me a careful letter to write to him and Probyn. He must be told by me and not by anyone else.'

'Probyn' referred to General Sir Dighton Probyn. The 56-year-old was Bertie's comptroller, in charge of the finances of the Prince of Wales' profligate household, but he was more than the official title, acting as a close confidant and protector. As an officer in the British Indian Army, Probyn had won Britain's highest military honour, the Victoria Cross, for courageous actions during the Indian Mutiny over thirty years earlier and was an honorary Sikh, which is why he often wore a turban, which, along with his very long and increasingly whitening beard, gave him a distinctive look.

Probyn originally lived at Bertie's London home, Marlborough House, but by 1889 was chiefly quartered at the royal Sandringham Estate in Norfolk, the prince's country residence. He was a favourite of Princess Alexandra after he saved her when she was thrown from a horse. In the Cleveland Street scandal, Probyn would act as emissary between Bertie and the Prime Minister Lord Salisbury.

Another person close to Bertie who Somerset would have to appease was Francis Knollys, aged 52, the prince's private secretary. He had held that position for almost twenty years by 1889, as well as being gentleman usher to Queen Victoria for even longer, although he wasn't a favourite of the queen as he would be for her eldest son. Bertie's biographer Jane

Ridley sketches Knollys as looking like an Italian waiter: 'a dapper little man with shiny black hair and a beard cut into a strip down his chin.'[2]

Knollys' family had long been in royal circles. His ancestral namesake had served as a key courtier to King Henry VIII in the sixteenth century and his own father, General William Knollys, had acted as a spy for Queen Victoria to monitor the younger Bertie after Prince Albert's death, reporting back to the monarch any improprieties, as well as being the prince's comptroller, the role later taken up by Probyn. And Francis Knollys' sister, Charlotte, had been bedchamber woman to Princess Alexandra since 1872, so his family was firmly embedded in Bertie's household.

Like Probyn, Knollys was essentially Bertie's protector, which the prince often needed because of his illicit and sometimes not-so-secret love affairs, for which Knollys acted as an enabler, finding suitably grand and discreet rendezvous points. Along with Probyn, Knollys also helped keep much of Bertie's extravagant spending from press and public scrutiny. He screened the heir to the throne's correspondence and ordered retractions by newspapers if any went too far when reporting on the prince.

Knollys knew where every one of Bertie's scandalous skeletons rattled. As part of his extended duties, he would also have to deal with shielding Bertie's eldest son, Prince Albert Victor, from discredit and disgrace. The implications of Eddy's whispered involvement in the Cleveland Street scandal would be a new test of the courtier's silky skills, after he and Probyn had personally investigated the gravity of the accusations around Lord Arthur Somerset's legal and social folly. Francis Knollys and Dighton Probyn were as close to Bertie as any non-royal could be and reassuring them was of paramount strategic importance to Somerset in his predicament.

PC Hanks was discreetly in place at the Duchess of Beaufort's funeral in Badminton on 8 October, ready to pounce on Somerset if the arrest warrant should come through, not knowing that the Lord Chancellor's opinion given on the previous day meant that no action could be taken against Somerset, yet again. Hanks even sent a telegram to Abberline in London just after midday, requesting permission to act. But in his final report of that day's events, he could only report that he 'saw Lord Arthur Somerset was present at the obsequies'.

Inspector Abberline had no choice but to order Hanks to return to London. The constable, like Abberline and their overall boss James Monro, was extremely frustrated, but powerless to act until higher authorities above them sanctioned Somerset's arrest, which was now seeming unlikely, at least while Somerset was accessible for enforcing a warrant. Monro had already made his feelings clear in a letter to the DPP, Sir Augustus Stephenson on 1 October, citing recent criticisms in late September in the *Man of the World*, *Reynolds's News* and the *North London Press*. In his opinion, the police were being 'most undeservedly blamed for inaction in this case'.

On 10 October, two days after the Duchess of Beaufort's funeral, with Somerset still walking free and by now back in London, Monro wrote twice to Hamilton Cuffe, Stephenson's number two, as Stephenson was still on holiday in Scotland. Monro first protested about the procrastinations of the highest authorities over Somerset: 'I can only deplore the delay which is being made in high quarters about this horrible case.' Second, Monro complained about the lack of action being taken against Arthur Newton for trying to get Algernon Allies out of the country.

The Met Commissioner also defended Abberline, angrily reacting to Newton's accusatory letters to the DPP regarding his inspector's handling of Allies:

> Mr. Newton's letters are simply bounce [bluster or swagger], and he may find this policy awkward yet. If he or his clients try force, they will find it be no remedy! If he tries any more of his objectionable letters, I suggest your referring him to the Police. We shall deal with him.

Cuffe was also uneasy about the way the scandal was being handled by the Establishment, and the next day he wrote to Stephenson, 'None of the bigwigs who are conducting this case are in town or accessible to one another which does not expedite matters [...] to go on picking holes in the evidence [...] seems to me incapable of justification'. Cuffe suggested sending the case to the War Office for decisive action, and this was put to the Attorney General, Sir Richard Webster, who agreed in principle. But when Webster wrote to the still holidaying Lord Chancellor, Lord Halsbury strongly vetoed the proposition.

Then, on 16 October, the Met Commissioner James Monro had two very distinguished visitors at his office in Scotland Yard. They were Sir Dighton Probyn and Francis Knollys, the Prince of Wales' comptroller and private secretary, respectively. Bertie had been informed about Somerset and the shocking implications of the scandal, including most probably about his son Eddy, whose name was being mentioned in association with the clubs.

Bertie's two closest aides were trying to press Monro to find out the true gravity of the situation. But Monro gave Probyn and Knollys nothing, telling them that the case was under the supervision of the DPP and neatly sidestepping a tricky political minefield. Probyn and Knollys immediately made for the Treasury to see the DPP, Sir Augustus Stephenson, but as he was still being deputised while on holiday, it was Hamilton Cuffe who had to deal with them.

Cuffe afterwards wrote a brief note to document the meeting, dated that day, in which he made it clear how difficult Bertie was finding it to accept his trusted friend Somerset's involvement in the scandal. He recorded that he had been informed by Probyn and Knollys that the 'P. of Wales was in a great state, didn't believe a word of it and wished he could come himself to clear LAS [Somerset], and must have something settled'.

The urgency to deal with the matter was made clear to Cuffe and the Assistant DPP was perturbed by the high-level escalation of the case. He held Bertie's emissaries off, explaining that he had to get advice from Stephenson. Cuffe told them that if they cared to return to see him the following day, 17 October, he might have some more information.

Probyn went off that afternoon to Sandringham, Norfolk, but Knollys stayed in London and later that day sent a telegram to Cuffe saying that he could meet him either at the Marlborough Club, the meeting place of Bertie's exclusive circle, or back at the Treasury the next day. Cuffe had to get advice fast and adrenalised by stress he rallied around, eventually locating Sir Richard Webster, the Attorney General. Luckily for Cuffe, Webster assumed responsibility, telling the Assistant DPP that he was not authorised to give any information about the case and the Attorney General was dealing with it. But Cuffe didn't contact Knollys, and Knollys didn't pursue the second meeting, probably instinctively knowing that he would get nothing from it.

It was becoming plain to both Knollys and Probyn that Somerset was in legal jeopardy. The lack of straightforward answers offered by the DPP's office, and the Attorney General's assumption of its burden, revealed that the case against Somerset was legally strong and ongoing. They would have to speak to Somerset directly. The justice system was holding itself up as much as it could under pressure, but whether it would ever allow Somerset to be arrested was another matter.

In fact, Probyn and Knollys had met Somerset, who had since returned to London, on the morning of 16 October, *before* they visited either Monro or Cuffe that day. In a letter to Reginald Brett that evening from the Marlborough Club, where he was staying, Somerset revealed what had happened in that meeting. It detailed Arthur Newton's close involvement and Probyn and Knollys' wariness of Somerset's lawyer. They had advised Somerset to replace him with George Lewis of the Lewis & Lewis law practice, who was adept at settling difficult cases involving notable people out of court. It also stated that Somerset was already aware of what had transpired in the courtier's meetings with Monro and Cuffe (if true, Cuffe's response under stress was less noble than he recorded) and that Inspector Abberline was also a key focus of concern as he was accused of trying to stir up the case in the press.

'Sir Dighton [Probyn] and Francis Knollys met me at 9.15 this morning and I suggested they should see Newton,' wrote Somerset:

> They agreed and I sent for him. He told all just as he had told Colonel Montagu [Somerset's commanding officer], and they went off to Monro. He told them nothing but they hunted him a bit and told

him it was a scandal that these rumours were entirely circulated by the police. He denied it, whereupon Sir Dighton said they were and as evidence he knew that Abberline had been to the *Pall Mall Gazette* and tried to make them write up the case and that two inspectors had told two gentlemen in society in the street all about the case. Monro pretended to be furious with Abberline, but then said the matter was in the hands of the Public Prosecutor, so off they went. Stephenson was out but they saw Cuffe who said, 'Of course I ought to tell you that I know nothing, but I know all about it but am telling you nothing. However now you have come to ask I think we shall manage to let you know all about it.'[3]

Cuffe, in fact, gave Probyn and Knollys nothing. And although Somerset also confided to Brett that he would think about replacing Newton, he added that he didn't want to upset his lawyer, whom he seemingly liked.

Somerset then met Francis Knollys for further consultation at the Turf Club, at No. 85 Piccadilly, on the afternoon of 17 October. In a letter to Reginald Brett written that evening, Somerset made it clear that he knew that his case and fate were in the hands of the prime minister and relayed that Probyn was to meet him again the following afternoon at Marlborough House, presumably after seeing Lord Salisbury.

Somerset was now in quite an agitated and despondent state, writing:

> I must say I wish they would look sharp and do something as these long constant interviews are very trying. By the time anything comes on, if it ever does, my nerves will be in such a state that I shall be unable to do myself and my case justice [...] All this is very difficult and unpleasant.

In fact, Probyn didn't meet Somerset at Marlborough House that afternoon – both Knollys and Probyn were there, but Somerset wasn't. He'd got his servants to pack his belongings for a trip, and they were ready nearby, stacked onto a hansom cab. The peer was spooked, and unless he had some news of a positive development – ostensibly that he wasn't going to be arrested – flight was now becoming more appealing than staying to fight for his name. Probyn had already arranged to have dinner with Somerset that evening at Marlborough House again, but Probyn would arrive very late for the 8 p.m. appointment and by then, Somerset had already taken flight.

Sir Dighton Probyn met Lord Salisbury in a rushed rendezvous arranged by telegram at King's Cross Station at 7 p.m. on 18 October, from where the prime minister was due to take a train back to Hatfield House, his family home in Hertfordshire. Probyn directly asked Lord Salisbury if there were any grounds to arrest those implicated in the scandal, mentioning the Earl of Euston and even Eddy, Prince Albert Victor. As he would later relay when pressed, the prime minister informed Probyn that only Somerset wasn't safe from arrest, but he had been advised that the evidence against Somerset was legally 'insufficient' for a successful prosecution.

This was no salve to Probyn's concern. The Prince of Wales would be sullied by the possible arrest and trial of his friend and equerry for committing 'unnatural acts', *if* it were to happen. And as for his eldest son, Eddy's association – that could be disastrous for the entire royal family, from Queen Victoria down. So, Lord Salisbury's admission that Somerset *could* be arrested was very worrying to Probyn.

As the author H. Montgomery Hyde highlighted, Probyn wrote a letter to Lord Salisbury the next day, 19 October, which shows his feelings and shock at the fact that Somerset could well be guilty of the offences he was accused of, meaning that an arrest was possible:

> I fear what you told me last night was all too true. Until I saw you last night, I always thought it was a case of mistaken identity. I would not let myself believe (and tried to check myself from thinking) that it was anything else. But after my conversation with you, I drove home a miserable man. I knew the story must be true.

Probyn, a military man to his core, had seemingly trusted or wanted to trust Somerset's protestations of innocence – the word of an officer and gentleman. There is no evidence that Probyn was assured of Somerset's guilt prior to his meeting with Lord Salisbury. This mirrors Bertie, the Prince of Wales' reaction and aghast inability to grasp Somerset's culpability when he was told of the allegations against his equerry.

There is also no direct evidence that either Probyn, Knollys or Lord Salisbury directly warned Somerset, so that he could get away, but the ever-punctual Probyn meeting the prime minister and not arriving on time for his meeting with Somerset at Marlborough House allowed the peer to read the ruinous runes. It's highly unlikely that either Probyn or Knollys, or for that matter Lord Salisbury, were genuinely surprised by Somerset's swift exit – they wanted him to disappear and remain out of the way. The steps on the pathway had been quietly trod for some time.

It had been more than three months since Somerset was first named as a client of the brothel at No. 19 Cleveland Street, time in which he was able to return to Britain twice from abroad. But it was the procrastination of the authorities, Lord Salisbury's government, to issue a warrant for Somerset's arrest that allowed the peer to make his escape from justice abroad, as noblemen faced with similarly socially disastrous accusations often did in the eighteenth and nineteenth centuries.

This lack of official action and confusion among the highest tiers of the legal establishment on how to proceed was undoubtedly exacerbated by Somerset's lawyer Arthur Newton's ploys, especially his introduction of Eddy's name into the disreputable fray. It was certainly the gossip and dragging of Eddy's name into the scandal – the second in line to the throne, no less – which exerted the real pressure on Lord Salisbury. And it was Bertie, the Prince of Wales, who wielded it.

Bertie, along with Princess Alexandra, was abroad during this time, moving on from Denmark to Greece, so there were no face-to-face meetings between the British authorities and the prince. Meanwhile, Eddy had embarked on a tour of British India that October, reaching Bombay (now Mumbai) on 9 November. It took in stops all over southern India, including Hyderabad, Madras (now Chennai) and Bangalore (now Bengaluru). The trip would last seven months, but most royal tours were long then, with travel by ship to many ports of call, and his father Bertie had done a tour of India of similar length back in 1875. On the way home, Eddy did a short tour of Egypt, taking in Aden, Cairo and

Port Said, then went on to Greece, before arriving back in Britain in the mid-spring of 1890.

It was perfect timing to get Eddy away from Britain as the scandal that implicated him ran its course, and this was commented upon by elements of the press that winter, especially abroad. But, in fact, as the author Andrew Cook has pointed out, the tour had been planned months before in the spring, so the scheduling was no more than very fortuitous for Eddy and the royal family.[4] It kept him out of sight, if not out of mind, in the clubs, wider society and sections of the press.

The ready-to-flee Lord Arthur Somerset finally escaped on that evening of 18 October, and by the next day, he was temporarily ensconced in Wimille, a small town just north of Boulogne in France. Somerset had slipped away with the help of his commanding officer, Colonel Oliver Montagu, as he told Brett in another letter dated 22 October, by which time he was in Rouen, north-west of Paris. Lord Arthur Somerset would never set foot in England again.

The exasperation of the police at the obstruction of their extensive and proactive inquiry into the Cleveland Street scandal was put into assertive words by James Monro in a letter to the DPP, Sir Augustus Stephenson on 21 October. This was five days after the Met Police Commissioner had been visited by Bertie's close aides, Probyn and Knollys. In the communication, Monro arranged his points in sections, requesting to be informed of the following:

a) Whether the charge against the nobleman in question [Somerset] with reference to which there is evidence in possession of yourself and the Police is to be proceeded with.
b) If so, what action is to be taken by the Police in proceeding with such charge.

c) If not, whether I am to understand that this charge is definitely abandoned and that no action is to be taken by the Police, either acting under your orders or of their own motion.
d) Whether the charge against the Solicitor's clerk and others [Frederick Taylerson, Arthur Newton, and perhaps, Adolphus de Gallo, for attempting to get Algernon Allies out of the country] to be proceeded with either by yourself or if not whether the Police are at liberty to take such proceedings in the matter as they may be advised.
e) Whether you desire the boy Allies as a witness for the Crown to be still secured against any attempt to remove him from this country, or Metropolitan Police District.

Monro ended by stating, 'I have to press for a very early reply to this letter.'

Sir Augustus Stephenson replied to Monro the very next day, with 'I am not in a position to give you any answers or any information on any of the matters on which you ask'. Stephenson also wrote that he had passed Monro's letter to the Home Secretary, Sir Henry Matthews, who would have to consult Prime Minister Lord Salisbury.

It would be almost three weeks before an arrest warrant was finally issued against Somerset, and this action was influenced by the persistent pressure from Monro on behalf of the police and the growing disquiet in the press about the peer having escaped justice. With an election to face at some point and Somerset safely away abroad, Lord Salisbury, an innately political animal, knew he had to be seen to act, however belatedly. This was despite softly applied, but undoubtedly keenly felt pressure being put on the prime minister. Bertie's emissary and close confidant, Sir Dighton Probyn, wrote a plea to Lord Salisbury just after Somerset fled on 18 October, telling him that he was keeping the prince fully informed of developments:

I write now to ask you, to implore of you if it can be managed to have the prosecution stopped. It can do no good to prosecute him. He has gone and will never show his face in England again. He dare never come back to this country. I think it is the most hateful, loathsome story I ever heard, and the most astounding. It is too fearful, but further publicity will only make matters worse. I have of course telegraphed to the Prince, and am writing full particulars of this disgusting calamity to HRH. The Prince will be terribly cut up about it [...] I do not write with a view of trying to save the man. He is gone, he is beyond punishment, or rather out of reach of the law. I only want if possible not to increase the fearful disgrace which has fallen on his family. For the man, in his defence, I can only trust that he is mad.[5]

Bertie had indeed been both mortified and disbelieving about the allegations against Somerset when he was first told of them by Somerset's commanding officer, Colonel Oliver Montagu, who had visited him at Bad Homburg in Germany. Bertie had written to Probyn with incredulity, saying, 'I won't believe it, any more than I should if they accused the Archbishop of Canterbury.' The Archbishop of Canterbury was then, as now, the principal bishop and leader of the Church of England.

And on 25 October, the Prince of Wales finally wrote to Lord Salisbury himself, having digested the news, and like Probyn, implied that Somerset must be insane. In the letter, from Piraeus in Greece, where the royal yacht *Osborne* had docked, Bertie wrote that he was 'glad [...] that no warrant is likely to be issued against the "unfortunate Lunatic" – I can call him nothing else – as, for the sake of the Family and Society, the less one hears of such a filthy scandal the better'.

Bertie could have been referring to not just Somerset's family, but also his own family here, a direct appeal to Lord Salisbury to minimise the damage already done by the scandal to the royal family, the pinnacle of British society. But the remainder of the letter shows that Bertie was also concerned about the impact on Somerset's close relatives. The Prince of Wales asked if Somerset would be free from apprehension by the police if he were to return just to visit his family at some point, emphasising that he had no inkling of where Somerset had escaped to or whether he would ever want to return to England. Bertie ended his letter by writing that, until he had Lord Salisbury's response, neither Somerset's father, the Duke of Beaufort, nor other members of his family 'shall ever know from me that I have been in correspondence with you on this painful subject'.

A contemporary newspaper illustration of No. 19 Cleveland Street.

Lord Arthur Somerset, the Prince of Wales' close aide and brothel client, who was at the very centre of the scandal. (*Vanity Fair*, 19 November 1887, by Sir Leslie Ward)

Prince Albert Victor, known as 'Eddy', eldest son of the Prince of Wales, who was implicated in the scandal. (*Within Royal Palaces*, La Marquise de Fontenoy, courtesy of the Library of Congress/Wikimedia Commons)

The Post Office messenger boys and rent boys who also appeared as witnesses. (*Illustrated Police News*, 18 January 1890)

Some key players in the Cleveland Street scandal, also known as the West End Scandal, as depicted in the media. (*Illustrated Police News*, 7 December 1889)

The radical journalist Ernest Parke, editor of *The North London Press*. (*The Sketch*, 25 April 1894)

A caricature of Henry Matthews, the Home Secretary. (*Vanity Fair*, 10 September 1887, by Sir Leslie Ward, courtesy of CCNY/ Wikimedia Commons)

The Cleveland Street scandal depicted in the *Illustrated Police News*, 25 January 1890. (*Illustrated Police News*, 25 January 1890)

Henry Labouchère MP, architect of the Labouchère Amendment and antagonist of Lord Salisbury's government over the scandal. (*The Bookman*, 1912)

Sir Richard Webster, the Attorney General. (Russell & Sons, Cassell's Universal Portrait Gallery, 1895)

Sir Augustus Stephenson, the Director of Public Prosecutions for England and Wales. (*Illustrated Police News*, 25 July 1885)

Prime Minister Lord Salisbury (the Marquess of Salisbury). (*Great Britain and Her Queen*, Anne E. Keeling, courtesy of Project Gutenberg/Wikimedia Commons)

Francis Knollys (later Lord Knollys) the Prince of Wales' Private Secretary and fixer. (Bain News Service, 1910)

W.T. Stead, the crusading journalist who had a significant behind-the scenes influence on the Labouchère Amendment. (E.H. Mills, 1905)

Sir Charles Russell, who led the prosecution for the Earl of Euston in his libel case against Ernest Parke, defended the bent lawyer Arthur Newton and his clerk, and acted for the Marquis of Queensberry in his libel action against Oscar Wilde. (Elliott & Fry, Cassell's Universal Portrait Gallery, 1895, courtesy of Wikimedia Commons)

Oscar Wilde, whose life and career were destroyed just five years after the Cleveland Street scandal ended, was a victim of the same social and political environment. (Napoleon Sarony, New York, 1882, courtesy of the Library of Congress)

Ten

As well as being fed the news, gossip and agenda-led opinion, readers of newspapers in Britain in 1889–90 were then, as in the twenty-first century, consumers above all. And advertising was thriving. For those with a sweet tooth, there was 'Fuller's American Confectionery – Pure, Wholesome, Fresh Every Day – English Ladies should be everlastingly grateful to Messrs. Fuller & Co. for introducing these delicious sweetmeats to their notice'. And after eating those sweetmeats, there was a remedy for gnasher hygiene:

> With what shall we clean our teeth? – 'I always use a Powder to clean my teeth.' – That's where you were wrong. – 'I always use a Liquid Dentifrice or Mouth Wash'. – That's where you were wrong. – 'I always use the Salvine Dentifrice, which is a Powder and Mouth Wash combined.' – That's where you were right.

And then there was 'Edwards' Harlene, World Renowned Hair Producer and Restorer – for Producing Luxuriant Hair, Whiskers and Moustachios, Curing Baldness, Weak and Thin Eyelashes, Dandruff, Scanty Partings, or Restoring Grey Hair'. And if a testimonial from Mr N. Steed of Weedon was to be believed, it worked: 'Dear Sir – My hair, which has been coming off for years, is now completely restored after using three bottles of Harlene.'

And if Mr Steed had fashionable facial hair and wanted to dye it, there was J. Carter's Nut Brown Hair Stain of No. 17 Fleet Street, which was 'Undoubtedly the most Simple, Perfect, and Effectual Stain ever produced in one liquid for changing Fair or Grey Moustaches and Whiskers to a permanent and natural Light or Dark Brown in a few hours. No previous cleansing necessary.'

Not that those men implicated in the Cleveland Street scandal were overly concerned about sweets, their hair, beards or moustaches as those same newspapers began to take a real interest in them that late autumn and early winter of 1889. The press began to slowly stir when the *London Gazette* recorded on 9 November that Lord Arthur Somerset had resigned his commission in the Royal Horse Guards. It didn't say that his 'services had been dispensed with', as soldiers who brought ill repute to their rank were written up in that official register, just as Somerset's fellow No. 19 Cleveland Street client, Lieutenant Charles Montague Barber, had been listed back in 1880. But Somerset's 'retirement', obviously smoothed over by his commanding officer, Colonel Oliver Montagu, was suspiciously noticed by some in both society and newsrooms, because the timing, in the midst of all the rumours about the peer, was just too perfect.

It was the *Birmingham Post* that jumped in first, with an editorial which was careful not to name or allude too closely to the exiled Somerset, whose arrest warrant was yet to become public knowledge – that would come on 12 November at the Marlborough Street Police Court. But the fact that it referred to Somerset was clear to those in the know:

> ... until the police authorities take action against those who are alleged to be the chief offenders to indicate plainly in print names which are on every lip in all the clubs of the Metropolis; but since the issue within the past few days of certain official announcements, these are being mentioned on the street corners as well.

The arrest warrant for Somerset charged him with committing acts of gross indecency with other male persons, namely Algernon Allies, Charles Swinscow and Charles Thickbroom; procuring Allies to commit similar acts with other male persons; and conspiring with Charles Hammond to procure the commission of such acts, contrary to the Criminal Law Amendment Act of 1885.

And on 14 November, two days after the warrant was issued, the Liberal politician Henry Labouchère wrote about the scandal in his radical journal, *Truth*, which he had founded back in 1877. The issue must have gone to the printer days earlier, as there was no mention of the arrest warrant against Somerset, but Labouchère was characteristically forthright in his views and fired a warning musket against Lord Salisbury's Conservative (Tory) government and its handling of the case:

> The facts are in the hands of the Home Office and of Scotland Yard, but as some of the greatest hereditary names of the country are mixed up in the scandal, every effort is being made to secure the immunity of the criminals. Indeed, I am credibly informed that the Home Office is throwing obstacles in the way of prompt action on the part of Scotland Yard, and trying to get the persons concerned out of the country before warrants are issued. Very possibly our Government of the classes is of the opinion that the revelations which would ensue, were the criminals put on trial, would deal a blow to the reign of the classes, and to the social influence of the aristocracy. Let them, however, understand that they will not be allowed to protect their friends. It would be really too monstrous if crimes which, when committed by poor ignorant men, lead to sentences of penal servitude, were to be done with impunity by those whom the Tory Government delights to honour. The names are known. I warn Mr Matthews [the Home Secretary] that if he does not take action in this matter, there will be a heavy reckoning when Parliament meets. It is full time that the severest examples should bring home to all that there are certain foul crimes (too prevalent of late, by all accounts) that we cannot tolerate amongst us, unless London is to be regarded as the disgrace and opprobrium of modern civilisation.

It was a direct censure of and threat to Lord Salisbury. Labouchère would be the key figure in keeping the authorities under scrutiny and attack in his journal, and more importantly, in Parliament in the coming months. He had also been the mastermind of the amendment in the law that enabled the arrests of those involved in the Cleveland Street scandal.

Henry Labouchère had just turned 58 when he published that issue of *Truth* in mid-November 1889. He was descended from Huguenots (French Protestants), who had escaped France due to religious persecution and moved to Holland. Labouchère's grandfather, Pierre, a banker, then settled in England, marrying the daughter of Sir Francis Baring, the co-founder of Barings Bank, one of Britain's oldest merchant banks, which survived until 1995, when it collapsed amid a fraud scandal. Pierre amassed an enormous fortune, largely derived from the Dutch bank Hope & Co. for whom he worked in London. The firm underwrote the financial survival of the French government after the Napoleonic Wars with a loan that gained it 9 per cent of its massive risk, just as the Rothschilds had grown their immense riches by providing loans to fund the building of the English fleet during those same wars.

Labouchère's father, John, was also a banker for Hope & Co., and later for another leading firm. Along with his mother, Mary, the daughter of an MP, Henry grew up at Broome Hall, a large mansion in Surrey (which was, much later, in the late twentieth century, the home of the actor Oliver Reed). Henry already had a template and connections for his future career in politics, as his namesake uncle was a prominent Liberal politician, who was awarded the title of 1st Baron Taunton and served as President of the Board of Trade, Chief Secretary for Ireland and Secretary of State for the Colonies. In his late 30s Henry Labouchère would inherit his uncle's very substantial estate in 1869, as Baron Taunton died with no direct male heir.

But before that, Labouchère went to Eton and then Cambridge University, where he gambled prodigiously, and, as his biographer Algar Thorold noted,[1] racked up debts of £6,000. After being accused of cheating in an exam, Labouchère never graduated. Instead, he was packed off abroad by his parents to look after family business interests in South America, but the idiosyncratic Labouchère had soon moved on to

Mexico, gained work in a circus and spent months living with a Native American tribe in Minnesota.

On returning to England, with the help of family connections, Labouchère began a career in the diplomatic service. While they were minor posts, they would last a decade with some success, with Labouchère serving in America and all over Europe, until he refused to be reposted to Buenos Aires. He wrote to the Foreign Secretary, the Liberal John Russell, saying that he preferred to remain in Germany, where he was then based, claiming that he could do his new duties from there, thousands of miles away. The insolent request was denied and he was dismissed from the service in 1864.

The next phase of Labouchère's odyssey saw him being elected in 1865 as the Liberal MP for Windsor in Berkshire at the age of 34. He supported Prime Minister William Gladstone, especially over home rule for Ireland, but he was always an outlier, being stubbornly opinionated, easily riled and provocative, and therefore a potential troublemaker. He lost his seat by a tiny margin in 1868.

The large inheritance from his uncle that came in the following year would make him independently rich, velvet-cushioning him for the rest of his life and allowing Labouchère to take financial, social and, later, political risks.

Theatre-lover Labouchère, along with partners, had a building in Long Acre in London's Covent Garden rebuilt and turned into the 4,000-seat Queen's Theatre, which opened in October 1867. The theatre's company included Henry Irving, later a leading late-Victorian Shakespearean actor and knight; the acclaimed actress Ellen Terry, whose career thrived into the Edwardian age; and the now much lesser-known actress Henrietta Hodson. The theatre would thrive for a time, but closed in 1878 after a disastrous staging of *The Last Days of Pompeii*, based on the novel by writer and politician Edward Bulwer-Lytton.

Henry Labouchère invested a great deal financially and emotionally in promoting Henrietta Hodson in the 1870s after he fell in love with her. Hodson was still married but estranged from her husband, Richard Pigeon, a reportedly abusive solicitor, with whom she had a son, when she embarked on a long affair with Labouchère in 1868. Labouchère and

Hodson would have an illegitimate daughter, Dora, in 1884, but they couldn't get married until her husband died in 1887.

After the Queen's Theatre closed, Labouchère and Hodson spent many weekends at their retreat, the large Pope's Villa in Twickenham, so named as it was once the site of the home of the poet and satirist Alexander Pope (although that building had been demolished and rebuilt by the late 1870s). It was at Pope's Villa in 1881 that Hodson would coach the young and future celebrated actress Lillie Langtry, who, within a decade, would be the mistress of Bertie, the Prince of Wales, and who was also a close friend of Oscar Wilde. Hodson and Langtry would later fall out while touring America.

In parallel with his theatrical interests, Labouchère also became a journalist, reporting from abroad and at home, mainly for the *Daily News*, which had been set up in 1846 by the writer Charles Dickens, who was also its first editor. In the early 1870s, Labouchère bought an interest in the paper and helped improve its circulation. After writing for the weekly *The World*, founded in 1874 and where George Bernard Shaw would later be the art and music critic, Labouchère set up his journal, *Truth*.

Like many of his class at the time, Labouchère was vehemently antisemitic and anti-feminist. As the academic Claire Hirshfield has spotlighted,[2] he used *Truth* to rail against the riches and influence of the 'Hebrew Barons' and campaigned against the fledgeling suffrage movement. He was also strongly anti-homosexual.

Truth was a vessel through which Labouchère could air his stringent views, and he used it to great effect to attack Lord Salisbury's government over the Cleveland Street scandal. The authorities saw Henry Labouchère and his journal as a serious threat, as well they should have done. In late February 1890, when Labouchère finally launched an incendiary tirade against the government in Parliament, the DPP, Sir Augustus Stephenson, wrote to the Attorney General, Sir Richard Webster, singling out no fewer than nine editions of *Truth*, published between mid-November 1889 and the beginning of that month, as containing broadsides against the authorities over their handling of the case.

By then, Labouchère had been an MP again for a decade, having in 1880 been elected as one of two Members of Parliament for

Northampton. The other was Charles Bradlaugh, the atheist politician and activist previously mentioned.

It was in 1885, five years after his return to the House of Commons, that Labouchère made his first and greatest impact on the way that the Cleveland Street scandal would play out four years later.

The Criminal Law Amendment Act of 1885 was brought into being by public pressure on the authorities to protect young women and girls from vice after the journalist W.T. Stead's staunch and socially incendiary campaign 'The Maiden Tribute'. The act had gone through several drafts since it was first proposed in 1881 by the Liberal politician Lord Ramsay, but it was Stead's investigation and campaign that got it over the line and into law in 1885, so much so that it was known colloquially as the 'Stead Act'. It offered far greater protection for females and originally had no stipulation or focus on male prostitution or homosexual acts in general.

It was Henry Labouchère's lobbying, instigated indirectly by his friend Stead, which led to Section 11, the revision of the act that allowed for the prosecution of 'gross indecency' in Britain, making it a specific crime and far more enforceable than the previous laws against sodomy. The morally irascible and deeply anti-homosexual Labouchère put forward his amendment at the eleventh hour, citing the 'outrages on decency' carried out by 'deviants', not just in public, but in private, which was a new legal angle and troublesome because what went on behind closed doors was difficult to prove.

As the academic William Fize has highlighted:

The Labouchère Amendment can thus be considered as exceptional in the sense that it permitted the prosecution of those involved in virtually any sexual act between men that fell short of sodomy (defined by the criminal law as a sexual act involving both penetration and proof of emission). It thus made prosecution of a whole category of individuals much easier and conviction potentially more frequent.[3]

After a little contention in the House of Commons over how what became known as the 'Labouchère Amendment' diverted the original purpose of the act to protect females from vice, Section 11 was added to the act and passed into law.

But it was Stead who had originally kindled the fire in Labouchère's soft belly by writing to him proclaiming the increase in homosexual activity in London and other large British cities, garnered from extra research he had gathered while looking into the wider issues of vice.[4] That was enough to ignite Labouchère's already entrenched concern about the matter, and Section 11 laid out in clear terms how 'acts of gross indecency' could be prosecuted:

> Any male person who, in public or private, commits, or is a party to the commission of, or procures, or attempts to procure the commission by any male person of, any act of gross indecency with another male person, shall be guilty of a misdemeanour, and being convicted thereof, shall be liable at the discretion of the Court to be imprisoned for any term not exceeding two years, with or without hard labour.

Henry Labouchère had originally pushed for a maximum of seven years for the offence, but the Attorney General, Sir Richard Webster (already in his post then) and the Home Secretary, Richard Assheton Cross, whittled that down to two years. And that was the law under which those few prosecuted for their actions at No. 19 Cleveland Street – George Veck, Henry Newlove and Charles Hammond *in absentia*, went to trial. It was also the same legislation that would lead to Oscar Wilde's imprisonment just six years later.

As for W.T. Stead, he was publicly very quiet about the Cleveland Street scandal. As his most recent biographer W. Sydney Robinson stated, strangely for such a high-profile crusading journalist, Stead 'conveniently ignored' the scandal.[5] But then Stead's 1891 book *Portraits and Autographs* reveals just how much Stead was a firm member of the late-Victorian Establishment, being able to secure the portrait and autograph of Bertie, the Prince of Wales, Lord Salisbury, along with his friend Henry Labouchère, among many others.

Perhaps after his spell in prison a few years earlier, which was by all accounts a relatively comfortable one, the zeal had left Stead. He didn't officially vacate the editorship of the *Pall Mall Gazette* until 31 December 1889, months into the scandal, but its sensationalism-sensitive owner, Henry Thompson, may have hampered his editor's output. Or was Stead just shrewd enough to know how far he could push an agenda, and with a royal implicated in the scandal, possibly had no desire to become socially ostracised himself?

Labouchère's threat against Lord Salisbury's government in the 14 November 1889 issue of *Truth* set off a run of newspaper coverage about the scandal that would last for months in Britain and as far afield as New Zealand, Australia and Belize, with publications in France and the United States particularly having a ferocious field day. Unhampered by the British libel laws, the foreign press was free to be more vociferous.

The *New York Times* had already published a long report in its 'London Gossip' column of 10 November, four days before the *Truth* issue appeared. But it still alluded to Labouchère's coming crusade against the British government and, more damagingly for the authorities and especially the royal family, the implication of Eddy, Prince Albert Victor, in the scandal. The paper's London correspondent had his ear pressed close to the clubland ground, writing:

> I dare say rumors and perhaps even explicit statements have reached America before this about the extremely painful and revolting scandal which is being unearthed here by the authorities, and which involves a large number of men in the highest circles of English society. This number is variously stated as between sixteen and forty, and the names which are mentioned embrace even royalty. The scandal is analogous in character to that exposed in Dublin Castle four years ago by William O'Brien [in which the rent boy John Saul was involved]. As in that case, some of the obscure parties to the crime have been arrested, and will apparently be brought to trial and punished, but tremendous

efforts are making to shield the titled culprits from exposure. Only one name of this class, that of Lord Arthur Somerset, a Major in the Horse Guards, and the third son of the Duke of Beaufort, is given with certainly, and he was allowed to get away. Current rumor says that Prince Albert Victor will not return from India until the matter is completely over and forgotten, but there are certain stubborn moralists [Henry Labouchère] at work on the case who profess determination that it shall not be judiciously burked, and the prospects are that the whole terrible affair will be dragged out into the light. The character of the threatened disclosures and the magnitude of personal interests involved may be gathered from the fact that a Privy Council meeting has been held to discuss the subject.

And on 18 November, in the *Cincinnati Commercial Gazette*, under the explosive headlines, 'Wales' Heir Involved' and subheading, 'Albert Victor, Two Removes from the Throne, a Vile Wretch', Eddy was brought firmly and clearly into the press coverage and public fray. And it was a brutal attack on the prince:

Everybody was talking about it and passing on distorted versions to his fellows. But there was a general feeling that it would never get into the Courts. Now the prospect is different. Mr. Labouchere has said frankly in this week's *Truth*: 'What if the matter is "Burked" by the authorities, it will be brought up immediately when Parliament meets, and ventilated to the very dregs in the House of Commons.' This threat, ominously enough, follows a paragraph alluding to the costly apartments being fitted up for Albert Victor in St. James' Palace, the expense of which the Commons will be asked to meet. No connection between these two paragraphs is suggested, but it is obvious to everybody that there has come to be within the past few days a general conviction that this long-necked, narrow-headed, young dullard was mixed up in the scandal, and out of this had sprung a half-whimsical, half-serious notion, which one hears propounded now about clubland, that matters will be so arranged that he will never return from India. The most popular idea is that he will be killed in a tiger hunt, but runaway horses or a fractious elephant might serve as well. What this really mirrors is a public awakening to the fact that this stupid, perverse boy has become a man, and has duly two highly precarious lives between him and the English throne and is an utter blackguard and ruffian. Heretofore people have not known much about him, save that he was a dull chap whose nickname was Prince Collars and Cuffs. The revelation now that he is something besides a harmless simpleton has created a very painful feeling everywhere. Although he looks so strikingly like his mother, it turns out that he gets only his face from the Danish race, and that morally and mentally he combines the worst attributes of those sons of George III at whose mention history still holds her nose. It is not too early to predict that such a fellow will never be allowed to ascend the British throne; that is as clear as anything can well be. It is equally clear that the suppression of the scandal in which he, with some dozens of young and middle-aged samples of nobility and gentry of England is involved, has become impossible, and that every day the attempt is further persisted in will do enormous damage not only to the Government but to the aristocratic social structure generally. There is more indignation and ruffling of the equanimity of the English mind just now than I have ever seen before. Very little more repression will be needed to bring it to fever heat, but, as I have said, the whole scandal is going to come out.

If this polemic came to their attention at the time, it must have given Bertie, Queen Victoria and Eddy himself palpitations. And Sir Dighton Probyn and Francis Knollys would have been very perturbed, as would Lord Salisbury and senior members of his administration.

Five weeks later, on 22 December, a letter titled 'The Policy of Hushing Up' would be written to the *New York Herald*, signed by 'A Member of Parliament', which firmly defended Eddy, then on his planned tour of India, and the royal family against the allegations and attacks recently published about him in the American press. The author H. Montgomery Hyde surmised that the writer of the letter was Charles Hall.[6] The MP for Holborn in central London, Hall was also a barrister, a QC and, most relevantly, Attorney General to Bertie, the Prince of

Wales, who dealt with the heir to the throne's legal affairs. Aged 46 in late December 1889, Hall had held that position since 1877 and would be knighted in May 1890, officially for representing Britain at an important conference in Washington DC. The letter, if it was indeed written by Charles Hall, would undoubtedly have been sanctioned by Bertie, and reveals that the royal family was very disturbed by the rumours surrounding Eddy.

After firmly stipulating that Eddy wouldn't return early from his scheduled tour of India due to pressure emanating from the scandal, the writer went on the attack against the damaging gossip about Eddy's alleged frequenting of No. 19 Cleveland Street, now published in print in America, which had in one publication included a portrait of the prince:

> There are some people who will believe anything, and there is never any telling how far slander may spread [...] a more atrocious or a more dastardly outrage was never perpetrated in the Press. Speaking with some knowledge of the charges in question, and of the persons who are really compromised by them, I assert that there is not, and never was, the slightest excuse for mentioning the name of Prince Albert Victor in association with them. A feeling of delicacy can alone have prevented this statement appearing in a form to command universal credence, but now that there are libellers who do not hesitate to assail the young Prince – at a safe distance – it is a mistake for the English press to maintain absolute silence on the subject.

The writer of the letter ended by saying that he wished that the editor or proprietor of an offending publication 'could be reached by the law', and that such attacks on the royal family could only result in 'strengthening the attachment which the English people are proud of entertaining for their Sovereign and her family'.

In Britain, the coverage of the scandal was less provocative and inflammatory, with names still unnamed and even insinuations about Eddy absent. An example is *The Echo* from 11 November, which was still going with the headlines 'The Painful Society Scandal' and 'The

Minor Suspects in Custody'. Some papers were reporting rumour and were often very wide of reality, such as the *Bradford Daily Telegraph* of 15 November, which claimed to have heard 'on good authority' that 'two men of social standing have been arrested by Inspector Abberline', and as Abberline had been spotted in 'the magistrates' private room', the cases of the two men might have been heard in public.

Eddy would never be named in the British press, but others connected to the scandal wouldn't be so lucky. It was Ernest Parke, editor of the *North London Press*, who carried out his earlier threat to name names. He published an article on 16 November that would have serious legal implications for himself and bring the whole scandal under much wider public scrutiny, both in Britain and internationally:

> In an issue of the 28th September we stated that among the number of aristocrats who were mixed up in an indescribably loathsome scandal in Cleveland Street, Tottenham Court Road, were the heir to a duke and the younger son of a duke. The men to whom we thus referred were the Earl of Euston, eldest son of the Duke of Grafton, and Lord H. Arthur G. Somerset, a younger son of the Duke of Beaufort. The former, we believe, has departed for Peru [Parke was wrong here – Euston was in London, living in his home at No. 4 Grosvenor Place]. The latter, having resigned his commission and his office of Assistant Equerry to the Prince of Wales, has gone too. These men have been allowed to leave the country [only Somerset had], and thus defeat the ends of justice, because their prosecution would disclose the fact that a far more distinguished and more highly placed personage than themselves [Eddy] was inculpated in these disgusting crimes. The criminals in this case are to be numbered by the score. They include two or three Members of Parliament, one of them a popular Liberal [these politicians are still unidentified].

With Somerset gone, it was the naming of the Earl of Euston, Henry Fitzroy, which would prove to be truly inflammatory. Euston was warned about the article, just before it came out, by his solicitor friend Edward Bedford, who had read that edition of the *North London Press*.

Ernest Parke was 29 years old in November 1889 and had been married for five years to Sarah Blain, originally from Manchester, the wedding having taken place in Parke's native Warwickshire. They had a young son and lived at No. 21 St Luke's Road in Clapham, south-west London. Born in Stratford-upon-Avon in January 1860, the son of Fenning Plowman Parke, Parke had a solid education at Stratford-upon-Avon Grammar School and began his working life in a bank in his hometown. But he soon decided to become a journalist and, aged 22 in 1882, became a reporter on the *Birmingham Daily Gazette*, where he stayed until joining the *Midland Echo*, also in Birmingham, as a sub-editor in 1884. After only a brief spell with that publication, Parke moved to London, working as a sub-editor on *The Echo* between 1884 and 1888.

His next move was to a financial newspaper, *Stock Exchange*, founded by Baron Grant, and he was made editor at the age of 28. But as Ernest would later say on 25 April 1894 in an interview in *The Sketch* in a series called 'Journals and Journalists of Today', he left that position as he 'hated the work'. Luckily for him, the politician Thomas Power O'Connor, an Irish Nationalist MP, set up a new publication, *The Star*, in 1888, its first issue appearing in January that year. O'Connor recruited Parke as his chief sub-editor, and it was on that paper that he would truly thrive, later editing it himself.

Based on Stonecutter Street, close to Ludgate Circus in the City of London, *The Star* was an evening newspaper, published six days a week. It was a broadsheet, which ran to just four pages and had an aggressive tabloid approach to news. It also reflected the values of O'Connor, who wrote in his first editorial, 'The rich, the privileged, the prosperous need no guardian or advocate; the poor, the weak, the beaten require the work and word of every humane man and woman to stand between them and the world.' George Bernard Shaw was among the many notable contributors to the paper.

O'Connor was a radical, and he would support Henry Labouchère when the latter took on the government over the Cleveland Street scandal in Parliament. But as well as being very political with a social conscience, O'Connor had a real nose for news and gaining readers, and by February 1888, within a month of its first appearance, *The Star* had a daily circulation of around 125,000. This would rise by the end of the year, with the newspaper's sensational coverage of the Jack the Ripper killings becoming a major reason for the surge. Ernest Parke wrote some of those articles, proclaiming in one piece early in the sequence of murders, his opinion that they were committed by just one man. In his memoirs, O'Connor later wrote about Ernest Parke, describing him as 'a young, flossy haired man, with a keen face, a lithe and agile body, a tremendous flair for news'.

Parke continued working for *The Star* as he set up the *North London Press* in the summer of 1889, and remained in its employment for years. O'Connor and the paper would prove loyal and support him throughout his travails during the Cleveland Street scandal.

The *North London Press* was based at 100 Central Street in the area of St Luke's, east London, and by the late autumn of 1889 had a weekly circulation of around 4,500. This was a very respectable number of readers considering that Ernest Parke had a very limited budget and had only founded it months earlier. Parke, a Marxist and anti-monarchist, was ambitious, driven and hungry. He went further than any other British editor or journalist in exposing the aristocrats in the scandal which, likely to his private glee, had now also taken on a directly royal dimension through Eddy's implication.

The Earl of Euston sued for libel a week after Parke named him in the *North London Press*, with an application for a libel writ issued to Mr Justice Field on 23 November 1889. Euston stated in his affidavit, 'The atrocious libel that I have been guilty of an impossible and unspeakable crime is absolutely without foundation.'

That very day, Parke, who had already heard through contacts what was coming, put out another pre-written editorial in his weekly, reasoning clearly about the predicament he faced but firmly holding his nerve:

If the charges we [the *North London Press*] preferred against Lord Euston are untrue, and were made without sufficient reason, we have no desire to escape the natural and inevitable penalty of misleading the public on so grave a matter. Nor shall we seek to lay the blame on nay shoulders but our own. We have taken our position; we shall stand by it.

And in the lengthy editorial, Parke articulately outlined the course of events that had led him, since late September, to repeatedly report and comment on the handling of the Cleveland Street scandal in the *North London Press*:

And first, it is necessary to recite a few facts as to which we challenge contradiction. The information affecting Lord Arthur Somerset, the man Hammond, and other persons, distinguished and undistinguished, was in the hands of the authorities at the end of July. In a paper dated 28th September, but issued on the 27th, we first gave the outlines of the scandal, though we mentioned no names except Hammond's.

But between the 25th and the 28th of that month, the name of Lord Arthur Somerset appears among the list of spectators of races at Newmarket. He afterwards disappeared, in obedience, as Mr. Labouchere says [in his journal *Truth*] to a hint from a high official at Court [Sir Dighton Probyn], and his resignation of his command and of his office of Assistant Equerry to the Prince of Wales was gazetted [*London Gazette*]. When the warrant against him was issued he was safe from arrest. In the same way Hammond, the keeper of the den of infamy at Cleveland Street, had been able to put himself beyond the reach of the law. He fled to France, whence at the suggestion of our own Foreign Office, he was expelled as a mauvais sujet [a bad subject, a scoundrel], and he has fled, it is feared, without any prospect of being brought to justice.

The result, therefore, of these extraordinary — these unheard of — delays in fulfilling the forms of law, and protecting the community against nameless crimes, has been that two of the chief offenders have disappeared. But that is not all. Two minor members of this vile conspiracy [Veck and Newlove] were committed for trial and pleaded guilty to the charge at the Old Bailey. Their cases were brought on at the end of the day's proceedings, when the spectators had left and when everybody supposed that the sitting was over. Hurried clandestinely into the dock, these guilty wretches, condemned out of their own mouths, were awarded sentences of four [Newlove] and nine [Veck] months respectively for offences for which, at a previous Sessions, a minister at Hackney [Charles Hart Burleigh, a deacon] had been condemned to penal servitude for life, with the special warning from the judge that he could have no hope of a mitigation of his dreadful doom.

Parke also went on to defend the police handling of the Cleveland Street inquiry, which would undoubtedly have pleased the Met Commissioner James Monro, Inspector Abberline, PC Hanks and the other officers involved:

Now we hasten to say that we acquit Mr. Monro of any part of the lot in what we solemnly declare to be a deliberate attempt to shield high-placed offenders. On the contrary, all our information is that Mr. Monro has spared neither himself nor his staff in his efforts to detect and punish [...] During his tenure of Scotland Yard, the Chief Commissioner has won universal esteem as an incorruptible servant of the public, and he has fully maintained his reputation during the preliminaries of this disgraceful case.

Finally, Parke laid down his gauntlet to the highest politicians in the land, passing the responsibility to the House of Commons:

It will be for Parliament to interrogate Lord Salisbury, Mr W.H. Smith [Leader of the House of Commons], and Mr. Matthews [Home Secretary] as to their knowledge of the nature of the charges, the date at which they were first made, the form in which they were first made, and the evidence taken in their support, the names of the incriminated persons – be they whom they may – and the aid the Ministry have given to Mr. Monro, a zealous, a discreet, and an experienced officer, in carrying out the measures recommended by him for the detection of crime. If we have in any way contributed to that result, we shall be well repaid for the cost, the anxiety, the grave personal risk we incur in doing – and doing alone among the press – what we believe to be our solemn duty to the public.

Mr Justice Field gave the go-ahead for Euston's writ on the same day, Saturday, 23 November, and within hours, a warrant for Parke's arrest was issued. After conferring with a good friend, who offered to put up a sizeable bail for him, a few hours later, Parke turned himself in at Bow Street Police Court. He had known about Euston's application for a libel writ for a week, and knew well that if it proceeded, he would be arrested, but he hadn't fled.

It was brave, but then again, Parke firmly believed in his printed assertion that Euston had been a client at No. 19 Cleveland Street, which would soon seem to be further confirmed by the veteran rent boy, John Saul. Parke knew that he just needed to prove the truth.

As it was a weekend and there was no magistrate available to deal with matters, Parke was held over in a cell at the court until Monday, 25 November. On that day, he was released on bail bonds totalling £100 and committed to stand trial at the next sessions of the Old Bailey, two weeks later. Interestingly, the *Illustrated Police News* reported on 30 November that 'Mr. C.F. Gill, barrister, and Mr. Arthur Newton, solicitor, appeared to watch the case on behalf of certain parties whose names have been mentioned in connection with the scandals'. Newton always assiduously monitored developments and Charles Gill had represented George Veck at his trial and helped engineer a light sentence for him back in September.

The Star newspaper, where Parke foremostly plied his journalistic trade, published a front-page editorial the same day that Parke was bailed, under the headline 'A Word on the Scandals'. It was both a statement of where the paper stood on the scandal and an attack on the government and the police. It read, '*The Star* had hitherto been silent. Silence is no longer possible [...] The topic is the conduct of the authorities. People do not hesitate to say that some of the worst criminals have escaped, and have been allowed to escape, by the connivance of the police.'

The Star also immediately launched a campaign on its chief sub editor's behalf. Led by the deputy editor, T.P. O'Connor's number two, Henry Massingham, who was a year Parke's junior, it was called the 'Fair Trial Fund' and by the end of the month had received pledges from readers totalling £300. Parke's potential plight in the jaws of the rich and aristocratic Euston won him a great deal of support among the lower classes in the coming weeks, including in working men's clubs, and most of his fellow journalists also sided with him, but outside of *The Star*, most of them did so quietly at this stage.

The solicitor representing Parke, Minton Slater, got busy on his behalf. Slater wrote to the Home Secretary, Sir Henry Matthews, on 28 November asking to interview the imprisoned George Veck and Henry Newlove. A few days later, Slater received a reply from the DPP, Sir Augustus Stephenson, saying that he could have the depositions (statements before the magistrates' court) of the two men, implicitly meaning that Slater couldn't visit them in prison and ask his own questions.

Slater also penned a letter to the Met Commissioner James Monro with a request to interview the police officers involved in the Cleveland Street inquiry. The assistant commissioner, Dr Robert Anderson, who had held that post since 1888 and been in overall charge of the Jack the Ripper investigation, asked Stephenson for advice on this, and the DPP replied that it was Monro's decision to make. The officers were not made available.

Legal meanderings meant that the libel trial wouldn't reach the Old Bailey until the middle of January 1890, six weeks after Euston's libel writ was approved by Mr Justice Field. In the early preliminary hearings before a magistrate, Parke entered his expected plea of 'not guilty' and he was bailed again, this time for the sum of £500, and this amount was put forward.

On 16 December, Euston appeared before a grand jury at the opening of the next session of the Old Bailey and Parke was formally indicted, to which Parke again entered a plea of 'not guilty'. The defendant was required by law to back up this assertion of innocence and state how he would defend it, and Parke's legal team submitted a report to the court which stated that five witnesses would testify against Euston. That number sensationally included the long-time rent boy John Saul, anonymous 'author' of the notorious *The Sins of the Cities of the Plain*, and a very young man called Frank Hewitt, who it seemed had originally introduced Henry Newlove (who was still in Pentonville Prison alongside the cod clergyman George Veck) to the pimp Charles Hammond.

With this new information coming forward, Euston's legal counsel requested that the trial now be heard at the next session of the Old Bailey. This was granted, so Parke remained on bail over the Christmas period and dangerously dangled until two weeks into the New Year.

But Parke continued to report on the scandal. The *North London Press* of 21 December had, under the banner headline 'The Scandals' and the sub headline 'The Hush Policy Failing', another, which read, 'Solicitor Newton and others to appear at Bow Street'. It was also revealed that Parke had somehow managed to get hold of some of Charles Hammond's letters, reported under another heading reading 'Hammond's Letter'. Parke relayed how Hammond 'demands £800 to take his family to America', followed by 'Who found the money?' In the article, Parke also made it clear that 'the letters themselves are at the service of the Public Prosecutor'.

Almost two weeks later, on 4 January 1890, the DPP, Sir Augustus Stephenson, took up the offer, writing to Parke and asking for the letters to be sent.

Running parallel in the build-up to Ernest Parke's forthcoming trial for libel, the preliminary criminal proceedings against Arthur Newton and his associates Frederick Taylerson and Adolphus de Gallo were indeed underway. And in early January 1890, a subpoena was issued by the Treasury for Parke to appear in the case against the three men. Parke duly appeared.

As the *Staffordshire Sentinel* reported on 11 January, 'Mr. Ernest Parke, editor of the *North London Press* produced on subpoena, and handed to the prosecution, letters alleged to be from Hammond, and also voluntarily gave up a number of other letters, photographs, and cards.'

Eleven

While Ernest Parke waited for his tussle in court with the Earl of Euston, which would soon open the scandal much more widely to the attention of the press and public, the police were working busily behind the scenes. Abberline, under James Monro's direction, was building a case for the possible prosecution of Lord Arthur Somerset's lawyer, Arthur Newton, and his accomplices, Frederick Taylerson and Adolphus de Gallo, for the intimidation and attempted removal of witnesses against Somerset. This had been triggered by Newton's bid to get Algernon Allies, who was still under police protection as a potential witness, out of Britain.

Taking further statements from the former telegraph messenger rent boys, who had now been dismissed by the GPO, Abberline, aided by PC Hanks, was dismayed to hear that one of his officers, PC Richard Sladden, was being implicated in wrongdoing and possible police corruption along with another constable who wasn't on the Cleveland Street investigation. Sladden, who had done most of the surveillance on No. 19 Cleveland Street over a ten-day period in July and had later spent some time helping identify Somerset as a client, had, along with the ubiquitous PC Hanks, been a key officer in Abberline's inquiry.

On 16 December 1889, 16-year-old William Meech Perkins, who had been procured at the GPO as a rent boy at the brothel by Henry Newlove, gave a revealing statement to Abberline. It seemed that after Perkins and the other boys had been fired by the GPO on Friday, 6 December, Perkins and Charles Thickbroom, aged 17, had gone to PC Sladden's home at No. 109 Whitfield Street, near Tottenham Court Road, to tell him and ask his advice. They, along with 15-year-old Charles Swinscow, had got to know Sladden a little when he went with them to Piccadilly and Hyde Park Barracks to identify Somerset months earlier.

But it was what Perkins said next that concerned Abberline. A while after Perkins and Thickbroom had called on and spoken to the policeman, Sladden's daughter called at Perkins' home with a note from her father, reading, 'Will you and Thickbroom meet me outside my house at 9.15 p.m. today as I have something important to tell you.'

Perkins called on Thickbroom, and together, the boys did as Sladden instructed. Perkins said that Sladden appeared in uniform and told them to follow him as somebody wanted to see them. They did so, and he stopped just off Portland Road and went ahead. After a short time, Sladden returned to them with a group of other police officers. Sladden came forward alone, telling the two boys to remain where they were as someone would come and meet them there at 10.30 p.m.

According to Perkins, Sladden informed them that 'a man' wanted to see them about going away to another country, adding, 'I think it is Lord Arthur Somerset's father doing it'. Sladden then went off and came back with a man he had spoken to. The man, who had 'ginger whiskers', told the boys to be at 'the public house at the corner of Marlborough Street and Poland Street' in Soho at 2 p.m. on the following Monday, 9 December.[1]

The man with the ginger whiskers to whom Sladden introduced Perkins and Thickbroom was recognised by them. Perkins said that he was the policeman who 'keeps the gate at Marlborough Street Police Court'. Abberline swiftly identified this man as PC John Walker, who he knew as carrying out that function, but who had no previous connection to the Cleveland Street inquiry.

On Monday, 9 December, Perkins relayed in his statement that he and Thickbroom had duly gone to the pub and the ginger-whiskered man had come up to them outside and said, 'Newton has been here but could not see you, I will go and tell him you were here'. Newton then appeared and took the boys to his offices nearby, offered them a new set of clothes, to fund their journey to Australia, and to pay them both a weekly sum for a considerable amount of time once they were there. Perkins ended his new statement by saying that he hadn't mentioned PC Sladden's actions to the police during the previous week as he didn't want to get the constable into trouble. Abberline took a statement from Charles Thickbroom, which corroborated everything that Perkins had said.

Three days later, on 19 December, Inspector Abberline called in both PC Sladden and PC Walker to make statements. Sladden's version of events, given to another officer, was different from that of Perkins and Thickbroom regarding his own involvement. He confirmed that the two boys had visited him at his home on 6 December at 1.45 p.m. to tell him that they had been dismissed by 'The Service' (the GPO). The policeman recounted how he told them he was 'very sorry' for them and they said that they were 'frightened' to go home before they left. Perkins and Thickbroom were no doubt anxious about the reaction of their parents about their firing from a secure and respected job. Although both sets of parents, and those of the other rent boys, already knew of their sons' involvement in the scandal, their dismissal over it would have compounded their shame.

Sladden said that he left his home at 9.30 that night to go on night duty and the boys were once again outside his front door. But he made no mention of the claim by Perkins that his daughter had delivered a message to him asking them to call back there that night. Sladden added that the boys said that they didn't know what to do and he persuaded them to go home.

Sladden said that on the following night, Saturday, 7 December, the two boys were once again at his door, and he told them that 'a gentleman' (undoubtedly Arthur Newton) had £1,000 to be divided between them and the money had come from the Duke of Beaufort, Somerset's father. Perkins and Thickbroom left, but came back to see him on Monday, 9 December, asking him if he had heard anything more. Sladden said that he told them to go round to Marlborough Street Police Court and see a man there. When pressed, Sladden said, 'I meant the man on the gate at the Police Court – a constable – his name is Walker – I don't know his number.'

According to Sladden, the boys went to Marlborough Street Police Court as directed and then came back to see him at home again that same day. They said that they had seen a man and it was Arthur Newton. Somerset's lawyer had 'offered to give them a new fit-out and pay their passage to Australia and give them £1 a week for three years'. The boys also told him that Newton also gave them both 5s.

Sladden said that he told them, 'That sounds very nice', but warned the boys not to 'take a leap in the dark'. Perkins and Thickbroom also told him that Newton had asked them to bring 'the other boys' (Charles Swinscow and George Alma Wright) round to see him the next day, to which Sladden said he responded, 'I shouldn't advise you to do that [...] I think the best thing you can do is not to go near him anymore'.

Sladden added that a few days later, on Thursday, 12 December, Perkins came to see him again, this time alone. Perkins said that he had been to see Newton with Swinscow and Wright, and Newton had given the three of them a sovereign to share. The boys had then taken lodgings on the Edgware Road in central London for the night.

Sladden reiterated his warning and said he told Perkins that all of them should stay away from Newton, and not doing so 'will cause a great bother'. Sladden said that he also told Perkins not to mention his name in relation to the case. And he firmly denied having anything to do with Newton directly: 'I have never had any conversation or seen or had any communication with Mr. Newton – nor received any money from anyone [...] The only words – the only person – I ever spoke to about the case was Walker, the Police Constable.'

Sladden was adamant in emphasising that he had no connection to Newton, whether directly or indirectly through Walker. 'Neither Mr. Newton or anyone from his office has ever attempted to communicate with me. Nor has Walker given me any message from Mr. Newton, he has never told me that Mr. Newton has told him to tell me anything.'

Sladden also expressed his sympathy and empathy for the ex-telegraph messenger boys and their situation:

What I done I merely done what I thought was for the boys' good […] I was with them many weeks keeping observation on different Club houses. I had a very bitter feeling towards them at first, but in time my feelings altered towards them through being in continual conversation with them. I found them very deficient in knowledge of simple things that surprised me that I came to the conclusion that they were ignorant of the crimes that they committed with other persons.

When asked why he had mentioned the figure of £1,000 being offered by Newton, Sladden said that he had heard that amount being bandied about in 'common talk' around the police court. And as to what PC Walker had told him about the case, Sladden said, 'I don't think he has told me anything in particular. He has spoken to me about the case. There is one thing I deeply regret and that is not sending the boys to Mr. Abberline when they came to me.'

Sladden additionally further implicated PC Walker:

I wish to add that it was Walker who told me that it was a gentleman that had the money for the boys – I won't be sure whether he mentioned any amount or whether he said one thousand or two thousand but have heard both one thousand and two thousand spoken of by persons about the court.

In his statement taken the same day, 19 December, PC John Walker denied everything:

My duty is that of Gatekeeper at Marlborough Street Police Court. I had not spoken to any boys to put them in communication with Mr. Newton. I do not know Sladden that I know of. I have heard no gossip about the case and the Courts.

PC Sladden was then brought into the room for identification purposes:

I have seen him at the Court. I may have spoken to him about it, but I don't remember what I said if I did. I never heard there was money for the boys. I've only heard that Newton made a lot of money out of the case. I don't remember any boys asking me for Mr. Newton or any gentleman. Mr. Newton has not asked me to do anything for him with respect to that case – nothing about money for these boys. I have said nothing to Sladden about money for the boys – £1,000 or £2,000 or any other sum – I can say this positively. I am positive I have not heard any conversation about Mr. Newton and any of these boys, or with them separately.

The DPP had been informed of the implications of police misconduct or corruption against PC Sladden and PC Walker, and a letter written by Sir Augustus Stephenson to the Attorney General, Sir Richard Webster on 18 December (the day *before* the two constables made their statements) makes this clear. After reading the statements of Perkins and Thickbroom of two days earlier, Stephenson wrote:

From this it would appear either that Newton has been corrupting Sladden, or somebody else has been doing so [...] Mr. Monro does not propose to take any action or call upon Sladden and the other Constables implicated by the boys for any explanation at present.

Over six weeks later, on 3 February 1890, at which time legal proceedings were in advanced preliminary progress against Arthur Newton and his associates, the Met Commissioner James Monro responded in a memo to a question from the Home Office about whether any action was to be taken against PC Sladden, 'Not yet. This pends the decision in the case of Newton. I have purposefully abstained from taking this up till the termination of the proceedings in that case.'

Arthur Newton, his managing clerk, Frederick Taylerson, and 'interpreter', Adolphus de Gallo had in fact been issued summons to present themselves at Bow Street Magistrates' Court on 16 December 1889, the very day that Perkins and Thickbroom made their new police statements, which had undoubtedly topped up the police's evidence against them. Newton and his two subordinates were called to appear at the court a week later.

The three men were accused that, at times, between 25 September and 12 December that year:

> [they] did unlawfully conspire, combine, confederate, and agree together to obstruct, pervert, and defeat the due course of law and justice then pending at the Marlborough Street Police Court and in the Central Criminal Court in respect of offences alleged to have been committed at 19, Cleveland Street, Fitzroy Square, in the County of London, and to obstruct, prevent, the due course of law and justice in respect of the said offences.

On 23 December, this time at Bow Street Magistrates' Court, there was another hearing, and it demonstrated that Inspector Abberline, as the detective in charge of the Cleveland Street inquiry, was going to play a central role in the proceedings against Newton and his associates and that he would come under heavy fire himself.

Abberline was in court that day. Charles Gill, who had represented George Veck, was now Newton's counsel and, as *The Times* of Christmas Eve 1889 relayed, he had Abberline removed from the court:

> Mr. Gill asked that Inspector Abberline, who was the chief police officer engaged in the case, whom he should have to severely cross-examine, and against whom he should have to make imputations should be ordered to leave the court. Inspector Abberline was then directed to withdraw.

On 7 January 1890, further proceedings against Newton et al. occurred at the same court, and it was reported at length in *The Times* the following day.

Thickbroom was cross-examined by Charles Gill. When he was asked if Inspector Abberline had told him not to mention Sladden's name in relation to setting up the meeting with Newton, he replied that Abberline hadn't done so. But Thickbroom told the court that Abberline 'had said he did not want to mention Sladden's name, as he did not want to see him get into a bother'.

Regarding the implication of Sladden, Inspector Abberline was reported as saying that Sladden 'must have been very stupid' in compromising himself, presumably by his desire to help the former telegraph messenger rent boys, with whom he sympathised. It seems that Abberline didn't see Sladden's actions as corrupt and tried to protect him, a member of his investigative team, out of professional loyalty.

There is no record of any police action, internally or externally, ever being taken against PC Sladden or PC Walker in this matter, but they would surely have been unofficially reprimanded.

Meanwhile, Lord Arthur Somerset had been moving from place to place, all over France and down to Monaco. Having decided not to ask his father, the Duke of Beaufort, for financial support, Somerset was desperately trying to find a job, or as he termed it in letters to Reginald Brett, 'an appointment'. It was upsetting to Somerset when his former boss and friend Bertie, Prince of Wales, unsurprisingly refused to give him a 'recommendation' or character reference through intermediaries.

Somerset's mother wanted him to return to England to face the charges. But after her husband spoke to Arthur Newton about their son's chances of acquittal, which the wily lawyer said would be very hard to achieve with the prima facie (pre-trial) evidence against Somerset being so strong, the duke and duchess realised that this would not be a viable option. Many placed highly in society and in London's clubs felt that Somerset's silence in his own defence in exile and his failure to quash the persistent rumours regarding Eddy, Prince Albert Victor, being a client of No. 19 Cleveland Street exacerbated the situation – particularly for Eddy, his father Bertie, and the royal family as an institution.

Somerset had no intention of returning, and while he never said that Eddy had been involved in the goings-on at the brothel, he was using the gossip about Eddy, who was on his tour of India, as something of a shield for himself. Somerset wrote to his most trusted confidant, Brett, on 10 December 1889:

I cannot see what good I could do Prince Eddy if I went into Court. I might do him harm because if I was asked if I had ever heard anything against him – from whom? – has any person mentioned with whom he went there etc? – the questions would be very awkward. I have never mentioned the boy's [Eddy's] name except to Probyn, Montagu [Somerset's commanding officer] and Knollys when they were acting for me and I thought they ought to know. Had they been wise, hearing what I knew and therefore what others knew, they ought to have hushed the matter up, instead of stirring it up as they did, with all the authorities.

In the same letter, Somerset, who saw himself as a scapegoat in the scandal, made it clear that he knew a lot that could be damaging to others, but he would never give over those secrets. However, there was a veiled threat that if he were antagonised and pushed to face his prosecution, he could possibly crack: 'Nothing will ever make me divulge anything I know even if I were arrested. But of course, if certain people laid themselves out to have me arrested and succeeded, I might possibly lose my temper and annoy them.'

Out of reach of Abberline and arrest, in the end, Lord Arthur Somerset would never have to tell what he knew. But at that stage, he still felt the need to justify his silence and refusal to return to England to Brett, that letter giving an insight into the turmoil of his disrupted life and mind:

Of course, it has very often, or may I say constantly occurred to me, that it rests with me to clear up this business, but what can I do? A great many people would never speak to me again as it is, but if I went into Court and told all I knew no one who called himself a man would ever speak to me again. Hence my infernal position [...] At all events you and Newton can bear me witness that I have sat absolutely tight in the matter.

Another letter to Brett on 23 December showed that Somerset had also been watching developments in the libel case brought by the Earl of

Euston against Ernest Parke, the latter of whom had named Somerset in his editorials too:

> I cannot see if he remains in England how Euston can get out of prosecuting Veck and Newlove [who were already incarcerated, but in new proceedings] and then there will be another long trial, but I take it he has not finished with Parke by a long way. Altogether the approaching winter looks stormy in England.

He added that he had read in *The Times* that Eddy wouldn't return from his tour of India 'before the original intended time'.

The prosecution being brought against his lawyer and friend Arthur Newton, who had then just been indicted, triggered a stronger reaction. Somerset was concerned that his name would be further pulled into the public fray around the scandal:

> Poor Mr. N [Newton]! ... I suppose it will be another opportunity to draw my luckless name before the public? [...] I should think they have tackled a strong and dangerous man in N. If they put him in a corner, he will very likely give them a nasty one.

Somerset additionally mentioned Charles Hammond, whom he called 'H' and 'that arch ruffian', saying, 'I should be delighted if they got at him and got him 5 years'. He also revealed that none of the telegraph messenger rent boys from No. 19 Cleveland Street, whom he called 'youths', had directly approached him for money, and 'I trust that Abberline is seeing that A [Algernon Allies] is comfortable for the rest of his life'.

Ernest Parke finally faced his libel trial brought by the Earl of Euston at the Old Bailey on 15 January 1890, before Mr Justice Hawkins. The 73-year-old Hawkins, then known as Sir Henry Hawkins, but later as the 1st Baron Brampton, had begun his career as a barrister in 1843, developing and becoming known for his skills in cross-examination. Among many other cases, Hawkins was prosecuting counsel, first junior and then senior, in one of the most famous non-capital cases of the Victorian period: the trials of Arthur Orton, the Tichborne Claimant, in the early to mid-1870s. Hawkins was ultimately successful when the impostor Orton was given a lengthy fourteen-year sentence for perjury after making a claim that he was the rightful heir to the Tichborne baronetcy.

Hawkins was made a judge in 1876 and had already presided over several famous murder trials and built a reputation as a 'hanging judge' because of the supposed harshness of his sentencing. He was not well thought of by some legal scholars or some of those who represented defendants before him. The writer H. Montgomery Hyde, a barrister himself, wrote in 1976 that Hawkins' nickname of 'Hanging Hawkins' was unfair, however, and he 'favoured leniency, particularly for first offenders'.

Hawkins would later go on to oversee the trial of the undoubtedly guilty prostitute-poisoning serial killer, Dr Neill Cream, in late 1892, handing Cream a sentence of death. It was one of the most infamous murder cases of the century. And in 1896, Hawkins notably sentenced Charles Thomas Wooldridge, a soldier in the Royal House Guards, to death for the murder of his wife, Nell. Woodbridge was imprisoned with Oscar Wilde in Reading Prison in Berkshire prior to his execution and Wilde dedicated his famous 1897 poem 'The Ballad of Reading Gaol' to him.

But over six years earlier, the *Earl of Euston vs Ernest Parke* libel trial would prove to be another notable milestone in Hawkins' judicial career. Parke, as expected, pleaded not guilty 'and justification', which basically meant that the libel was true. This would be outlined in the defence put forward for him by Frank Lockwood QC, the Liberal MP for York, aged 43, who will resurface later in this story in the trial of Oscar Wilde, less than five years later, this time for the prosecution. Lockwood, later a solicitor general, was deputised by 27-year-old H.H. Asquith, subsequently widely known as Herbert Asquith, the Liberal prime minister between 1908 and 1916.

Euston's prosecution team was led by the very experienced Sir Charles Russell QC, aged 57, who would later succeed Sir Richard Webster as Attorney General in 1892 for a second stint in that role and, shortly after being elevated to the judiciary, become Lord Chief Justice in 1894. Highly successful as a lawyer, he was reputedly earning around £16,000 a year by 1890.

According to the *South Australian Chronicle* of 2 February 1890, more than a month after its London correspondent sent his dispatch about the trial on 17 January, Russell was paid 500 guineas for his work prosecuting Ernest Parke for libel. Russell was aided by Charles 'Willie' Mathews, who had defended Henry Newlove at his trial the previous year, and Lionel Hart.

Sir Charles Russell opened proceedings with a solemn reminder that the charge against Parke was a serious one and reiterated what the Earl of Euston had said in cross-examination at an earlier hearing at Bow Street Police Court in late November 1889 – that he had only been to No. 19 Cleveland Street once and only because he had been misled as to what took place there. Euston claimed that he had been in Piccadilly one evening in late May or early June 1889 and a card was pressed into his hand. This was an everyday occurrence in that busy area of central London, where cards advertising services were aggressively proffered to passersby, especially those who were obviously well heeled. Euston said that when he later looked at the card, it read, 'Poses Plastiques. Hammond, 19 Cleveland Street'.

As the cultural studies academic Nicole Anae has written:

A Victorian performance style known as poses plastiques mastered the art of manipulating the body into highly stylised and apparently motionless attitudes to resemble so-called living statues. Most favoured adopting Classical stances in the garb of Greek and Roman deities, and a number of its female technicians titillated audiences with costumes giving the appearance of almost complete nudity.[2]

Euston admitted that he decided to make a trip to No. 19 Cleveland Street about a week later, but he was under the impression that he would be seeing a show of nude or semi-nude posing women, a form of pornography, heterosexual in nature, and one much more acceptable to Victorian society.

Euston had testified that he had arrived at the brothel at around 10.30 or 11 p.m.:

> I rang the bell, and the door was opened by a man of medium height, clean shaven except for a dark moustache, and with hair that was getting thin on top [Charles Hammond]. He took me into the first room on the right of the passage. He asked me for a sovereign, which I gave him, and then I asked him where these poses plastiques were going to take place. He said, 'There's nothing of that sort here,' and then stated the real character of the house. I asked him what he meant by saying such a thing as that to me and told him if he did not let me out, I should knock him down.

Euston said that he left immediately and never returned to the house again.

Sir Charles Russell emphasised the point that Euston had admitted to going to No. 19 Cleveland Street *once*, using that fact as proof of the earl's honesty, as he could have denied going there at all. But most importantly, Russell was attacking the key thrust of the 'justification' put forward for the libel in Parke's defence: that Euston had visited the house on *multiple* occasions. The burden would be on Frank Lockwood and his team to produce evidence that Euston had indeed been there more than once.

Russell elected not to call Euston as a witness until after the defence witnesses had given their testimonies and only called three other witnesses. Firstly, there was Edward H. Bedford, a solicitor and friend of Euston who, after reading it, had alerted the earl to the 16 November 1889 edition of the *North London Press*, which he claimed to be libellous. Bedford said that he had met with Euston two days later, and they had both gone to the legal firm of Lewis & Lewis at Ely Place, near Chancery Lane in London, where the solicitor George Lewis was given instructions to proceed with a claim for malicious libel.

The prosecution's other two witnesses were Mr Walter Shepherd and Mr E. Adams, who had overseen the printing of the 4,500 copies issued. Their testimony amounted to little more than to confirm that Ernest Parke was the editor of the *North London Press* and that they acted as printers for the publication.

As he began his defence of Parke, Frank Lockwood then laid out his case, as the *South Australian Chronicle* summarised:

> Mr. Lockwood commented on the course pursued by the prosecution in keeping the Earl of Euston out of the witness-box until there should have been a chance of discrediting by cross-examination the witnesses in support of the plea of justification. He agreed with Sir Charles [Russell] as to the seriousness of the charge, and as to the seriousness of the plea put on the record by the defendant; but he proposed to place evidence before the jury which would satisfy them that Lord Euston had been in the habit of visiting 19 Cleveland Street. Some of the evidence might be open to the charge of being tainted, but it was obvious that in a case of this kind it was only evidence of that class that they could expect to find.

Lockwood consequently called several witnesses who seemed to be able to identify Euston as a visitor to the house. As the *Daily Telegraph* of 16 January 1890 reported, there was John O'Loughlin, a coal dealer and greengrocer, who had shops at No. 43 Saville Street and at No. 49 Tottenham Street. O'Loughlin told the court that his shop in Tottenham Street was about 27 yards (24.6m) from No. 19 Cleveland Street. On 'about 20th May' the previous year (1889), O'Loughlin testified that he was standing on the corner of Cleveland Street at about seven or eight o'clock in the evening talking to John William Smith, who worked as a porter at King's Cross potato market. O'Loughlin recounted that Smith drew his attention to a man getting out of a carriage in front of and between Nos 21 and 23 Cleveland Street. The gentleman was then seen entering No. 19 Cleveland Street.

Under friendly examination by Lockwood and then more sternly by Asquith and Russell for the prosecution, O'Loughlin proved irrepressible and raised many laughs in the court. A particular instance was when he asked for Euston to stand up and walk around so that he could examine his gait, which the earl did. Later in his cross-examination by Russell, O'Loughlin expressed surprise that Euston's walk was 'not the walk of a gentleman who had never done any hard work. He reminded me of a low policeman who had done twenty years on the stones [the beat].' That made many in the court titter.

But while O'Loughlin identified Euston as the man he had seen getting out of the carriage, he admitted under pressure that his eyesight was poor and had been deteriorating for about ten years. And perhaps most importantly, the man he had seen the previous May in Cleveland Street was around 5ft 9in–5ft 10in (1.75–1.77m) in height, while the very tall Euston was 6ft 4in (1.93m). O'Loughlin had been taken by an unnamed man to identify Euston at Hyde Park Corner before the trial commenced. (This man was, in fact, Captain Webb, a private detective, hired by Ernest Parke and his defence team to gather witnesses and test their reliability.) O'Loughlin also complained, to more laughter in the court, that he had only received the equivalent of around 10*s* in drinks and fares for his trouble.

O'Loughlin's friend and fellow witness, the potato market porter John William Smith, was then called to give evidence. He corroborated O'Loughlin's account and added that he had seen the same man (Euston) knock and enter No. 19 Cleveland Street 'a week or two' *before* he had witnessed the same scene with O'Loughlin. On that occasion, said Smith, the earl had arrived at around one or two o'clock in the afternoon. Smith then professed to have seen Euston six or seven other times in Cleveland Street over a period of eight or nine months but admitted that he might be mistaken as to identification. Smith triggered giggles when he said that he recognised Euston by the striped trousers he wore, and when Russell asked how he could identify the earl in court that day without seeing his trousers (Euston was seated), Smith replied that 'perhaps he is like me and got more than one pair'. Like O'Loughlin, Smith said that the man he had seen in Cleveland Street was around 5ft 8in tall (1.73m), 8in (20cm) shorter than the Earl of Euston.

Next up for the defence was O'Loughlin's son Michael, a barman, who had been unemployed for two months. He testified that the private detective Captain Webb had first approached him regarding giving evidence in the case about two months earlier, presumably in late November 1889 after the libel writ was issued. Michael O'Loughlin stated that he had seen Euston in Cleveland Street on three occasions, the first time being at the end of May or in early June 1889, when he was coming back from the nearby Middlesex Music Hall at around 11 o'clock at night. He had gone on a recce to Grosvenor Place (Euston lived at No. 4 Grosvenor Place) alone but under Captain Webb's direction, to identify Euston, which he did when he saw him. Asked if he had been paid for his time spent on the case, O'Loughlin said that he hadn't yet, but 'I dare say I shall get something' and 'I should not care to work for nothing', which led to some more laughter in court.

Hannah Morgan, who had previously lived at No. 22 Cleveland Street until late December 1889, then gave evidence. Her home was directly opposite No. 19. She said that she had seen Euston going into No. 19 Cleveland Street on several occasions between 12 p.m. and 1 p.m., and he wore a blue pilot topcoat with a velvet collar and was tall. Like Michael O'Loughlin, she had made a trip to Grosvenor Place to identify Euston there, which she did. Morgan said that she had seen around fifty or sixty 'persons' going in and out of the brothel, but that she could only identify one of them: the Earl of Euston. Euston was asked to stand up in court and Morgan identified him as the man she had seen. Asked by Russell if No. 19 Cleveland Street had 'a very bad name', she replied, 'Yes sir, very bad indeed'.

Frederick Grant, a barman who lived at No. 221 Euston Road, north of Tottenham Court Road, was called to testify next. A friend of Michael O'Loughlin, he confirmed O'Loughlin's statement about seeing Euston in Cleveland Street as they returned one night from the Middlesex Music Hall. Like O'Loughlin and Morgan, Grant had been shown a book of photographs for identification purposes by Captain Webb, in which one photograph was of Euston. When Russell asked for the book to be produced in court, the leading defence counsel, Frank Lockwood, said that he couldn't produce it as it wasn't in his possession.

Grant identified Euston as the man he had seen in Cleveland Street by pointing to him in court.

The defence's final witness had by far the biggest impact on the trial. It was John 'Jack' Saul, the veteran Irish rent boy who had, almost six years earlier, been caught up in the Dublin Castle scandal involving homosexual orgies. Dublin Castle was the seat of the English government in Ireland (until 1922) and the scandal was exposed by William O'Brien, an Irish Nationalist, in his radical journal *United Ireland*. It involved 'homosexual activity amongst the staff at Dublin Castle' and especially implicated James Ellis French, the Director of the Detective Department at the Royal Irish Constabulary (RUC), and interestingly, considering the involvement of GPO telegraph messenger boys at Cleveland Street half a decade later, Gustavus Cornwall, Secretary of the Dublin branch of the GPO.

Saul, who had moved to London by the time the Dublin Castle scandal erupted, was recalled from London as a Crown witness, along with another rent boy called John Daly. But Saul's testimony was never used because the events he described were seen as too old. As the cultural historian and LGBT history specialist Rictor Norton highlighted in his sourcebook of articles, *Homosexuality in Nineteenth-Century England*, Saul's evidence went back almost a decade to the mid-1870s, when he had been a sexual partner of Martin Kirwan, who was by 1884 a captain in the Royal Irish Fusiliers but had been a lieutenant when Saul was involved with him.

As previously mentioned in this story, Saul was also the 'anonymous' author of the controversial 1881 book, *The Sins of the Cities of the Plain*. Saul, who was born in poverty in a Dublin tenement on 29 October 1857, was 32 and much older than the other rent boys involved in the Cleveland Street scandal. He had lived quite a life and was an ebullient, confident character, completely unafraid to speak his truths, which were then considered taboo to the prurient ears of late-Victorian society. Examined by Frank Lockwood, Saul introduced himself to the court:

[Saul:] I live at 15, Old Compton Street, Soho. In May 1879 I met a man named Charles Hammond, who was then living at 25, Oxenden Street, off the Haymarket, and two weeks afterwards I went to lodge with him there. We both earned our living as sodomites. I used to give him all the money I earned, often £8 a week. He moved to 19, Cleveland Street just after Christmas, 1886. At about the end of March [1887] I went to live there. During the time I was there I remember many persons coming to the house.

[Lockwood:] Do you see any person here in this court whom you have seen in Hammond's house, 19 Cleveland Street, at any time?

[Saul, pointing at Euston:] One gentleman I recognise that I took there myself if I am not thoroughly mistaken.

[Lockwood:] When was that?

[Saul:] Some time at the end of April or the beginning of May 1887.

[Lockwood:] Where did you meet this person?

[Saul:] In Piccadilly, not far from the Albany Courtyard, near Sackville Street [coincidentally, where the No. 19 Cleveland Street client and stockbroker Hugh Weguelin lived], nearly opposite the Yorkshire Grey [a pub]. He laughed at me, and I winked at him. He turned sharp into Sackville Street.

[Lockwood:] Go on. Tell me what happened.

[Saul:] The Duke, as we called him came near me and asked me where I was going. I said 'Home' and he said, 'What sort is your place?' 'Very comfortable,' I replied. He said, 'Is it very quiet there?' I said yes it was, and then we took a hansom cab there. We got out by the Middlesex Hospital, and I took the gentleman to 19, Cleveland Street, letting him in with my latchkey. I was not long in there, in the back parlour or reception room before Hammond came and knocked and asked if we wanted any champagne or drinks of any sort, which he was in the habit of doing.[3]

Then there was some disturbance in court. As the *Daily Telegraph* recounted on 16 January 1890:

> As the witness [Saul] was proceeding to give evidence of a character which renders it unfit for publication, there was some demonstration of disapproval from that portion of the court allotted to the public. Mr Lockwood said he hoped his task would not be rendered more difficult by such exhibition of feeling. Mr Justice Hawkins said that if this sort of thing was repeated, he should order the court to be cleared. The evidence was filthily brutal and disgusting, but it was necessary to hear it. So far as this witness was concerned, he afforded a shocking spectacle.

No record exists of exactly what Saul said about his encounter with Euston in this part of his testimony. No contemporary newspaper in Britain or abroad reported those details, for reasons of public decency and, more importantly, fearing prosecution for obscenity. And the records of the proceedings of the Old Bailey provide no details either, except for recording the names of the judge and the respective counsels and the outcome of the trial. It may well be that this section of Saul's evidence wasn't even transcribed in court or that part was deleted after the proceedings had finished.

But Saul's statements to Abberline, made first on 10 August 1889 at Scotland Yard and added to two days later, do still exist. In them, Saul said that he did not have penetrative sex with Euston, as Euston had other tastes: 'He is not an actual sodomite. He likes to play with you and then spend on your belly.' Saul also said of himself, 'I am still a professional Mary-ann. I have lost my character and cannot get on otherwise.'

Saul went on to tell Lockwood at the Old Bailey that Euston had left a sovereign for him on a dressing-table at No. 19 Cleveland Street on that first visit in April or May 1887. Saul also added that he had later seen Euston at the house on another occasion when Frank Hewitt and Henry Newlove were there (Frank Hewitt was the boy who had originally introduced Newlove to Charles Hammond). Saul said that he finally fell out with Hammond at the end of May 1887 and left the brothel.

Saul was then cross-examined by the chief prosecuting counsel Sir Charles Russell:

[Russell:] Where are you living now?

[Saul:] Since just before Christmas [1889] I have been living at Akerman Road, Brixton with a very respectable man named Violet, who is taking care of me. I gave my evidence to Inspector Abberline at the beginning of August [1889]. I met Violet at the private inquiry office in Westminster [Captain Webb's detective agency, hired by Parke and his defence team].

There were some gasps in court at the mention of Saul giving his statement to Abberline. In fact, it was made to Abberline's clerk more than five months earlier, as Saul later told Lockwood in court in a brief re-examination to clarify that point after Russell's cross-examination. Why hadn't Abberline and the police acted sooner? This procrastination by the police was seemingly wilful, but in truth, it was due to the dithering and obstruction in the case by higher authorities. But it would be an accusation heartily hurled at Abberline and his fellow officers by the lawyer Arthur Newton's defence counsel at Newton's trial five months later in May 1890.

Saul additionally informed the court under questioning from Russell that he had gone to live in Brixton with Violet after he had given his statement to Abberline, and for the previous five months had been receiving 10s a week from Captain Webb's agency, a portion of which he sent to his 'very poor' mother in Ireland:

[Russell:] Have you any means of earning your bread?

[Saul:] No, sir.

[Russell:] I see you have a ring on your finger?

[Saul:] It's not my fault, or it would have been gone long ago. It's only paste.

There was some laughter in court.

[Russell:] And a silver-headed cane?

[Saul:] Oh, that's not much, 1s 6d no more. I bought it in the Brixton Road. Mr. Violet lets me have money sometimes and supplies me with whatever I want. I was concerned in committing an indecent act in Dublin in 1875 [which later resurfaced in the exposure of the 1884 Dublin Castle scandal] and since I have been in London I have tried to earn an honest living but have not been able to get a character [reference]. The police and detectives have always been kind to me here [which reveals that officers in London then largely turned a blind eye to everyday rent boy dealings, when there was no extra political or social pressure such as in the Cleveland Street case, thereby accommodating homosexual activities]. I offered my evidence in Dublin some years ago, but it was not used. I was employed a little while at Drury Lane Theatre in *The Royal Oak* [a romantic drama in five acts put on in September 1889 as the scandal was developing – Saul may well have worked backstage, and if onstage, his name wasn't recorded]. I expressed my willingness to give evidence for Mr. Parke, but for nobody else.

Saul went on to say, when asked by Russell, that he didn't know Ernest Parke, but he thought Parke 'was acted very unfair with'. He also said that he had no idea who the Earl of Euston was when he first met him in Piccadilly and went with him to the brothel. Additionally, Saul made a reference to a man called 'Carrington', who he said he'd been shown a photograph of in Captain Webb's office, but Russell cut him short, saying that he did not want to introduce new names into the case and he regretted that Saul had done so. Mr Justice Hawkins agreed with Russell and Saul's testimony moved on to other matters, but Saul went on to mention 'Carrington' again, saying that he was a friend of his and was nicknamed 'Lively Poll'.

Saul said that he had seen Euston in Piccadilly several times since he was with him at the house and saw him again at No. 19 Cleveland Street but had never spoken to him since that first visit. This was, Saul told the court, because when Euston left after visiting the brothel with him for the first time in the early summer of 1887, after leaving the sovereign for him and just before he departed, Euston turned to him and said, 'Be sure, if you see me, don't speak to me in the street'.

Regarding his falling out with Hammond, Saul explained that a key reason was that the pimp made him work hard providing services to clients and took most of his earnings, and he wasn't fed well when his earnings sometimes temporarily dipped. Asked if he had lived for a while with a woman known as Queen Anne in Church Street, Soho, Saul said that Queen Anne was a young man called Andrew Grant, who was there in court, and Grant knew Hammond, as well as 'a lot of the aristocracy'.

And there Saul's testimony and that of Parke's defence ended. The fact that John Saul was never subsequently prosecuted himself, after admitting in court to the same acts that saw others prosecuted in the Cleveland Street case, shows just how much the authorities wanted the scandal to 'go away'. As the writer Theo Aronson has pointed out, Saul could have made many further damaging revelations about those highly placed in late-Victorian British society if he had been forced into the dock to defend himself – it was a risk too great to take.[4]

Lord Euston himself was then called to give evidence, and in his examination by Sir Charles Russell, he reiterated his version of having gone to No. 19 Cleveland Street under false pretences, and just once. Under cross-examination by Frank Lockwood, Euston stated that the first time he had heard of a rumour connecting him to the house was on 26 October 1889. That gossip, Euston told the court, had come to him from his friend, the solicitor Edward Bedford, who would also draw his attention to the edition of the *North London Press*, which named him around three weeks later. Euston relayed that he had then told Bedford his story about visiting the house very briefly to see a show of poses plastiques.

Lockwood said that such a nude display was 'filthy', and when questioned as to whether he felt shame about wanting to see such a presentation, Euston replied that he did not feel ashamed. But when asked why he hadn't told any of his other friends about his visit to the brothel prior to his name becoming connected to it in rumour, Euston said, 'I thought I was well out of it. It was a beastly sort of thing, and I thought I would not mention it to anybody.'

Lockwood got Euston to admit that he knew Lord Arthur Somerset, which was unsurprising as they belonged to some of the same clubs, although Euston said he had no idea when Somerset left England. Mr Justice Hawkins queried this line of questioning, but Lockwood assured the judge that he had an objective for doing so and went on to press Euston as to whether he had visited Somerset after he had fled to France. Euston vehemently denied this.

Lockwood summed up the defence case for the jury and criticised Euston's moral position on not feeling ashamed of wanting to see some poses plastiques. He also said that Euston had only admitted to going to No. 19 Cleveland Street once because he feared that he had been seen. Lockwood asked the jury to reject Euston's 'story' without hesitation, and apart from testing the credibility of John Saul, Sir Charles Russell had failed to undermine the credibility or respectability of any of the other defence witnesses.

Russell then stood up and in his closing statement asserted that the libel against his client, Euston, had been proved, adding that Parke had failed to establish his plea of justification. As the *Daily Telegraph* reported, Russell said:

> There had been laid before the Court loose and most unsatisfactory evidence of identification in connection with the alleged visits to Cleveland Street, while the foully tainted testimony of John Saul was such that no one would imperil the life even of the meanest of God's creatures upon it. If a man's life were involved in this case [for a capital crime] he felt sure that the jury would not accept it. Throughout this matter Lord Euston had behaved as an honest and straightforward man would behave.

It was by then 6.40 p.m. and the court was adjourned, returning the next day, 16 January, for the judge's summing up of the case. Ironically, it was the day before Ernest Parke's thirtieth birthday.

The court was packed to the beams again as Mr Justice Hawkins began by saying that no evidence at all had been presented to prove that the Earl of Euston had left England in fear of arrest. This was a reference to Parke writing in his editorial of 16 November 1889 in the *North London Press* that Euston had done so.

The judge then turned to the defence's identification witnesses, individually going through each of their testimonies, and to summarise, he said that none of them were satisfactory identifications, especially as to the height of the man they had seen, who was said to be much shorter in height than Lord Euston. He also made a point of saying that the way in which Captain Webb and his employees had shown the witnesses photographs of Euston and asked if he was the man they had seen was unethical, as those giving evidence should be given 'the opportunity to rely on their own knowledge' rather than 'refreshed' with a photograph or portrait.

Regarding the evidence given by John Saul, whom Hawkins referred to as 'that creature', the judge said that he could not envisage 'a more melancholy spectacle or a more loathsome object'. He added that he wished for the Metropolitan Police's honour that Saul's evidence that they had turned a blind eye to his activities was untrue. As to Saul's testimony that he had seen Euston at No. 19 Cleveland Street twice, Mr Justice Hawkins told the jury:

> Of course, you only have the oath of Lord Euston against the oath of this man. It is necessary for me to speak out, and you will have to ask yourselves which oath you prefer: the oath of a man, who according to his own account, if he has spoken the truth, is liable to be prosecuted and sent to penal servitude, or the truth of the prosecutor.

The judge expressed his great surprise that Saul himself hadn't been prosecuted yet for his own activities or 'crimes', as he termed them. And if Inspector Abberline (whom he named) had known about Saul's activities since August of the previous year, Saul should have been arrested and charged. Hawkins said that as a member of the public himself, he wished to know, and he was sure the jury would like to know, why Abberline hadn't acted against Saul.

Hawkins then went on to attack Abberline: 'It should be the first duty of those who are the guardians of peace and morality, if they had evidence of crime like this, to bring the criminal to light, no duty can be more obligatory.' The judge then backtracked slightly, giving Abberline some benefit of doubt by saying, 'On the other hand, if Saul did not tell Abberline, or if he did, and Abberline could not believe the story or could get no corroboration of it, I do not wonder at no proceedings being taken'.

Mr. Justice Hawkins then moved on to question why Henry Newlove and others (certainly Veck, although he wasn't named), who spent time at No. 19 Cleveland Street hadn't been brought before the court to give evidence. Finally, Hawkins reminded the jury that they had to reach a decision on two points: if a libel had been published by Parke reflecting on Lord Euston's character, and if that were the case, if that libel was justified by the facts.

At 1.05 p.m., the jury duly retired to determine its verdict, but it returned after just forty minutes. The jury's foreman stood and gave the verdict as guilty and added that the justification put forward by Parke and his defence was not proven.

The prosecution junior counsel Charles Mathews stood up in court and highlighted to the judge that on 16 November of the previous year, Parke had written in the *North London Press*, 'If the charges he had preferred against Lord Euston were not true, and were made without sufficient reason, he had no desire to escape the natural and inevitable consequences of misleading the public on so grave a matter'. Mathews added that on 30 November, despite being committed to face trial four days prior, Parke had further published a portrait of Euston next to ones of Lord Arthur Somerset and the pimp Charles Hammond. Hawkins replied that he didn't think that anybody would have recognised Euston from the portrait, but Mathews stipulated firmly, that 'may not have been the intention' of Parke.

Parke himself was then allowed to address the court, saying that throughout the whole case he had acted in good faith and had published what he thought to be in the public interest. He added that he hadn't printed without having evidence to support it, but what that evidence was, he couldn't say. It is impossible to say who gave Parke the information on which he based his editorials, but it seems highly likely that it came from a police officer who had the inside track on the case.

As the *South Australian Chronicle* reported over a month later on 22 February 1890, 'As a last straw too, police assistance suddenly dried up, and poor Parke had to choose between going to prison and violating the confidence of the detective who originally supplied him with the story.' If true, who was this policeman? Was it somebody on Abberline's investigation team? Or another officer in the force who was indirectly privy to what was going on in the inquiry?

There followed exchanges between Mr Justice Hawkins and Parke in which the judge gave Parke every chance to present more evidence in his defence:

[Hawkins:] The libel is an exceedingly bad one; but if you would like to have until tomorrow to give me any information which you think would alter my view of the matter you shall do so, but at present as the evidence stands, I see none that was in your possession at the time the libel was published.

[Parke:] I can only state that I had evidence in my possession.

Mr Justice Hawkins said that it was a very 'serious matter' to publish in a paper with a circulation of 4,000 or 5,000 copies 'imputations of a horrible character'. Parke said that he would have to abide by the verdict of the jury, but he had published the portrait of Euston for the same reasons as many other papers had subsequently, and at the time he had published his articles, he'd had in his possession a statement from John Saul as evidence.

Hawkins replied:

At the present moment I fail to see any evidence that would justify, morally, the publication of the libel upon which the jury have returned a verdict of guilty [...] I do not think that I could allow you to remain under the impression for a moment that anything in your statement shows you honestly believed the libel was true when you published it. As a matter of course, I could not be satisfied with your bare statement. At present it stands in my mind as a very atrocious libel.

The judge went on to reiterate that Parke could have until the following day to present further evidence or to communicate with his counsel. But Parke's defence team declined this opportunity for further time, obviously at Parke's instruction, as he would not name whoever else had given him evidence apart from Saul.

Mr Justice Hawkins proceeded with his closing statement before passing sentence. At the end of his summation of the case and trial, Hawkins said, 'In all the circumstances I feel it to be my duty to pass upon you a sentence which I hope, besides being a punishment to you, will be a warning to others not to publish atrocious libels upon others without justification.'

He sentenced Parke to twelve months' imprisonment, without hard labour. According to the *South Australian Chronicle*, Parke 'received his sentence with composure, and was removed to the cells'.

Parke's defence had failed to prove that Euston had been a client at No. 19 Cleveland Street to support and justify what Parke had published about the earl. John Saul's testimony had been inherently by far the most directly damaging to Euston. But as Saul was perceived to be of very low character, as exemplified by Hawkins referring to him as 'that creature', the jury did not believe it, and this was also guided by Mr Justice Hawkins' summing up before the jury retired. As the *Auckland Star* of New Zealand frankly reported on 6 March 1890, 'The Judge summed up dead against the defendant'.

But was Euston truly a client at No. 19 Cleveland Street?

There was an interesting piece of information from the trial implicating Euston that was never covered in the British newspapers but it was reported in at least two American publications. It must have been raised by Frank Lockwood and Parke's defence team. The *Boston Globe* of 15 January 1890 documented that 'Veck [Hammond's right-hand man, then in Pentonville] interviewed in prison, admits that he knows Euston, and that he has been at his Lordship's house in Grosvenor Place, but declines to say for what purpose'. The convicted and roguish Veck was unsurprisingly never called to give evidence.

And *The Plain Speaker* of Hazleton, Pennsylvania, reported the following day:

> Two businessmen of unblemished reputation will also be called aver [to declare] that they had an interview with Veck at the Cleveland Street house. They were engaged with him in a certain business speculation. Veck closed the interview by remarking that he would not detain them longer as he was expecting a visit from Lord Euston. On going out they met in the doorway a tall man whom they have since identified by photographs as Euston. The date of this incident was a month subsequent to the occasion when the plaintiff (Euston) admits that he called on Veck [in fact, Hammond, although Veck may well have also been there when Euston said he mistakenly called there to see some poses plastiques].

Neither of the two businessmen were called to give evidence. The reasoning for this didn't escape the notice of the switched-on London correspondent of the *South Australian Chronicle*:

> It is only fair to Mr. Parke's intelligence and to the common sense of his legal advisors to explain that when he embarked on the plea of justification he fully expected to be able to produce a number of witnesses [...] Where they disappeared to and who provided them with funds to go the luckless journalist had not been able to ascertain. He soon found indeed that a much longer purse than this would be necessary to make any sort of a fight against the prosecution. The private inquiry agents he employed [Captain Webb's detective agency] were no kind of match for Mr. George Lewis [Euston's solicitor].

Had Lewis bought off witnesses who were due to offer evidence against Euston, as Arthur Newton had previously done for Lord Arthur

Somerset? Newton had no direct connection to Euston, and by now had his own serious legal travails so certainly wouldn't have been involved in making those standing against Euston disappear, but Lewis could well have done the same for his client, using Euston's considerable funds.

It has never been definitively proven that Euston was a client at No. 19 Cleveland Street. At the 1890 libel trial, Parke's defence team failed to prove that the earl had been there more than the one time that Euston admitted. This was not helped by the patchy testimonies of witnesses in Cleveland Street, especially regarding the wildly disparate height of the man seen there pulling up in a hansom carriage many times and entering the locally well-known house of ill repute.

But on balance, John Saul's evidence to the police in August 1889 and at Parke's trial five months later has the detailed ring of brazen truth. It's also important not to forget the fact that the No. 19 Cleveland Street GPO employee, rent boy and procurer Henry Newlove had, independently of Saul, named Euston as a client of the house on his arrest by PC Hanks on 7 July 1889. That was over a month before Saul made his first statement to the police.

And another indirect assertion suggests that Euston was indeed involved in the veiled late-Victorian London homosexual scene and could well have been a frequenter of the brothel, just like Somerset and others who attended there. As the author Neil McKenna has highlighted in his book, *The Secret Life of Oscar Wilde*, the rent boy and homosexual blackmailer Robert Cliburn, who knew Oscar Wilde, later 'boasted that he had rented [performed paid sexual acts with] the Earl of Euston, who had figured so prominently in the Cleveland Street Scandal'. Cliburn was of dubious character, but he had nothing to gain from that boast – there's no record of him ever extorting Euston.

If this is the probable truth, that Euston had been to No. 19 Cleveland Street more than once, and for sexual services, the only piece of information which Parke published and got wrong, as emphasised by Sir Charles Russell in his prosecution, was that Euston had escaped to Peru.

Ernest Parke served his sentence in Pentonville Prison, where both George Veck and Henry Newlove had earlier been sent. Parke's health suffered in prison, and after appeals to the Home Secretary, Sir Henry Matthews, he was released on 7 July 1890, having served almost half of his sentence. As the *Daily Telegraph* briefly detailed on the following day, 'He has completed twenty-five weeks of his sentence, during which he has lost nearly a stone in weight. Mr. Parke says he has been well treated throughout his period of detention, both by the governor and medical staff. He is going away for a long holiday.'

After his break, Parke would resume his successful career as a journalist at *The Star*, where, the following year, he would rise to be the long-standing editor before co-founding another newspaper, the *Morning Leader*, in 1892. But the *North London Press* wasn't resurrected and he never took such a radical position in print again.

Twelve

On 23 January 1890, a week after Ernest Parke was found guilty and sent to prison, Somerset's lawyer, Arthur Newton, was back at Bow Street Magistrates' Court, along with his associates, Frederick Taylerson and Adolphus de Gallo, as the legal proceedings against them continued. This hearing was significant, as Newton's counsel, Charles Gill, went on the attack against the increasingly persecuted Abberline.

The inspector had been singled out for criticism by the judge in the Euston libel trial and asked to leave the court at a previous hearing in the case against Newton, et al. on 23 December the previous year. On that day in court, exactly a month earlier, Gill had said that he would be making 'imputations' against Abberline, and now he began to make them. *The Times* of the next day, 24 January 1890, relayed what Gill said:

> Counsel pointed out that by July 4 [1889] the Post Office officials, and through them the police, had received all the information it was possible to obtain in this matter. Inspector Abberline had on that date all the information in his hands, but for some reason he did not act. Counsel considered that the whole cause of the mischief that had arisen through the spread of these disgraceful scandals, which touched both high and low, was the conduct of Inspector Abberline in allowing in July the man Hammond to leave the country. It might, and very reasonably, not have been thought right or desirable to institute

a prosecution on the evidence of such boys as had been called in this case; but it also was clear that it had not occurred to Abberline even to have Hammond watched. When this man was out of the country Abberline strolled – 18 hours after the statements had been made to him by the boys – up to the police-court, and then for the first time asked for a warrant. On the next day he arrested Newlove, Newlove not being, as Hammond was, in a position to leave the country [...] The learned counsel then proceeded to deal in detail with the circumstances under which Allies was looked after by Hanks and Abberline, whose conduct throughout the case he strongly denounced, and on whose evidence he threw the gravest doubt.

It was an aggressive and calculated ploy by Charles Gill to paint the police, through Abberline, as the Cleveland Street case's investigative lead, in broad and detailed strokes as the cause of the procrastinations and ineptitude in failing to apprehend Charles Hammond, and, along with PC Hanks, in their protective handling of Algernon Allies as a witness. By casting a shadow on Allies' evidence against Newton and his associates, the strongest potential testimony against his clients, Gill was paving the way to sway a jury against Allies when the actual trial eventually got under way.

By doing this, Gill sought to make Arthur Newton's actions, which amounted to the charge of 'conspiracy to defeat the ends of justice', appear ethical, legal and proportionate. But the reality was that Abberline and his overall boss, the Met Commissioner Sir James Monro, had been frustrated and hampered at every turn in trying to act in their inquiry and affect arrests. And this had been caused by the dithering, both the unintentional and wilful, of Lord Salisbury and his government under the velvet-gloved pressure exerted by the Prince of Wales and his emissaries, and the entrenched power of the royal family.

By making Abberline and the police the culprits in the mishandling of the case, a take that had already had some traction in the press, Gill was attempting to create a simple and tangible scapegoat to exonerate Newton and his illegal misdeeds. Time would tell if this strategy would prove successful.

Meanwhile, on 30 January, Henry Labouchère, the Liberal MP for Northampton, architect of Section 11 of the 1885 Criminal Law Amendment Act and editor of the radical journal *Truth*, published an attack on John Saul. Labouchère venomously protested the fact that the long-time rent boy wasn't to be prosecuted for the allegations he had made against Euston in court, which the jury found to be untrue:

> The Public Prosecutor [Augustus Stephenson], apparently, has made up his mind not to prosecute the creature Saul for perjury. If this be so, a more scandalous decision was never taken. A jury had decided that the 'creature' committed one of the most horrible perjuries on record – a perjury for which the longest sentence permitted by the law would not be sufficient. An eminent judge has endorsed the opinion of the jury. And the Public Prosecutor takes no action!

Labouchère also made an equivocal defence of the illegal actions of the lawyer Arthur Newton, which was on the surface inexplicable but fitted perfectly with Labouchère's anti-Establishment agenda. It also enabled Labouchère an opportunity for a backhanded, if mostly deserved, condemnation of Lord Salisbury's government's inaction and class-based, prosecutorial prejudice over the scandal to protect the royal family.

Above all, Labouchère had already been introduced to Newton, earlier in January. Somerset's friend, Reginald Brett had engineered a meeting between them to see if they could mutually aid each other. For Labouchère, Newton could supply details that could help him in his crusade against the government, and Newton would have wanted the support of the crusader. Labouchère's pleading in mitigation of Newton's actions in *Truth* may have been part of that quid pro quo support:

> As regards Mr. Newton, had I been his counsel I should have sought to show that the Government had made it manifest that their endeavours to prosecute Lord Arthur Somerset were not bona-fide, and that, consequently, my client was aiding, and not impeding, the actions of

the guardians of the law by getting witnesses out of the way. I regard these guardians of the law as far more culpable than Mr. Newton; for what can be more outrageous than for the Executive to allow the police to bring obscure persons to justice [Veck and Newlove] and to take very good care that persons socially eminent should escape? No matter. Parliament meets in a fortnight.

In fact, it would be a month later when the Cleveland Street scandal reached its political climax. In the House of Commons on 28 February 1890, Labouchère went into battle and finally launched his concerted castigation of Lord Salisbury and his government's handling of the case in Parliament. As *The Times* reported the following day, Labouchère had not warned those he was accusing of his attack, but craftily created the grounds for it by riding on the back of another debate, where the granting of government funding was being decided:

> The question was again put that a sum not exceeding £3,725,103 be granted on account to defray [pay for] charges to the Civil Service and Revenue Departments. Mr. Labouchère said he rose to move the reduction of the vote, and he based the motion on the fact that certain official persons whose salaries were included in it had conspired together to defeat the course of justice.

That was enough. Labouchère got some of the exact dates in the timeline of the unfolding of the scandal wrong, but he had a remarkable grasp of events, many of which took place far away from public or journalistic scrutiny, just months after they had occurred. As both a politician and journalist, Labouchère was extremely well connected, and his sources were strong. *Hansard*, the official report of all parliamentary debates, as always, recorded the proceedings word for word:

> [Henry Labouchère MP:] I was saying that practically my charge is that certain official persons confederated together to defeat the course of justice by interfering to prevent their friends being put on trial for a crime in regard to which two persons were tried and convicted.

Before stating the facts, I wish to call attention to the present position of the law in these matters. There is no doubt that of late years a certain offence – I will not give it a name – has become more rife than it ever was before. Before 1885 the law was insufficient to deal with it, because the offence had to be proved by an accessory, and many other offences very much of the same nature were not regarded as crimes at all.

In 1885, when the Criminal Law Amendment Bill was before a Committee of the House, Mr. [W.T.] Stead – who, it will be remembered, took a very active part in urging that Bill on the attention of the House – sent me a report with reference to this offence, giving particulars and evidence which went to show the extent of its prevalence. I was requested to read this report to the House, but I did not think it desirable to do so, although I thought the case was pretty well proved. I proposed the addition to the Bill of a special clause which I took from the French Code, and this clause was submitted to the Attorney General and Lord Cross, and, with some verbal alterations, accepted and incorporated in the Bill, and is now the law of the land. Therefore, in 1885, Parliament armed the guardians of public morality with full powers to deal with this offence. In doing so, they recognised that the offence was on the increase, and they expressed their desire that it should be stamped out; and, presumably, it was I intended that the law should be used equally against high and low ...

The sentence on Veck was scandalously inadequate ... If ever a man deserved the full sentence of the law this man Veck did ... Whether this inadequate sentence was a condition of these men pleading guilty, or whether, as they did plead guilty, it happened that the depositions at the Police Court were not shown to the Recorder, and he did not know how monstrous the case was, I do not know. But I think it is pretty clear that the real object was to stop all further disclosures, hush the matter up, and get these men out of the way.

I believe that Newlove and Veck would never have been prosecuted had it not been for the action of the Postmaster General and the secretary of the Post Office. The matter occurred in the Post Office, and they – I honour and respect them for it – insisted that action should be taken in the matter. The Solicitor to the Treasury, who is, I believe, under the orders of the Right Hon. Gentleman the Home Secretary, and the Treasury – and I dare say the Home Secretary also – knew perfectly well by this time that certain persons had frequented this house in Cleveland Street; they knew that the police had got certain clues; they knew certain names had been mentioned; and they determined, so far as they were concerned, that if they were obliged to prosecute these two men the case should go no farther if they could prevent it. Having thus arranged matters in regard to these two men, what, the House will wonder, had become of Hammond, the proprietor of the house? If Hammond had been arrested, he would no doubt have been able to make revelations ...

Perhaps I may be allowed to explain that my case is that the Government wish to hush this matter up. Now, I think I have proved my case. The house is in no obscure thoroughfare, but nearly opposite the Middlesex Hospital. Surely it must have been known to the police, and if it was not known to them it ought to have been. In no other city in the world are such abominations openly carried on. Parliament has done its best to put down houses of ill-fame, but compared with this place a house of ill-fame is respectable. If it were desired to make an example of the offenders, why was not a policeman stationed at the house to follow the persons who came there? The obvious answer is that it was not desired to follow them up and punish them. One person guessed the police were on his track. I do not wish to mention any names except those which have already been made public, but I will give the name of this person because a warrant is out for his arrest. It is Lord Arthur Somerset. A warrant is out for his arrest, and he has fled. I am not certain whether the police got on his track by seeing him come to the house or whether his name was given by one of the boys, or by Veck or Newlove, but in any case on the 23rd of July several of the boys were taken to Knightsbridge Barracks, where Lord Arthur Somerset was quartered, and the boys identified him as a person who had been with them in the house. I know that evidence of informers is generally tainted, but the evidence of the boys is not nearly so tainted as would have been the evidence of one of these professional wretches.

These boys were employed at the Post Office. They have been more sinned against than sinning, and it is not likely that they would have identified Lord Arthur Somerset unless they honestly believed he was the man who tempted them ... The object of the Treasury was to hush up the matter, not to have prosecutions ... Instead of making every effort to punish offences, as far as I can see every effort has been made to hush up the matter. I do not know what the defence of the Government may be, but I venture to advise them not to put up any lawyer with a brief in his hand, who will by special pleading and evasive chicanery defend this charge.

[There were then cries of 'Order!' and 'Withdraw!' in the chamber.]

Very well, then, I will say not by the same tactics as those pursued with regard to the Special Commission—that means the same thing to us on this side of the House [the Liberal side].

My first charge is that Lord Salisbury and others entered into a criminal conspiracy to defeat the ends of justice. I ask for a Committee to investigate this charge and allegation, and if it is granted, I am perfectly willing to withdraw my Amendment, but I will not, and I do not think that many in this House will, be satisfied with a mere *ex parte* denial [done with respect to or in the interests of one side only or of an interested outside party] on behalf of the incriminated persons. If the Committee is not granted Lord Salisbury and the others stand condemned by their own Code of ethics ... If the Government refuse this investigation, either they admit their guilt or they have two Codes of ethics – one for an Irish leader and another for a Conservative leader.

If the Government plead guilty, I shall deem it my duty to divide the House, because I think that this House ought to disconnect itself from any condoning of abominable offences of this kind, and ought to stand up for the principle of equal justice between man and man. If they do not admit their guilt I shall divide, because a man cannot be Judge, jury, and defendant in his own case. If those charges, openly made in this House, are not in some way investigated a heavier blow will be dealt to the good name of the country and to the cause of law and order than anything that his been done for many and many a year.

I appeal to the whole House, to Hon. Members sitting on both sides, to support me in the action I have taken. I appeal to them, not as followers of this Ministry or of that, but on the broad ground that they are English gentlemen. I appeal to them because I know that they loathe these offences as much as I do, and I hope that they will stand by me in the only course that ought to be pursued in this matter, and the only course which will lead to the thorough and efficient prevention of such crimes.

Aside from letting Bertie, the Prince of Wales and the royal family off the proverbial hook, it was a lengthy and brave diatribe against the Prime Minister Lord Salisbury and his government and the way they had handled the Cleveland Street scandal. But it was Labouchère's reference to 'the criminality of Lord Salisbury' and the assertion that 'Lord Salisbury and others entered into a criminal conspiracy to defeat the ends of justice' that would cause him trouble.

After Sir Richard Webster gave his extensive defence of Lord Salisbury and the government, as he had to do as a prominent member of it, there were interactions in the debate by several Members of Parliament, which became heated. During these exchanges, Labouchère was given support several times by Thomas Power O'Connor, the Irish Nationalist MP, who, as mentioned previously, was also the editor of *The Star* newspaper and the now imprisoned Ernest Parke's boss there.

Labouchère offered to give the name of his source who had told him about the meeting between Lord Salisbury and Sir Dighton Probyn, during which, he said, the prime minister had tipped off Probyn about Somerset's impending arrest, which Probyn then passed to Colonel Oliver Montagu, who in turn, warned Somerset, allowing him to flee.

Labouchère wrote the name of his source on a piece of paper, but his submission was declined by the chairman. As the *Daily Chronicle* reported the following day, 1 March 1890, Labouchère then 'tore up the piece of paper on which he had written the name and scattered the fragments on the floor. An industrious member [of Parliament] picked up the pieces and put them together. And in a few minutes the name was in everyone's mouth.' Sadly, there is no record today that names Labouchère's source.

But then the chairman of the debate asked Labouchère to withdraw his comments about Lord Salisbury, and Labouchère declined to withdraw them twice. Then a question was put forward, asking if Labouchère should be suspended from the House of Commons. A vote was taken and 177 of the Members of Parliament present voted for Labouchère's suspension, while 96 voted for him to remain. The motion to suspend was carried by a majority of 81 votes, and there were some cries of 'Aye!' and cheers.

The Speaker of the House announced, 'The Ayes have it. I have now to call on the Honorary member for Northampton to withdraw.'

Labouchère replied, ever defiant in his position but having to obey the rules of the House of Commons, 'I beg, Sir, to withdraw, expressing at the same time my regret that my conscience would not allow me to say I believed Lord Salisbury.'

There were loud cheers from those members in support of Labouchère.

Henry Labouchère immediately left the House of Commons. He was suspended for a week. But he had managed to land a mighty blow and bloody the nose of Lord Salisbury and his government. And above all, Labouchère put the allegations he made about the way the authorities conducted the legal proceedings regarding the Cleveland Street scandal on the parliamentary record forever.

Thirteen

Meanwhile, the long string of legal hearings against the lawyer Arthur Newton, his clerk, Frederick Taylerson, and 'interpreter', Adolphus de Gallo, for 'conspiring to defeat the ends of justice' in the Cleveland Street case were still far from coming to a head that winter of 1890. From Monday, 6, to Friday, 10 January 1890, a great deal of evidence had been heard from multiple prosecution witnesses at Bow Street Magistrates' Court.

Algernon Allies was the first, repeating the testimony he had given at Marlborough Street Police Court in the proceedings against George Veck and Henry Newlove in September, the previous year. Again, he identified Somerset as the man who had posed as 'Mr Brown' and confirmed that he had destroyed letters he had received from Somerset after receiving an anonymous letter asking him to do so. Allies additionally identified Taylerson as the man who had visited him and tried to persuade him to go abroad to prevent him giving evidence and he said that Newton had sent Taylerson for that purpose.

The ex-telegraph messenger rent boy Charles Thickbroom appeared next and spoke about PC Sladden's introduction to another man who arranged a meeting with Newton, who promised him and William Meech Perkins that he would fund them, along with Charles Swinscow, to go to Australia and give them a weekly stipend. Perkins then fully corroborated Thickbroom's evidence.

George Alma Wright and Charles Swinscow, the latter of whom had kicked off the whole Cleveland Street inquiry when he opened up as PC Hanks interrogated him for petty theft back on 4 July 1889, gave evidence next. They both repeated the evidence they had given at Marlborough Street Police Court months before. But Swinscow, under cross-examination, revealed that he had lied to PC Hanks in one important detail in his first statement – he had said that he had visited No. 19 Cleveland Street twice, when in fact he had been there on five occasions.

Inspector Abberline was called to the stand, and he confirmed that on the Cleveland Street inquiry he 'took instructions' from the Commissioner of the Metropolitan Police (James Monro) and the Assistant Commissioner (Dr Robert Anderson), as well as the Treasury (essentially the DPP, Sir Augustus Stephenson and the Assistant DPP, Hamilton Cuffe). Abberline was brief and professional in his answers, his long policing experience of giving evidence in court palpable. He could also at times be curt when he was asked a question that he felt was inappropriate. An example was when he was asked if he had wished that more publicity had been given to the case, to which he replied, 'Certainly not. Nor did I say anything of the kind.'

Regarding not bringing back Charles Hammond from abroad, Abberline firmly repeated more than once that it was to do with the extradition treaty with France and legal issues. He remained professional and showed no frustration at how his investigation had been hampered by the dithering and obstruction of higher authorities.

On the subject of Swinscow being dishonest in his initial statement to PC Hanks in early July 1889, Abberline said that when Swinscow had confessed this to him, 'I told Swinscow that it was very wrong for him not to have told the truth and that he must correct his statement at the first opportunity.' When pressed by the presiding magistrate, Mr Vaughan, as to why he hadn't taken Swinscow directly to a magistrate to have his existing statement altered, Abberline replied that he knew that Swinscow would have to appear again before a magistrate anyway, so he would have the chance to admit it then.

PC Hanks was the final key witness for the prosecution. Hanks backed up Abberline in every respect and spoke about the handling of Allies in police protective custody. Regarding Arthur Newton and whether he knew him, Hanks said that he did, by sight, as Newton had previously cross-examined him in the proceedings of another case at the police court, where Newton carried out most of his legal work. When Newton's defence counsel Charles Gill asked him if he 'did not like' Newton, Hanks replied, 'I had a great respect for him – at one time.'

The case against Newton and his two associates was then adjourned, and brief hearings would continue in the coming three months, with many legal manoeuvrings orchestrated by Newton's defence team. This included an unsuccessful attempt to get the case against the three defendants thrown out altogether.

But at a Grand Jury hearing at Bow Street Magistrates' Court on 3 February, the charges against Adolphus de Gallo were dropped, with the jury deciding that there was insufficient evidence to prosecute him, and he was discharged. While he was undoubtedly involved in witness harassment on behalf of Newton, the evidence against de Gallo had always been peripheral and somewhat shadowy, like the man himself.

And Newton and his legal representatives also managed to get the main trial to be heard not at the Old Bailey but at the Royal Courts of Justice in the Strand, where it meets Fleet Street, which had been opened by Queen Victoria just eight years earlier. Legally, this was felt by the defence to be more favourable to Newton and Taylerson.

Long before going to final trial, Henry Labouchère, who had defended Newton in his journal *Truth* on 30 January, had written to Reginald Brett, outlining how he thought Newton's defence should be handled. This very much suited Labouchère's agenda against Lord Salisbury's government and its prosecution of those accused in the scandal and mirrored what he had published in *Truth*. Labouchère wrote in his letter to Brett that Newton 'can only fight by showing that the government sought to hush up the affair and that consequently he had a full right to suppose that there was no bona fide intention to prosecute Lord Arthur Somerset'. Labouchère added that this was supported by the plea bargain afforded George Veck and Henry Newlove at their trial in September 1889, by the police, who he said had 'aided and abetted' Charles Hammond in his escape to Europe and eventually to America, and how the police had procrastinated in arresting Somerset, enabling him to flee.

The trial of Arthur Newton and Frederick Taylerson finally began at the Royal Courts of Justice on 16 May 1890 before Mr Justice Cave. Sir Lewis Cave was 57 and had been a judge since 1881. In 1882, he had notably presided over the trial in Leeds of the poisoner Kate Dover, who had dosed her boss and lover Thomas Skinner – she was his housekeeper – with arsenic. She was only convicted of manslaughter, however, and received a life sentence. Incidentally, Dover was defended by Frank Lockwood, Ernest Parke's counsel in his libel trial, who would also go on to prosecute Oscar Wilde in 1895.

Newton and Taylerson were prosecuted by the Attorney General, Sir Richard Webster and three juniors, including Horace Avory, who, as junior treasury counsel, had given the DPP, Sir Augustus Stephenson, advice on the prosecution of Henry Newlove and the possible prosecution of Somerset, and had been on the prosecution team against Veck and Newlove in September 1889. Somerset's former lawyer and his clerk were defended by Sir Charles Russell, who had successfully prosecuted Ernest Parke for libel just four months previously.

There were six charges against Newton and Taylerson, to all of which they had both pleaded 'not guilty' in previous hearings. Taylerson kept the same pleas, but Newton, knowing that he couldn't escape punishment for the sixth charge – of knowing that 'divers male persons' had committed certain offences under the 1885 Criminal Law Amendment Act – and knowing that prosecutions being brought would allow them to escape prosecution, pleaded guilty to that count. His defence was that he was merely protecting his client (Somerset) from possible blackmail and that he (Somerset) was not then charged with any offence. But in fact, Newton had also helped Charles Hammond to escape to America, and Hammond had been charged by that time. And Newton had tried to spirit Allies, Thickbroom, Perkins, Wright and Swinscow out of the country.

On the first day of the trial, as *The Standard* of London reported on 21 May 1890, a special jury had found Frederick Taylerson 'by consent' not guilty of all charges, and he was discharged. Sir Richard Webster didn't insist that the first five charges were persisted with and Newton was found not guilty on those counts, so just his guilty plea for the sixth charge remained.

On Tuesday, 20 May, Mr Justice Cave summed up, directly addressing Newton:

> Arthur John Newton, you have pleaded Guilty to conspiracy to obstruct, pervert, and defeat the due course of law and justice, and to prevent the due prosecution of certain persons for certain acts of gross indecency. Now, that offence is one of very considerable magnitude, because I can conceive nothing which would tend more to discredit the administration of the law in the eyes of the public generally than the notion that a wealthy criminal might, by his bribing witnesses to remove themselves out of the jurisdiction, escape punishment.
>
> Your Counsel [Sir Charles Russell], addressing me on your behalf, made a very eloquent appeal to me, founded upon certain statements which you had made to him, and upon certain facts which had come out in the course of the investigation. He appealed to me to take a lenient view of your case, on the ground that he thought you were rather shielding men from infamous charges dictated by infamous motives, than doing anything that would impede the actual course of justice, and that your offence should rather be imputed to the indiscreet act of a zealous solicitor, than to a desire or intention on your part knowingly to interfere with and impede the course of justice.
>
> The learned Attorney General [Sir Richard Webster], in the speech he addressed to me, made a remark upon that subject which I have some little difficulty in appreciating altogether the force of. He said he wished to accept what had fallen from Sir C. Russell, that you were acting for some persons who were charged, and – he felt bound to say this was consistent with the evidence before him – that you might have been led away by zeal for your clients into acts which you ought to have considered more carefully, and for the consequences of which you must be held responsible. It was suggested on your behalf that you were endeavouring to shelter clients from blackmailing, and he said there was nothing in his instructions to negative that view, and

assuming that I accepted that statement, he had to observe that there was nothing in the evidence inconsistent with it.

I cannot see in your attempt to remove Allies out of the jurisdiction anything else than an attempt to get rid of in the course of inquiry – because everyone knew at that time that further inquiries were being made – of witnesses who might give evidence which would be inconvenient. Similarly, I am unable to understand your conduct with regard to Hammond. I place little reliance on what took place with regard to the four other boys [Thickbroom, Perkins, Wright and Swinscow]. There is nothing to show that you really did intend to remove them out of the jurisdiction of the court.

The punishment for this offence consists of fine or imprisonment at the discretion of the court. This, however, is one of those cases in which a fine would be no punishment at all. The case is too serious. An attempt to defeat the law is a matter which throws too much scandal upon the administration of the law, and which, if it were successful, would have such an extremely bad influence, that I must pass upon you a sentence of imprisonment, and that is, that you be imprisoned for six weeks.

Newton's junior defence counsel then asked the judge if the defendant 'would be treated as a first-class misdemeanant', which meant that Newton would receive lenient treatment in prison. Mr Justice Cave said that he would consider that, and Newton was immediately taken into custody.

The legal community generally thought that the sentence of six weeks was too severe, and this was backed up by a petition to the Home Secretary, Sir Henry Matthews, citing the perceived harshness of the punishment, which was presented on 29 May. The petition was signed by no fewer than 250 London law firms and called for a reduction in the sentencing, or for Newton to be treated as a first-class misdemeanant.

Newton served his sentence in Holloway Prison in north-east London. In the end, he wasn't given first-class misdemeanant status and received no special leniency. On 11 June 1890, when he had been there for three weeks and served half his time, Newton petitioned the prison governor for early release. He complained that he had 'intense pains in his head', 'an acute attack of diarrhoea', was 'unable to sleep at night' and was in 'a very depressed, low condition'. But neither the petition by the legal fraternity nor his own pleas secured an early release and Newton served the full six weeks.

Arthur Newton received no professional reprimand – the Law Society didn't suspend him, let alone strike him off the legal register, although the latter would happen much later in his colourful career for a different offence.

Legal reports in contemporary newspapers show that Newton was back practising as a solicitor in the police courts by the early autumn of 1890, two months after his release. It is highly questionable how Newton could be sentenced to just six weeks in prison for the harassment of and attempting to remove multiple Crown witnesses from the country, while Ernest Parke served six months (reduced from the original sentence of one year) for libelling the Earl of Euston. But that was how the late-Victorian British authorities and legal system operated, set in reinforced granite in the hypocritical values and mores of that society.

Meanwhile, over 4,700 miles (more than 7,500km) away, there were developments concerning Charles Hammond in America, which would lead to insider details about No. 19 Cleveland Street being publicly revealed.

The pimp had by now moved on from Philadelphia and settled in Seattle, Washington State, living at 22321 Front Street. The entrepreneurial Hammond had only been in Seattle for a short time but had already opened a bar there, the Haymarket Saloon, which was soon doing good business. Hammond had presumably chosen that name because he had lived in the Haymarket area of Central London in the late 1870s.

And within months of arriving in Seattle, Hammond was also making threats in the American press that were nothing short of blackmail – attempts at the extortion of those about whom he held dangerous secrets in connection with his former brothel in London. The *New York Herald* of 10 March 1890 reported:

> Charles R. Hammond, who knows more than anybody else about the London scandals, said today that unless certain people prominent in London kept faith with him and cabled money to him by Tuesday of this week, he would say something then that would place them in very bad light.

The newspaper then went on to quote Hammond directly, the former pimp and now extortionist saying:

> The time for denials from one side and the other is past, and if Lord Euston and Hugh Weglen [sic] knew what was to their interest they would communicate immediately by cable [...] Weglen is the son of the man who occupies an exceptional position in the financial world of the British capital.

Hammond was now beginning to name names to increase pressure for the payment of hush money. Euston had, as we know, already won his libel trial against Ernest Parke in a civil case, but did Hammond have more dirt on him, which could expose Euston to possible criminal prosecution? And it was the first time that the stockbroker Hugh Weguelin had been named publicly in connection with the scandal, even if Hammond had failed to give the reporter the correct spelling of his name. Did either of them, or any others, pay up? There is no evidence that they did, but former clients of No. 19 Cleveland Street must have been troubled.

Then, eight months later in November 1890, Hammond was arrested, charged with grand larceny and placed in the county jail. Hammond was accused of stealing the belongings of Augusta Simons (wrongly reported as 'Simmonds' or 'Simmons' in some contemporary US newspapers), 'a barkeeper's wife'. The *Evening Mail* of Stockton, California, reported on 25 November 1890, 'The principal witness for the prosecution is Hammond's former bartender, Alexander Todhunter.'

It seemed that Mrs Simons had been drinking with Hammond in his Haymarket bar until 2 a.m. on 1 October, then became drunk and wanted to go home. The *Seattle Post-Intelligencer* of 26 November 1890 gave more details on what was said to have occurred:

> Alexander Todhunter, the bartender, saw Hammond leave the saloon with the woman and also noticed that the woman was without her sealskin sacque. Mrs. Simmons [sic] claims that Hammond took her home, and once in the house she had a hard time to make him get out. Her husband was not at home. She became deathly sick from the liquor she had drunk and knew nothing until 6 o'clock in the morning. It was then she missed her gold watch and chain. At 5 the same evening, she discovered that her sealskin sacque was also missing. She never knew whom to suspect of taking the articles and kept quiet until Monday, when Alexander Todhunter came to her and said he had had a row with his employer [Hammond] and wanted to send him 'over the road' [to the penitentiary]. He then told her what purported to be the correct story of how the articles came into the possession of Hammond.

Alexander Todhunter claimed that Hammond had later admitted to him that he had stolen the items belonging to Augusta Simons.

Hammond couldn't raise his $1,000 bail, so remained in prison while he awaited trial. The US Superior Court ruling and rejection of Hammond's appeal later stated that Hammond was convicted of stealing:

> One sealskin sacque, three-quarter length, lined with brown surah silk, and having sealskin covered buttons, of the value of two hundred and fifty dollars, and one lady's gold hunting case watch and gold chain, of the value of seventy-five dollars; and all of the aggregate value of three hundred and twenty-five dollars, and of the value of more than thirty dollars, of the personal goods and property of one Augusta Simons.

It was a sizeable haul for Hammond if he did do it, the total value being around $350. Many American newspapers reported on the Hammond grand larceny trial because of his involvement in the Cleveland Street scandal, reminding readers that he was wanted by Scotland Yard in London for his central involvement in the case. The name of Eddy, Prince Albert Victor was sometimes also included in the reporting in connection with the brothel and the fact that Hammond was thought to possess important documents which he carried in 'a small case'. The inference was that these papers could incriminate many important people back in London.

Hammond was convicted on 17 December 1890 and sentenced to two years in the Walla Walla Penitentiary, Washington State, which had opened less than four years earlier, but for now, he remained in the county jail while his appeals were launched.

But was Charles Hammond guilty of grand larceny? And was Augusta Simons truly his victim? Two days later, on 19 December 1890, the *Fresno Weekly Republican* questioned if Hammond had been framed and under the headline 'Is it a Conspiracy?', reported:

> The recent developments in the case indicate that Hammond is the victim of a conspiracy, of which Alexander Todhunter is at the head. Todhunter is supposed to be an English detective, and failing to get Hammond on British soil, charged him with stealing a sealskin sacque from Mrs. Augusta Simons, whom Todhunter induced to visit Hammond's saloon. Hammond claims that there is $250,000 at his disposal [yet strangely, he couldn't find his $1,000 bail a year before] on deposit at the Bank of California and other banks, which has been placed thus by wealthy Englishmen as hush money. Hammond has been in Seattle more than one year and has abundant means. He refused to talk but admitted having threatened to return to London. He said that parties there are trying to prevent his return, and in order to do so had Todhunter trump up the charge against him. He expects to get a new trial and says he will return to London and take the consequences but refuses to betray the men who patronized his Cleveland Street house.

The *Los Angeles Herald* of 1 January 1891 reported:

It is claimed that Todhunter is an English detective trying to get Hammond into the penitentiary at the instance of the wealthy Englishmen who patronized Hammond's Cleveland Street house, and who are tired of paying hush money. Hammond claims he is the victim of a conspiracy and that Todhunter had been paid to get him out of the way.

Then, on 7 January 1891, there was an unexpected and explosive development. With Hammond now in prison, his 'secretary' Herbert Ames, who had lived at No. 19 Cleveland Street and escaped with Hammond to Europe in early July 1889 and then on to America, felt safe enough to reveal what he had witnessed at the brothel and in his life abroad with Hammond since.

Herbert John Ames was born in February 1872, so he was then almost 20, but when he first began working for Hammond he was 16 years old. Ames made his 'confession' in an affidavit, sworn in the presence of three witnesses, including a notary public. His lengthy statement ran in the *San Francisco Chronicle* under the headline 'Hammond's Secrets – New Revelations about his London Den' on 8 January 1891, although it was reported very widely in newspapers across America. The newspaper highlighted that before his boss was put under lock and key, Ames had been 'afraid to tell his story because of Hammond's threats of personal violence'.

This is Ames' statement in full:

In June 1888, Thomas Conway, a boy 19 years of age, told me of the existence of a house kept by Hammond on Cleveland Street in London, and induced me to go there with him. As the life was an easy one and money was plenty, I remained there until June 1889 [in fact, July 1889], at which time a discovery of the nature of the house compelled Hammond and myself to leave London. I was told by Hammond that he had been running the place between three and four years, and during the year that I was there about twenty men visited the house regularly.

Many of these were introduced into the house under a false name, and the names of some were never known either to Hammond or myself. Seven of the men I became personally acquainted with, and their names were: the Earl of Euston [so was he really a long-standing client?] residing at 11 Grosvenor Place [actually No. 4], London; Lord Arthur Somerset, residing at Hyde Park Barracks; Robert Jervoice [Jervoise], Queen's officer at Winchester barracks; Dr Maitland, of Harvard, a suburb of London [this man cannot be traced, and no London suburb sharing the name of the American university has ever existed]; Percy Stafford, a capitalist of London [also cannot be traced]; Hugh Waglin [Weguelin], banker [stockbroker], of 56 Sackwell [31 Sackville] Street, London; and Captain Barbey [disgraced former Lieutenant Charles Montague Barber] of the army.

All the visitors to the house were from the higher class and they were always liberal with their money. Then the exposure occurred which caused the house to shut down. Hammond took me with him and went to Calais and then to Paris. In Paris we stayed three weeks with Mrs. Hammond's sister and then we went to Langley, France. At Langley, Hammond was met by Arthur Newton, a lawyer acting in the interests of the visitors to the Cleveland Street house, and he wanted us to go to America at once. On the following day [official sources show that this happened in early September, not July 1889] two English detectives [not including Inspector Abberline, who had already returned to England after his trip to France chasing Hammond in August] had Hammond expelled from the country. They told him to leave by noontime.

In July [early September] 1889, we left France and went to Belfast, and then to Halanzy [Luxembourg] where we stayed three weeks. While in Halanzy, Newton, the lawyer, sent word to Hammond to go to Antwerp, where he would meet him and arrange matters. We met Newton at Brussels, and in a room in one of the hotels there, Newton asked Hammond what he would take to go to America. I was in the room at the time, and Hammond told him that he would have to have £5,000 to start with. The matter was finally compromised between them for £800. We sailed, under fictitious names, on the steamer Penland [SS *Pennland*] for New York, and when we arrived there a man named Harris, who had been sent by Newton to see that we arrived all right, paid $4,000 over to Hammond.

Hammond cannot write, and since he has been here, I have done that work for him. I have written letters for him demanding money from the Earl of Euston, Lord Somerset and Robert Jervoice [sic] since we have been here, and within the past month I wrote and registered a letter to Jervoice [sic] demanding £100 for Hammond, who stated that he was in trouble. Whether or not Hammond ever received any return I cannot positively state.

While Hammond was running the Haymarket Saloon [in Seattle] I once asked him for money. He was very pleasant and offered me some whisky to drink, but I did not touch it, as there was a substance in the bottom of the glass which looked like poison.

The names revealed by Ames caused a stir. Gossip about the scandal intensified and press coverage was widespread, but as detailed earlier in this story, no action was taken against any of those whose identity was now divulged, except of course Somerset, who had been allowed to escape his arrest and into exile. The most interesting aspect of Ames' statement is perhaps in revealing just how hands-on Arthur Newton had been in helping to facilitate Hammond's escape beyond reach to America, and that he had travelled to both France and Belgium to do so. Newton was fortunate that Ames hadn't exposed these details *before* his trial the previous year.

Newton faced no further prosecution over his conduct during the Cleveland Street scandal. Much to the police's frustration, the higher authorities of the royal family and Lord Salisbury's government saw the scandal as being over. Apart from occasional murmurings in the press and undoubtedly in the clubs of London, the affair was safely asleep, just as they wanted it to be. And both British institutions of monarchy and sitting government in Parliament had done what they could to ensure that it was 'put to bed' as quietly as possible and stayed there.

But back in America, on 10 January 1891, the imprisoned Charles Hammond sent a cease-and-desist letter to his lawyers who then passed it to the *Seattle Post Intelligencer*. It was aimed at the American press generally, which was most probably in reaction to Ames divulging so many details about No. 19 Cleveland Street just two days before. The newspaper reported the letter in full the next day:

> Having been informed that certain newspapers have contracted with divers persons, to me unknown, for publications purporting to come from me concerning my business affairs at No. 19 Cleveland Street, London, England, please state on my behalf that any and all such statements are utterly false and without any foundation, for I have never made known to any person, either verbally or otherwise, anything connected with my affairs in England, and I pronounce any written instrument with my name attached to it, concerning my Cleveland Street affairs, a forgery. I hereby warn all papers against impostures of this character.

Were other forces at work against Hammond? Was Hammond being pressured or threatened by those he could damage with his secrets?

This was somewhat hypocritical, since Hammond himself had named the Earl of Euston and Hugh Weguelin to the press back in March 1890. Nobody but Hammond or Ames knew those names in America, and Ames certainly wouldn't have leaked them as he feared Hammond, who was still at liberty at that time. The unscrupulous and manipulative Hammond was most likely covering himself and trying to obscure the truth, while reminding those whose secrets he held that he still had them.

At this time, Hammond was in yet more trouble, this time in a civil case, when he was sued for fraud. He had sold the fixtures and fittings of his bar, the Haymarket Saloon, for $1,600, having assured the buyers that there was no money owed on them, when in fact there was still $227.40 outstanding. He had to come up with that amount plus costs. And although Hammond was incarcerated, he was still creating headlines. In early March, the *Chicago Tribune* received information from Portland, Oregon, that the Cleveland Street pimp's 'letters' had been stolen:

An English detective named Partridge recently secured possession of the famous English letters of Charles Hammond, but was a few days ago robbed of them by a man named Tyrell. Partridge says he came direct from London with instructions to secure the letters at any price and at all hazards. He followed his man to Australia, then back to California, and finally located him there. A dicker [negotiation] was made, and a compromise effected wherein the blackmailers were paid several thousand dollars for the letters in question, a number of which were from noted persons in England. While at San Francisco Partridge met a man named Tyrell, who introduced himself and stated he had been sent out from London to aid Partridge. He produced a photograph of the latter, by which means he said he identified him, and presented credentials and testimonials. By these he gained his confidence. Partridge explained to Tyrel how matters stood, saying the affair had been compromised, but still, he had hopes of getting a cinch [firm grip] on Hammond and his gang. While at Sacramento, these papers, which were kept locked up in a tin box and zealously guarded, mysteriously disappeared one night with the 'slippery' Tyrrel, who was the only person who knew what the box contained. Partridge was in a hole. He came North and notified a Tacoma [Washington State] detective agency. A man answering the description of Tyrell was seen to leave Tacoma on Wednesday for Portland, and the officers claim they will capture him tomorrow.

Then the *Seattle Post-Intelligencer* of 16 March 1891 reported that one of its reporters had spoken to Hammond, who was still at the county jail in Seattle, and shown him the report. Hammond was quoted as saying that no such theft of his letters had taken place and he lengthily bemoaned his circumstances, sounding both dejected and desperate:

There is no truth in this, whatever. I have no letters hidden in a tin box. I have no letters where anyone can get them [but he wasn't denying that he had such letters somewhere – his extortion capital]. Judging from the reading of that item I make up my mind that it was sent out from Seattle. I believe that it originated with a man who is now in this town and is partly to blame for my imprisonment [Hammond wouldn't name him when asked, but he presumably meant Alexander Todhunter].

I do not care about mentioning any names until I am clear of my present trouble [a canny reminder to those involved with No. 19 Cleveland Street that he had their names to mention]. I have had offers to sell letters which have been reported to be in my possession, but I have none that I care to part with. A detective who claimed to be from San Francisco called to see me not long ago, and said he wished to work up my case. I was afraid of him and would have nothing to do with him. I have been deceived by everyone I trusted and will put my trust in no one hereafter. I am as innocent of the crime of which I am held and have been sentenced as a newborn babe. I am a victim of numerous enemies. I am not perfect. I have my faults, so has everyone, but that is no reason why people should frown on me unjustly because I am down.

My money is now gone. At the time of my arrest, I was doing a good business – making as much as $60 a week. Now I am destitute, and my family is without means. Up to a week ago I kept them, but between my attorneys, of whom I have had many, and the expenses of my family, I have nothing left and the county must take care of my wife and child. My wife lay on a bed of sickness all last week. Yesterday she recovered sufficiently to get up, and she came down to see me. She is afflicted with heart disease and can do nothing for herself, and what can my boy of 13 years do for her? I am not a petty thief. I have my faults, but I never stole anything in all my life. I believe someone is tampering with my mail, for I am receiving no more letters. All I can say is that I am in sore straits.

Both Partridge and Tyrell seem to have existed, but who sent them? Was Partridge hired on behalf of the notable Englishmen incriminated in the letters over their involvement in the Cleveland Street scandal? Was Tyrell then paid by Hammond to get them back from Partridge? The truth about the farrago of Hammond's missing letters and whether they were ever stolen or not was never learnt.

On 7 August 1891, the *Seattle Post Intelligencer* briefly mentioned that Hammond had caught pneumonia in the county jail and as he was gravely ill, he had been moved to 'the poor farm' under guard. 'His escape in his present condition would be an impossibility, but the sheriff will not take any chances, and the prisoner will be closely watched until he either dies or is well enough to be returned to the county jail.' Hammond did recover in time and was indeed escorted back to prison.

But was there a conspiracy against Hammond in the grand larceny case? No evidence can be found that Alexander Todhunter, Hammond's barman, and the principal witness against him, was a private detective. But could he have been paid by anxious and well-heeled former clients of No. 19 Cleveland Street to silence Hammond? And if so, could Somerset's fixer and lawyer Arthur Newton have been involved in such a conspiracy? Would a conviction for theft have been enough to calm the wealthy conspirators? Surely, if they wanted to remove the risk of extortion or blackmail, social ruin and possible legal prosecution, they would plan to silence Hammond more permanently.

Could Alexander Todhunter just have been a lone operator? An English grifter in America trying to get control of Hammond's Haymarket bar in Seattle, or just vengeful, holding a grudge after a falling-out with his boss? Or could Todhunter have seen what he claimed – the manipulative and criminally inclined Hammond having stolen Augusta Simons' possessions?

Whatever the truth, what happened next casts doubt on the veracity of Alexander Todhunter's accusations against Hammond. Not long after his final appeal failed, a petition with many signatures, including those of the Mayor of Seattle, George W. Hall, and other leading city figures, was presented in support of Hammond's innocence in the grand larceny conviction.

Hammond, who had been in the county jail for around fifteen months, was pardoned by the incumbent Governor of the State of Washington, Elisha. P. Ferry. Four reasons were given for Hammond's pardon: 'That the petitioners believe that he was not guilty; That they fully believe that the ends of justice have been subserved by the imprisonment already sustained; That he has a family in destitute circumstances, dependent solely upon him for maintenance; That he is in failing health.'

Hammond was set free on 6 February 1892 and disappeared from press and public scrutiny. The next day, the *Seattle Post-Intelligencer* reported that Hammond's son, Manty, the future actor, was 'overjoyed' at his father's release and had gone to the county jail to welcome him back to freedom. It also relayed that Hammond's 'face is white and bleached from long confinement' and that he was 'somewhat thin from ill health'. The newspaper stated that the Seattle police were sure that Hammond was innocent of the grand larceny charge, and his accuser Alexander Todhunter had left Washington State. It was believed by those who had investigated the matter that Todhunter was indeed 'a detective employed by certain persons high in English society for the sole purpose of placing Hammond, who formerly ran the notorious Cleveland Street house in London, behind the bars'.

Charles Hammond then forever disappeared from press and public scrutiny.

Inspector Abberline officially left the Cleveland Street inquiry on 6 December 1889, but he had, as detailed, made court appearances in the Newton and Taylerson police and magistrates' court hearings in the first months of 1890. On leaving the inquiry, Abberline claimed expenses of £58 17s 11d. When he had come off leading the Jack the Ripper on-the-ground investigation in late 1888, he had received expenses of just over £30, but Abberline had been on the Cleveland Street case much longer and had travelled to France chasing Charles Hammond.

In 1890, Abberline was promoted to chief inspector and given mainly desk duties at Scotland Yard. He had risen to a very high rank, and if he had enjoyed administrative work he could have risen even higher in the police hierarchy, but Abberline was an officer who liked to be on the ground, and he was stultified in this hands-off new role.

In that same year, Abberline's overall boss, the Metropolitan Police Commissioner James Monro, who had fought hard to allow Abberline to carry out his duties in the Cleveland Street inquiry, resigned his position on 21 June. This was due to Monro's difficult relationship with the Home Office, led by the Home Secretary, Sir Henry Matthews. Since his appointment in November 1888, Monro had been at odds with government authorities over the number of officers at his disposal and the quality of their uniforms and equipment. As time went on, these differences became more political and there was a row about the promotions of high-level officers; Monro wanted them to be recruited from within the ranks, rewarding time-served officers, while Matthews wanted to install his own choices. (As of 2024, Monro is still the commissioner with the shortest tenure in the Metropolitan Police's history, at nineteen months.)

The repeated obstruction and procrastination that Monro had endured at the hands of his political superiors while attempting to prosecute the Cleveland Street case must also have irked him, especially as his force was unfairly pilloried and criticised so much in the press. Abberline undoubtedly shared these frustrations at the thwarting of the inquiry and was disillusioned at his inability to do the difficult and high-profile job given to him. Just under two years later, in early June 1892, Abberline also retired. He had served for twenty-nine years and had received eighty-four commendations and awards – an astonishing number. This was despite his two biggest cases, the Jack the Ripper and Cleveland Street cases, being respectively unsuccessful and only partially successful.

Abberline was 49 years old, and many officers retired after thirty years' service, so he was short by one year, but he was able to leave the force on a full pension as the 1890 Police Bill made provision for early retirement after twenty-five years of service. So, disillusionment and a feeling that he had gone as far as he thought he could in his policing career was probably a key factor in his decision to retire then, but it was also financially practical.

On 8 June 1892, a leaving dinner was held for Abberline in the City of London, close to his old stomping ground of the East End, where he had served for much of his career. The *Sunday Dispatch* reported the event on 12 June, under the headline 'Presentation to a Detective':

An interesting ceremony was performed on Wednesday night at a complimentary dinner given at the Three Nuns Hotel, Aldgate, to Mr. F.G. Abberline, late Chief Inspector of the Criminal Investigation Department, New Scotland Yard, on his retirement from the police force [...] To mark their sense of the value of Mr. Abberline's services to the community, a number of subscribers joined in the presentation to him of a valuable tea and coffee set, weighing in the aggregate 140 oz [almost 4kg]. Mr. Abberline warmly thanked the company for their handsome gift. In the course of the evening constant reference was made to the loss which the Detective Department had sustained by the retirement of this much-respected officer. Many of his former colleagues were present.

Abberline would go on to work as a private detective and was employed for three seasons at the casinos in Monte Carlo. He never wrote his memoirs, but at the insistence of his friend Walter Green, who also lodged with Abberline and his wife Emma, he made a press-cuttings book about some aspects of his career. This has become known as 'Abberline's Scrapbook' and is twenty-eight pages in length, all handwritten. Abberline details a missing persons case he worked on as well as twelve pages about his private enquiry agent role in Monte Carlo. There's no mention of the Cleveland Street and Jack the Ripper inquiries, by far his most prominent cases. But the reason for this can be gleaned from Abberline's own words in the scrapbook:

At the time I retired from the service the Authorities were very much opposed to retired officers writing anything for the press as previously some retired officers had from time to time been very indiscreet in what they had caused to be published and to my knowledge had been called upon to explain their conduct and in fact they had been threatened with actions for libel.

Abberline only ever spoke to the press about his thoughts on the identity of Jack the Ripper once, after the persistent and professional encouragement of another lodger, John Philip Collins, a journalist on the *Pall Mall Gazette*, which published his limited insights in March 1903, as detailed in the prologue of this book. Abberline would always keep his discretion about the Cleveland Street scandal and his deep frustrations in leading the inquiry to himself.

Fourteen

The Early 1890s

Picture the scene. At Pagani's Restaurant on Langham Place, just off Great Portland Street in London's West End, once you have passed the arched and pillared art-nouveau frontage, the decor inside is luxuriously soothing. The pale-blue wallpaper with matching curtains, the electric lamps with shades and the bow window at the back of the room whisper understated and nonchalant elegance. But this is the downstairs public room. Upstairs, the rather more exclusive Artist's Room accommodates private parties, and on this day, it hosts three of the most famous faces in London, indeed in many parts of the world. The bearded and already corpulent Edward, Prince of Wales, known as Bertie, is seated next to his former mistress, the actress Lillie Langtry, and Oscar Wilde, the acclaimed playwright, poet, wit and author of the recently published novel *The Picture of Dorian Gray*.

Oscar has known Lillie for around fifteen years, since the late 1870s. He has already dedicated two of his poems to her and rumour has it that he wrote his wildly popular play *Lady Windermere's Fan* for her, which is still on at the St James's Theatre. There's also gossip that the married with children, yet likely homosexual, Oscar has a deep love for Lillie, and not just in a platonic sense.

The three sit in the private dining room with its deep-red velvet curtains and draping above the ornate fireplace, the walls around them decorated with drawings and paintings under glass and the signatures of many legendary artistic patrons, including the toast of Covent Garden, the Australian soprano, Nellie Melba; the French actress, Sarah Bernhardt; and the American painter, James Abbott McNeill Whistler.

The ever-attendant waiting staff are especially attentive when serving the Prince of Wales, Queen Victoria's eldest son, next in line to the throne reigning over the biggest empire in the world. The mood is joyful and playful at the table, as the illustrious guests feast on lark and steak pie and calf's brains, with the finest wines and liquor being decanted, and Oscar entertaining the lovers.

Oscar remembers the Cleveland Street affair well, but probably has little idea that Bertie had used his considerable power to hush up an explosive homosexual scandal emanating from a house not far away from where they sit. Bertie had acted to protect his own eldest son, Prince Albert Victor, second in line to the throne, who had been implicated in the scandal, as had one of his closest aides and other aristocrats, the very men that ruled Britain and a large swathe of the globe. It had been a close-run thing, with the top of the hierarchy tarnished but surviving.

Nor did Oscar know that the same scandal had set the tone and template for his own public disgrace and destruction, which was to befall him within the next few years. There was no hint that evening of what was to come. Oscar sat there in all his finery and at his zenith, not yet 40 years old, but his perfectly curled hair would later become flaxen and limp, his soft delicate skin coarsened and haggard. The stage was already set for his downfall, which would break him and lead to his early death, and Bertie, like most others, would soon ruthlessly turn his broad back on Oscar when he was arrested, convicted and imprisoned.

When, in July 1890, Oscar Wilde published his 50,000-word gothic novel *The Picture of Dorian Gray* in the American *Lippincott's Monthly Magazine*, an advance blurb was supplied by *The Christian Leader*, proclaiming, 'Mr. Wilde has performed a service to his age'. This endorsement by a leading religious publication may seem ironic now, as the short novel would soon cause outrage, including in the large-circulation *Daily Chronicle*, whose book critic wrote on 30 June 1890 that it would 'taint every young mind that comes in contact with it' and that the novel was 'heavy with the mephitic odours of moral and spiritual putrefaction'.

The story of its hedonistic and murderous eponymous protagonist and his Faustian pact, the selling of a soul for eternal youth, along with perceived and undoubtedly intended taboo homoerotic overtones, drew moralistic fire. Passages in the novel, such as this one, where the leading character Sir Henry Wotton admires Dorian Gray, were provocative to late-Victorian sensibilities:

Lord Henry looked at him. Yes, he was certainly wonderfully handsome, with his finely-curved scarlet lips, his frank blue eyes, his crisp gold hair. There was something in his face that made one trust him at once. All the candour of youth was there, as well as all youth's passionate purity. One felt that he had kept himself unspotted from the world [...] He was made to be worshipped.

The *Scots Observer* of 5 July attacked hard, its critic writing:

Why go grubbing in muck heaps? The world is fair, and the proportion of healthy-minded men and honest women, to those who are foul, fallen or unnatural is great. Mr. Oscar Wilde has again been writing stuff that were better unwritten; and while *The Picture of Dorian Gray*, which he contributes to *Lippincott's*, is ingenious, interesting, full of cleverness, and plainly the work of a man of letters, it is false art – for its interest is medico-legal; it is false to human nature – for its hero is a devil, it is false to morality – for it is not made sufficiently clear that the writer does not prefer a course of unnatural iniquity to a life of cleanliness, health and sanity. The story – which deals with matters only fit for the Criminal Investigation Department or a hearing *in camera* – is discreditable alike to author and editor.

But it was the final paragraph of that review which openly referenced Wilde's allusions in the novel to the Cleveland Street scandal, which had recently reached its public denouement: 'Mr. Wilde has brains, and art, and style; but if he can write for none but outlawed noblemen and perverted telegraph-boys, the sooner he takes to tailoring (or some other decent trade) the better for his own reputation and the public morals.' The reference to 'outlawed noblemen' arises from Basil Hallward, who paints Dorian's portrait, saying to Dorian in the novel, 'There was that wretched boy in the Guards who committed suicide. You were his great friend. There was Sir Henry Ashton, who had to leave England, with a tarnished name. You and he were inseparable.'

For Sir Henry Ashton, read Lord Arthur Somerset. Wilde was writing his novella in late 1889, when Somerset's name and his escape abroad were all over the press, not to mention the London clubs, some of which Wilde frequented. And Wilde was an acute and sensitive observer of all around him, his literary antennae always tuned in and alert. Wilde was commissioned to write the novel by Joseph Marshall Stoddart, the editor of *Lippincott's*, at a dinner at the Langham Hotel in central London on 30 August 1889, when the Cleveland Street scandal was beginning to attract newspaper interest and was already a key subject of gossip in London clubland. Sir Arthur Conan Doyle was present at the dinner and Stoddart also commissioned Doyle's Sherlock Holmes novella *The Sign of Four*, which appeared complete in the magazine in February 1890, five months before *The Picture of Dorian Gray*. Stoddart would make his own adjustments to the latter manuscript before publication, restraining some homoerotic elements.

But it wasn't enough for the British readership. In response to the critical moral furore, W.H. Smith, then Britain's foremost bookseller and a presence at most railway stations, pulled all copies of the offending British edition of *Lippincott's* from its bookstalls.

Wilde would make more changes to the novel for its book publication in 1891, and the fervent emotion and admiration of male beauty was further toned down. He had no choice, as some were calling for his prosecution. As Alex Ross pointed out in the *New Yorker* in 2011, the *St. James Gazette* 'suggested that the Treasury or the Vigilance Society might wish to prosecute the author'. Wilde's London publisher, Ward, Locke & Co., wouldn't have risked going ahead without the alterations.

Just four years after *The Picture of Dorian Gray* was published in book form, it would be used against Wilde in court as proof of his 'degeneracy', the novel being called 'perverted'.

Wilde's troubles all began on 18 February 1895, when the irascible Marquis of Queensberry, the father of Wilde's lover – Lord Alfred Douglas, known as 'Bosie' – left a calling card at a club the writer frequented, the Albemarle in Mayfair, central London. Written on the card was 'For Oscar Wilde, posing Somdomite', a misspelling of 'sodomite'. Such a social insult in mid-1890s Britain was intended to provoke Wilde into defending his reputation, and it did just that.

A few decades earlier, there might have been a duel, but Wilde, at the encouragement of Bosie, who had an exceedingly difficult relationship with his father, headed to the libel court – unwisely, as it happened, because the insult was based on fact. The affair between the married Wilde and Bosie was tumultuous and their lifestyle indiscreet, and there were many other young men in their orbit. As Wilde's biographer Richard Ellmann highlighted,[1] in another echo of the Cleveland Street scandal, the noted illustrator Aubrey Beardsley, a friend and associate of Wilde, wrote to Wilde's close friend Robbie Ross in November 1893, 'the numbers of telegraph and messenger boys who came to the door was simply scandalous'.[2]

Just as Ernest Parke was arrested in 1890 when the Earl of Euston took out a libel writ against him, so was the Marquess of Queensberry on the morning of Saturday, 9 March 1895, once Wilde had issued a private writ for defamatory libel. Like Parke, Queensberry could only win if he could prove that what he had written on his calling card was true, namely that Wilde was a sodomite, and he soon had private enquiry agents digging into Wilde's lifestyle, writings and past to gather evidence.

On 23 March 1895, Wilde paid a visit to Mrs Robinson, a palm reader who had 'society' clientele, and they met at her London home in

Mortimer Street, central London. Wilde was looking for guidance on whether to stay and fight and risk arrest if his libel writ was unsuccessful or flee abroad, as Lord Arthur Somerset had done just over five years earlier. What Mrs Robinson told Wilde at that meeting is unknown, but on a visit to her in the previous year, she had reportedly relayed to him that 'I see a very brilliant life for you up to a certain point. Then I see a wall. Beyond the wall I see nothing.' Whatever he was advised at his second reading, Wilde decided to stay and fight rather than admit disgrace and fade away in exile.

By 1895, Lord Salisbury was no longer the prime minister, having been beaten by the Liberal politician and former premier William Gladstone, the Liberal politician, at the General Election in 1892. When Gladstone resigned in 1894, Lord Rosebery became prime minister. Incidentally, Bosie's elder brother Francis died in a hunting accident in October of that year – he was found shot dead. Francis was rumoured to have been in a relationship with none other than Lord Rosebery. The cause of his death was seen by many to be suicide, because he was fearful of public disgrace. This could have only increased the Marquis of Queensberry's anger and homophobia, motivating him further to rescue his younger son from Wilde's clutches.

The Home Secretary was now Herbert Asquith, the future prime minister, who had been a junior defence counsel at Ernest Parke's libel trial five years previously. Hamilton Cuffe, who had been Assistant DPP during the Cleveland Street scandal, had been promoted and was now the DPP.

The Marquess of Queensberry appeared at the Old Bailey on 3 April 1895 to defend himself against Wilde's libel writ. Twenty-four-year-old Bosie was seated in court, close to where the judge entered. The proceedings were presided over by Mr Justice Collins, an Irishman. Wilde's prosecution team consisted of Sir Edward Clarke QC, aged 54, who had been Solicitor General in Lord Salisbury's government until 1892; Charles Mathews, who had been a junior prosecution counsel against

Ernest Parke at his libel trial, five years earlier; and Travers Humphreys, who would go on to be junior prosecution counsel in several prominent trials, including against Dr Crippen in 1910, the poisoner Frederick Seddon in 1912, the 'Brides in the Bath' killer George Joseph Smith in 1915 and Sir Roger Casement for treason in 1916.

Queensberry was defended by the 41-year-old meticulous Irish barrister and politician Edward Carson QC, who later became Solicitor General and then Attorney General for England. Carson was deputised by Charles Gill, who had represented both George Veck in 1889 and Arthur Newton in 1890, during the Cleveland Street scandal.

The *Evening Sentinel* of 6 April 1895 reported, 'There was a crowded attendance of the public. On taking his place in the dock, Lord Queensberry answered the indictment by pleading first not guilty, and secondly that the libel was true, and was published [on his calling card] for the public benefit.'

The prosecution read excerpts from *The Picture of Dorian Gray* and the contents of an Oxford University undergraduate literary magazine called *The Chameleon*, which only lasted one issue, in which Bosie had published two homoerotic poems. One of those poems, *Two Loves*, contained the now famous and then incendiary line 'the love that dare not speak its name'. There was also a sexually provocative short story by the editor, John Bloxham, called *The Priest and the Acolyte*, which Wilde, who was a friend, had encouraged Bloxham to publish.

Edward Carson and Gill managed to portray Wilde to the court as seedy and amoral, exposing his lifestyle in the homosexual underworld in London, Worthing, in Sussex, and Paris. Included was Wilde's friendship with Alfred Taylor, who Carson said was Wilde's procurer. Taylor had been arrested in a raid on a brothel in Fitzroy Square the previous year and would go on to be Wilde's co-defendant in the following criminal trial. It was the same milieu of rent boys as seen in the Cleveland Street scandal, although, unlike in the goings-on at that brothel, none of the 'boys' that Wilde was alleged to have sexual relations with was under the age of 16.

The press at the time reported that the young men who had relations with Wilde were aged between 18 and 23, although close reading of the libel trial proceedings reveals, as others have noted, that one,

Alphonse Conway, was 16. Although the age of consent under the Criminal Law Amendment Act of 1885 was 16, Henry Labouchère's Section 11 Amendment of that legislation, stipulating 'gross indecency' as an offence would soon put Wilde in criminal jeopardy.

The murky mural that Carson painted before the court of Wilde's 'secret' life was damaging to his character. Under cross-examination, Wilde was witty and almost characteristically, as in his writing, epigrammatic in his answers, such as 'I have never given adoration to anybody except myself'. The court sometimes descended into laughter.

But Carson managed to unsettle Wilde once, when he was asked if he hadn't kissed a boy because he was 'too ugly', a description of the young man given by the writer. 'Why mention his ugliness?' said Carson, trying to elicit from Wilde that he would have kissed him if he had been attractive.

Wilde erupted angrily, saying, 'Because you sting me by insolent questions!' before adding, 'Calmly, I say you sting me, and try to unnerve me in every way, and I say things flippantly that I would not say seriously.'

At no small cost, Queensberry's private detectives had done their job, and on what would be the final day of the libel trial, Friday, 5 April, Carson announced that he would be calling several male rent boys – who were probably coerced through fear of prosecution themselves – to give evidence against Wilde to prove Queensberry's assertion.

After a subsequent conference with his lawyers, Wilde did not appear again in court and left by hansom cab. His chief counsel, Sir Edward Clarke, had recommended that Wilde withdraw his libel writ against Queensberry because the coming witness testimony against him would lose him the case. Carson returned to court and said that he wished to withdraw from the prosecution after consulting with Wilde. He was content for a verdict of not guilty to be passed based on the evidence put forward against Wilde by the readings from *The Picture of Dorian Gray* and *The Chameleon*. Edward Carson had to accept that a verdict of not guilty would mean that his client was liable for prosecution for sexual offences. Mr Justice Collins then told the jury that bringing back a verdict of not guilty would also mean one of justification.

The North Star relayed on 6 April:

The jury after a moment's consideration returned a verdict of not guilty against the Marquess of Queensberry, the foreman adding that what he had written was published for the public benefit. The judge thereupon ordered the Marquess of Queensberry's discharge from custody and certified for costs. The Marquess on descending from the dock was heartily congratulated by his friends, and the court rapidly cleared.

Wilde would be liable for Queensberry's legal fees and costs, and this would soon bankrupt him.

Wilde had made his way to the Holborn Viaduct Hotel, close to the court and where he had stayed during the trial. On hotel stationery, Wilde wrote to the *London Evening News* an explanation of his withdrawal, as the verdict would soon be all over the press. It read:

> To the Editor – It would be impossible for me to prove my case without putting Lord Alfred Douglas in the witness-box against his father. Lord Alfred Douglas was extremely anxious to go into the box, but I would not let him do so. Rather than put him in so painful a position I determined to retire from the case, and to bear on my own shoulders whatever ignominy and shame might result from my prosecuting Lord Queensberry.

That same evening, Sir Edward Clarke made it known to friends that before he had accepted his retainer to represent Wilde, he had sought assurance that the charge made against him by Queensberry was 'utterly without foundation'. Clarke reportedly said that Wilde had given him that assurance.

The Press Association approached Queensberry's solicitors, Messrs Russell and Day, and asked if Queensberry intended to follow up with criminal proceedings against Wilde. Queensberry's legal representatives answered:

> It was not his lordship's intention to take the initiative in any criminal prosecution of Oscar Wilde, but after the finding of the jury this morning in the libel action, the whole of the documents, with proofs

of the evidence upon which the defence had intended to reply, were forwarded to the Public Prosecutor the Hon. Hamilton Cuffe.

But *The North Star* reported on 6 April:

An application had been made at Bow Street by, it is understood, Mr. Charles Russell, Lord Queensberry's solicitor [...] and Mr. Angus Lewis, of the Treasury, for a warrant for the arrest of Wilde, and the application was granted by Sir John Bridge [Chief Metropolitan Police Magistrate], and placed without delay in the hands of the police. A description of Wilde was afterwards issued.

Meanwhile, the same paper relayed that Queensberry had sent a message to Wilde immediately after the libel trial ended, saying, 'If the country allows you to leave, all the better for the country; but if you take my son with you, I will follow you wherever you go, and shoot you.'

Wilde, whose play *The Importance of Being Earnest*, which many consider his theatrical masterpiece, had premiered at the St James's Theatre on 14 February, was now facing arrest. Although he knew Bertie, the Prince of Wales and many other society figures personally, Wilde wasn't an aristocrat like Somerset and his arrest wasn't damaging to the royal family. He chose not to flee immediately after the libel trial on 5 April, despite close friends advising him to escape to France as Somerset had done, saying, according to his biographer Richard Ellmann, 'The train has gone. It's too late.'

Little time would be wasted on executing the warrant on Wilde. By then, Wilde was ensconced in the Cadogan Hotel, not too far from his home in Chelsea's Tite Street. It was there, on the same day that his libel prosecution of Queensberry had collapsed, that Wilde was arrested at about 6 p.m., by Inspector Richards and Sergeant Allen of Scotland Yard. *The North Star* described Wilde's arrest and charging:

He seemed somewhat surprised when the charge was read over to him, but made no reply, and was immediately taken to New Scotland Yard and handed over to Inspector Brockwell, who held the warrant. After remaining for some time at Scotland Yard, Oscar Wilde was placed in a four-wheeled cab and conveyed to Bow Street, where he arrived at 8.10pm, in custody of Inspectors Brockwell and Richards. On alighting from the cab, Wilde walked up the steps to the door of the police station briskly with his hands in his pockets, and was at once placed in the dock, and charged by Inspector Digby with committing acts of gross indecency [under Section 11 of the Criminal Law Amendment Act 1885] with certain male persons [...] While the charge was being read, the prisoner leaned over the dock still keeping his hands in his pockets, and appearing unconcerned. The prisoner did not make any reply to the charge, and he was removed overnight to an ordinary cell. Soon after Wilde had been removed to the cells, a man [probably Wilde's butler or close friend, Robbie Ross] drove up in a hansom cab bearing a portmanteau containing some of the prisoner's clothes, etc. He carried the bag into the station, but the police would not permit him to leave it, and he had to carry it away again.

Wilde's plays, *An Ideal Husband* and *The Importance of Being Earnest*, were still running at the Haymarket Theatre and St James's Theatre respectively on 5 April. The press reported that audiences were smaller than normal, and when Worthing was mentioned in the performance of *The Importance of Being Earnest*, some murmurs were heard from the gallery seats. Wilde had been accused of committing gross indecency with a rent boy in that Sussex town during the libel trial, the details of which were already all over the evening newspapers. *An Ideal Husband*, at the end of its planned run, moved to the Criterion Theatre in Piccadilly for thirteen more performances and would close on 27 April, while *The Importance of Being Earnest* had its last performance on 8 May. Meanwhile, Wilde was moved on remand to Holloway Prison, where Bosie would visit him every day.

Wilde went on criminal trial at the Old Bailey on 26 April 1895, alongside his friend Alfred Taylor, both accused of twenty-five counts of gross indecency and conspiracy to commit those acts. Both men pleaded not guilty.

The trial judge was Mr Justice Charles, aged 56, who would retire from the bench just two years later because of ill health. Wilde's legal team was the same as at his libel trial, while the prosecution was led by Sir Frank Lockwood QC, the Solicitor General and defender of Ernest Parke at his 1890 libel trial; Charles Gill, the defender of George Veck, and Arthur Newton and Frederick Taylerson in 1889 and 1890 respectively; and Horace Avory, who had advised the DPP over the ramifications of the Cleveland Street scandal, a member of the Veck and Newlove prosecution team who had acted in the same role against Newton and Taylerson.

It was agreed by opposing counsels and the judge that Wilde and Taylor would be tried separately, one after the other. Taylor was defended by Mr J.P. Grain, who was widely known on the London legal circuit. Incredibly, none other than Arthur Newton had instructed him on behalf of Taylor.

On the stand during the trial, Alfred Taylor introduced himself:

I am 33 years of age. I am the son of a cocoa manufacturer, whose business is now being carried on as a limited liability company. Up to the age of 16 or 17 I was educated at Marlborough School, and afterwards I went to a private tutor at Preston, near Brighton. I then entered the militia, going into the 4th Battalion of the Royal Fusiliers, City of London Regiment. My original intention was to go into the army, but on coming of age in 1883 I came into a fortune of £45,000 and have since that time had no occupation but have lived a life of pleasure.

Charles Gill, for the prosecution, read and referred to *The Picture of Dorian Gray* and Bosie's poem 'Two Loves', published in the *Chameleon*, as in the libel trial, asking Wilde on the stand the meaning of the key line 'the love that dare not speak its name'. After expanding on the 'great affection' felt between older and younger men through history going back to Plato, Wilde referred to his present predicament:

It is in this century misunderstood, so much misunderstood that it may be described as 'the love that dare not speak its name', and on that account of it I am placed where I am now. It is beautiful, it is fine, it is the noblest form of affection. There is nothing unnatural about it. It is intellectual, and it repeatedly exists between an older and a younger man, when the older man has intellect, and the younger man has all the joy, hope and glamour of life before him. That it should be so, the world does not understand. The world mocks at it, and sometimes puts one in the pillory for it.

On the second day, 27 April, Charles Gill asked to remove the charges for conspiracy from proceedings, explaining that keeping those charges would make it difficult to call witnesses to the box to give evidence. But the core charges of twenty-five counts of gross indecency against Wilde and Taylor remained.

The following day, after Mr Justice Charles had summed up, agreeing that not guilty verdicts should be returned on the charges of conspiracy for both Wilde and Taylor, the jury retired at 1.35 p.m. The jury returned at 5.15 p.m., having been unable to reach a verdict.

Both Wilde and Taylor were bailed to await retrial. Wilde's bail was set at £5,000 and this was only for the three weeks until Wilde's second criminal trial was scheduled. Half of the bond was put up by the Reverend Stuart Headlam, an Anglican priest with a love of the theatre whom Wilde didn't know personally, with the rest being met by Wilde's friends. The writer went to stay with two old friends, the writer Ada Leverson and her husband, Ernest.

Wilde and Taylor were left dangling for almost a month until the next court sessions. The defendants and the same legal teams reassembled in a crowded Old Bailey on 20 May, but this time the judge was Mr Justice Alfred Wills, 66 years old, who was a noted mountaineer in the Alps in the 1850s and served as President of the Alpine Club in the mid-1860s.

The prosecution then made allegations against Taylor, as they did with Wilde, to stain them with the stigma of homosexuality and effeminacy. The following is a sample of Taylor's cross-examination by Charles Gill:

[Taylor:] It is untrue that I was expelled from a public school for being caught in a compromising situation with a small boy in the lavatory. It is true that I used to have a number of young men living in my rooms and sleeping in the same bed.

[Gill:] Is it true that you ever went through a mock marriage with Mason?

[Taylor:] Absolutely untrue.

[Gill:] Had you a woman's dress in your rooms?

[Taylor:] An Eastern costume.

[Gill:] A woman's dress?

[Taylor:] Yes.

[Gill:] A woman's wig?

[Taylor:] I will explain. It was …

[Gill:] Had you women's stockings?

[Taylor:] Yes.

Wilde had little to add to the evidence he had given in the libel and first criminal trial, and when Sir Frank Lockwood asked him if there was any truth to the charges against him, in line with his not guilty plea, he unsurprisingly replied, 'None whatsoever'.

At the end of the trial, both Wilde and Taylor were found guilty of gross indecency and sentenced to two years in prison with hard labour, the maximum under Section 11 (the Labouchère Amendment) of the Criminal Law Amendment Act of 1885. On sentencing, Mr Justice Wills said that the sentence was 'inadequate' and that it was 'the worst case I have ever tried'. Wilde and Taylor had been handed terms much more severe than those given to George Veck and Henry Newlove for the same offences in the Cleveland Street scandal – nine and four months, respectively. And Lord Arthur Somerset and Charles Hammond had been allowed to escape, while others involved in the activities at the brothel evaded any legal scrutiny completely. But then Veck and Newlove had been given an engineered plea deal by the Establishment to avoid further revelations, and those who managed to avoid trial were able to do so because of the pressure applied by the royal family, via the government.

Wilde and Taylor had no official protection and no such fortune. And hard labour in a late-Victorian prison for two years changed all and destroyed some.

Wilde was first briefly held in Newgate Prison before being moved to Pentonville Prison and then Wandsworth Prison, all in London. Finally, he was incarcerated in Reading Prison, Berkshire, to serve out his sentence. Wilde's conduct inside was reported as 'good', but he suffered physically because of the austere diet (oatmeal and brown bread) and hard physical work, picking oakum (hours on end, hitting lengths of heavy rope with a hammer to separate the tar covering it) or walking a treadmill for six hours a day. At one stage, Wilde fell over and ruptured his eardrum.

And Wilde was financially ruined. As the *New York Times* reported on 25 September 1895, on the previous day Wilde was transported from prison to the bankruptcy court in London in a hansom cab, although he didn't have to take the stand. Proceedings were adjourned that day, but Wilde's debts were said to be £3,581 and his counsel had subscribed £1,500 towards the liquidation of that amount. The remainder would be found, so that 'twenty shillings on the pound', the whole amount, was paid.

By July 1896, Wilde had been 'relieved of oakum picking', allowed more books to read and more exercise – walking in line in the fresh air of the prison yard – than other prisoners, according to a Visiting Committee Book of that date which assessed his welfare. But Wilde suffered badly from diarrhoea and lost weight. When he entered prison, he was recorded as being of 'bulky and flabby physique' and weighed 190lb (86kg), although he was 6ft 2in (1.91m) tall. It's hardly surprising that Wilde shed weight. He had spent years as a pleasure-seeking and sedentary writer, eating rich food, drinking alcohol and doing little physical exercise. The meagre prison diet and hard labour would have been a great shock to his system.

Wilde's mental state was declining too. As early as 4 June 1895, just ten days after going to prison, the *Pall Mall Gazette* reported that Wilde had 'become insane' and was being held in a padded room. Both assertions were untrue, but Wilde had become depressed. Just over three months later, on 11 September, the governor of Wandsworth Prison wrote to the Home Office about Wilde, likely in response to the reports about his mental health in the press:

> When he first came down here from Pentonville he was in an excited flurried condition and seemed as if he wished to face his punishment without flinching. But all this has passed away. As soon as the excitement aroused by the trail subsided and he had to encounter the daily routine of prison life, his fortitude began to give way and rapidly collapsed altogether. He is now quite crushed and broken.

A handcuffed Wilde was transferred from Wandsworth to Reading Prison on the afternoon of 20 November 1896, passing through Clapham Junction Station in London en route out of the capital. Wilde would later write in *De Profundis*, while at Reading, about the abuse he suffered on the station platform, a crowd taunting and spitting at him, reducing him to tears and from which it took him a long time to recover. Today, there is a blue plaque at the station marking the event.

That November, just over eighteen months into his two-year sentence, Wilde petitioned for early release. An official at Reading Prison relayed to the Home Office that Wilde 'reiterates his plea as to the cause of his crime as indulgences but urges release on the ground of his imprisonment tending to madness'. Wilde had many friends and supporters petitioning on his behalf too, but the official response to Wilde's request was, 'The prisoner's fear of mental breakdown or a decay of his literary capacity is expressed in too lucid, orderly and polished a style to cause apprehension on that point.' There would be no early release.

Wilde's sentence officially expired on 19 May 1897, but his friends implored the Home Office for him to be released on another date close to it, to evade 'the curiosity and interference of the press' and avoid 'the persecution of certain disorderly persons, to which he was actually subjected to upon his release on bail' in early May 1895. The authorities denied the request, and Wilde was released on the scheduled date. Oscar Wilde immediately took a boat to Dieppe in France, and never went back to Britain again.

Rooted in Labouchère's Section 11 of the 1885 Criminal Law Amendment Act, the legacy of the Cleveland Street scandal, which set the template for Oscar Wilde's trials and conviction half a decade later, had a momentous effect on the way that homosexual men were treated under British law until the late twentieth century. By 1954, almost seventy years after the Labouchère Amendment became active, more than 1,000 men were being imprisoned annually for gross indecency. In that year, due to mounting protest and pressure, Winston Churchill's second Conservative administration established the Wolfenden Committee, led by John Wolfenden, then Vice Chancellor of the University of Reading, to investigate how homosexuality and prostitution were addressed legally.

The Wolfenden Report, published in October 1957, concluded that there 'must remain a realm of private morality and immorality which is, in brief and crude terms, not the law's business' – basically, that sexual acts between two consenting men should be decriminalised. A parliamentary debate was held in 1960 and the motion in favour of that finding lost, but the public debate around its recommendations increased during the 1960s as British culture became increasingly liberal.

Finally, in 1967, the Sexual Offences Act was passed, which legalised consensual sexual acts between men aged over 21 in England and Wales, making the Labouchère Amendment and the earlier Offences Against the Person Act of 1861 extinct. However, decriminalisation didn't come to Scotland until 1981 and Northern Ireland in 1982.

But the impact on the way that homosexual acts were perceived by the public had been greatly influenced by those two late-nineteenth-century laws which had criminalised and made it easier to prosecute sexual acts between men. Attitudes en masse take far longer to change than the law, and in this way, both the Cleveland Street scandal and Wilde's imprisonment have left a lasting, if gradually fading, mark on British culture.

As the journalist Patrick Kelleher has highlighted, 'Wilde was one of an estimated 50,000 men who were pardoned by the British government for the "crime" of gross indecency'[3] under the Policing and Crime Act. It was 122 years since Oscar Wilde's conviction and 128 years after PC Luke Hanks interrogated Charles Swinscow at the headquarters of the General Post Office, which set the Cleveland Street scandal in motion.

Coda

Frederick Abberline

After working as a private detective in the casinos of Monte Carlo, in 1898 Abberline joined the European branch of the famous Allen Pinkerton's Detective Agency. In 1904, at the age of 61, Abberline retired, and with his wife Emma, left their home in Lambeth, London, and moved to the seaside town of Bournemouth in Dorset, not too far from where he was born. They first lived in Methuen Road and moved a short distance to No. 195 Holdenhurst Road in 1911. Abberline died on 10 December 1929, aged 86, and was buried in an unmarked grave in Wimborne Road Cemetery. Emma died several months later and was buried alongside him. In 2001, a commemorative plaque was placed on the outside of their house in Holdenhurst Road and six years later, a headstone was donated to mark Frederick and Emma's graves.

Algernon Allies

After testifying in court, Allies emigrated to America in the early 1890s and by 1897 was living in Chicago, Illinois. He married Louise Priscilla Wagner on 31 January 1900. He died on 28 October 1925 in Al Capone's Chicago.

Herbert Ames

Charles Hammond's 'secretary' disappeared into obscurity after revealing the secrets about his life with the pimp and No. 19 Cleveland Street. He remained in America, and died aged 55 in Oregon City, Oregon, in January 1928.

Charles Montague Barber

After evading any police action over his frequenting and probable procuring at No. 19 Cleveland Street, Barber was summoned to the Royal Courts of Justice on 17 February 1893, as reported in the *London Gazette*. With others, he faced a writ of summons 'of the sum of £443 and 3 shillings'. He was at that time living at the Ridgeway, Wimbledon, then in Surrey. Both Barber's wife Anne and daughter Isabel were living in Hampstead, north London between 1891 and 1901 without him.

The Earl of Euston

Just over a decade after the Cleveland Street scandal, Euston was made an aide-de-camp to Bertie when he became King Edward VII in 1901. But the following year, the earl was in court over financial matters, mixed up with the ubiquitous lawyer, Arthur Newton. As the *Cardiff Times* reported on 12 July 1902, moneylenders had acted:

> ... against the Earl of Euston, as the acceptor, and Mr Arthur J.E. Newton, as the drawer, of a bill of exchange for £3,000, which had been dishonoured [...] Lord Euston said that the bill in question was [...] security for advances made by the plaintiffs to Mr Newton. Motives of simple friendliness led his Lordship to accept the bill. The bill was the last of a series which Newton used for loans raised entirely for himself.

The moneylenders claimed that Euston was 'liable for nearly £15,000 on bills which he had backed for Newton while the latter was acting as the Earl's solicitor'. They had tried to retrieve the money from Newton, but the lawyer couldn't pay it, so they held Euston responsible.

Newton had gone to Euston in 1899 asking for help in securing loans, promising that he expected to receive £10,000 from his father. This led the judge to remark, 'Ah, many a man has said that before', which prompted laughter in court. Newton had also promised Euston that he was taking no financial risk, as even if Newton died, he was insured for £30,000. In the witness box, Newton denied that he had committed any fraud:

> ... because he had told him of the policies, and of the large income he was making. 'And Lord Euston does not say there was fraud either,' he added. He pointed out that Lord Euston had not, up till now, been called upon for a farthing.[1]

The judge found that no fraud had been committed. But in April 1903, as relayed by the *Evening Express*, Euston was made bankrupt, owing £54,269, and his assets were valued at £174. Euston was made Deputy Lieutenant of Northamptonshire in 1907 and lived in the villages of Passenham and then Potterspury in that county. He died aged 63 on 12 May 1912.

Luke Hanks

After his work on the Cleveland Street inquiry in 1889, PC Hanks had left the Metropolitan Police by the spring of 1891. In April of that year, he was working as a shirt and collar dresser and living at No. 13 Amhurst Road, in Hackney, east London. By December 1891, he was employed as a detective with the London, Tilbury & Southend Railway Company. On 11 August 1892, his wife Helen gave birth to a daughter, Agnes, in West Ham, then in Essex. But Hanks evidently had a serious alcohol problem by this time, and on 17 October 1893, he was arrested and charged with being drunk and disorderly in the East End and taken to Bethnal Green Police Station, where he died later in a police cell. The cause of death was given as 'Serious effusion of the brain, resulting from pneumonia or weakness from large indulgence in liquor'.

Hanks was 39 years old, but newspaper reports gave his age as 43. The *Nottingham Journal* of 20 October 1893 reported that after being taken to the police station, 'Later in the day, information was received that the man was dead, having been seized by a fit in his cell'. The *Barking & East Ham Advertiser* relayed on 21 October that Hanks was separated from Helen:

> The news of her husband's sad death greatly upset Mrs. Hanks and on Wednesday morning, when it was confirmed by a police constable on Upton Park railway bridge, she suddenly fainted and fell heavily to the ground. The poor woman was restored to consciousness and taken home.

At the inquest on 25 October, it emerged that Hanks had been suspended from his job as a railway detective on account of his 'drinking habits'. He had been drunkenly violent when arrested and tried to attack two constables, and four constables were needed to take him to the police station. The *Illustrated Police News* of 28 October 1893 reported:

> It is stated that for twenty-three years Hanks had been a teetotaller, but since June he had been drinking heavily – in fact, he had been behaving so badly that his wife would not live with him. It was no more than a week ago since she left him, and since then he had eaten scarcely anything.

Robert Jervoise

By 1891, Jervoise, a No. 19 Cleveland Street client, was living as a boarder in central London 'on his own means'. He died in London on 11 April 1896, aged 38.

Colonel Oliver Montagu

Lord Arthur Somerset's commanding officer in the Royal Horse Guards and Bertie, Prince of Wales' former equerry died of cancer in Cairo on 23 January 1893, aged 49. His death left his close friend Alexandra, Princess of Wales, heartbroken, especially as she was already in mourning after the recent death of Eddy, Prince Albert Victor.

James Monro

After resigning as the Commissioner of the Metropolitan Police in mid-1890, Monro returned to India, where he had previously been employed in the Indian Civil Service, and worked as a missionary. He established a Christian Medical Mission in the city of Ranaghat, West Bengal, before retiring back to Britain and living in Chiswick, west London. Monro died, aged 81, on 28 January 1920.

Henry Newlove

After serving his prison sentence for his role as rent boy and procurer at No. 19 Cleveland Street, Newlove went back to live with his mother, Margaret, in Camden, north London. Margaret died in January 1907, aged 74, and by 1911 Newlove was working as a railway clerk, living as a boarder with his brother William and sister-in-law Eliza. He was still employed as a clerk in the spring of 1922 and then lived in St Pancras, north London, but was soon discharged to St Pancras Hospital in the St Pancras Workhouse. By the outbreak of the Second World War in September 1939, he was retired and living in Tottenham, then in Middlesex. Newlove died, aged 74, in July 1945.

Arthur Newton

Lord Arthur Somerset's lawyer and fixer, a major player in many of the events in the Cleveland Street scandal and the solicitor for Oscar Wilde's co-defendant Alfred Taylor in the 1895 trial, Newton went on to work on many famous murder cases. By this time, Frederick Taylerson had been succeeded by Lino Novissimo as Newton's managing clerk. Novissimo was adept at gaining clients for his unethical boss by 'cell lobbying' – approaching those accused of murder in their cells and offering them legal representation. In 1899, he instructed the rising barrister Edward Marshall Hall to defend Annie Dyer for the murder of her illegitimate baby. Dyer was acquitted, with the jury not even needing to leave the court for deliberation. And in 1907, he was part of Robert Wood's defence team in the 'Camden Town Murder' trial, the murder of Emily Dimmock, in which he again engaged the now-famous Marshall-Hall. Wood was also sensationally acquitted.

But in 1911, Newton was suspended by the Law Society for twelve months for selling to newspapers false death cell confession letters from murderers sentenced to be executed. One of these was purported to be written by Dr Crippen, who was hanged for the murder of his wife, the actress Cora, whose stage name was Belle Elmore, in 1910. Largely due to the transatlantic steamship chase to catch him, the Crippen case became one of the most infamous in British history. Crippen took Newton on as his solicitor and Newton sold Crippen's 'confession' to the *Evening Chronicle* for 500 guineas, which temporarily increased the newspaper's circulation tenfold.

Another publication to which Newton sold a death cell confession letter was the magazine *John Bull*, run by the fraudster and Member of Parliament Horatio Bottomley, who also incidentally contributed £200 to Crippen's defence fund.

Then in 1913, Newton was sentenced to three years in prison for land fraud. As detailed in *The Observer* of 19 October 1913, Newton had conspired with an Austrian count to defraud Dr Hans Torsch, also an Austrian and heir to a large fortune.

When Newton went to prison, his son took over his legal practice but it soon folded. On his release, Newton set up a marriage agency and worked as a private enquiry agent. He died in 1930, aged 70.

Ernest Parke

After serving six months for libelling the Earl of Euston, Parke went back to being a sub-editor on *The Star* newspaper, and then in 1891 rose to editor, a position he remained in for almost twenty-seven years until March 1918. He became a member of the Institute of Journalists in 1892 and was made a fellow in 1910. He also co-founded and became the editor of the *Morning Leader* in 1892 and became the managing editor of the *Star and Morning Leader* until 1912. He was a director of the *Daily News and Star* between 1912 into the early 1920s.

He remained living in Clapham, south-west London, until he and his wife Sarah moved back to his native Warwickshire, where they lived at Moorlands in Kineton. In later years, Parke was a director of the *North of England Newspaper Co.*, the *Sheffield Independent Press* and the *Northern Newspaper Co.*

Sarah passed away in 1937, and Parke died aged 84 on 21 June 1944.

Bertie, Prince of Wales

Not long after the Cleveland Street scandal died down, Bertie was forced to give evidence in court in June 1891 for taking part in an illegal card game in September 1890, which became known as the Royal Baccarat Scandal; it was covered closely by the press but did him little damage. Almost ten years later, in April 1900, Bertie was nearly killed when he was shot at by a teenage would-be assassin in Belgium, who was protesting about Britain's actions in the Second Boer War, which was then in full flow.

On the death of his mother, Queen Victoria, on 22 January 1901, which closed the Victorian epoch, Bertie became King Edward VII.

Historians generally see his reign as a successful one, and he was a largely popular monarch. Bertie died, aged 68, on 6 May 1910, bringing the Edwardian age to an end after less than a decade.

Eddy, Prince Albert Victor

Following his return from touring India, Queen Victoria tried to marry Eddy off to the German Princess Alix, his cousin, but she turned down Eddy's proposal. She went on to marry Tsar Nicolas II of Russia in 1894 and was murdered along with him and their children by the Bolsheviks in July 1918. More matches for Eddy were explored, and finally, he was engaged to be married to Princess Mary of Teck and the wedding set for February 1892. But it never took place.

Eddy died of pneumonia on 14 January 1892, aged 28. Princess Mary later married Eddy's younger brother, George, who became King George V on Bertie's death and reigned until January 1936. Bertie was grief-stricken by Eddy's early death, the second child who he and Princess Alexandra had outlived.

George Ripley

Ripley, a likely client of No. 19 Cleveland Street, was living at No. 39 Paultons Square in Chelsea, London, in 1893, renting two furnished rooms for 'over 21 shillings a week'. He died aged 49 on 17 March 1895 and left £6,076 7s 10d to his brothers, Edward and Frederick.

John Saul

No more was heard from Saul publicly after his testimony against Euston and the furore surrounding it. He eventually returned to his native Ireland and died at the Old Lady's Hospice, Harold's Cross, in the south of Dublin, on 28 August 1904. He was 46 years old.

Lord Arthur Somerset

Somerset remained in exile for the rest of his life, and he finally settled in Hyères on the Côte d'Azur in France. As the writer Simon Heffer has highlighted, he lived with James Neale, also from England. Somerset died there, aged 74, on 26 May 1926.[2]

Charles Swinscow

After he inadvertently kicked off the Cleveland Street scandal in early July 1889, Swinscow was dismissed by the General Post Office in December of that year and gave evidence at the Arthur Newton and Frederick Taylerson court hearings in early 1890. Swinscow managed to adapt back into normal life once the notoriety had faded.

On 13 April 1900, Swinscow married Evelina Mabel Cecelia Joy in Islington, north-east London (then in Middlesex). He was 27 and worked as a clerk, and she was 23 years old. They went on to have a daughter, Pearl, who was born in 1901. They lived with Swinscow's mother, Emily, and his siblings in Islington. Another daughter, Maude, was born in 1907.

By 1911, Swinscow and his wife and children had moved into their own place and lived in a flat in the newly built Samuel Lewis Buildings in Liverpool Street, Islington. Swinscow was by then employed as a pattern card maker but would later become a clerk in the Civil Service. He died in early September 1945, aged 71, in Islington, where he had lived his whole life.

Frederick Taylerson

After his acquittal in the May 1890 trial, Newton's managing clerk left the lawyer's employ and went on to marry Clara Bailey on 10 October 1891. Taylerson died aged 36 on 15 September 1902 in Dr Stock's Home, an asylum in Surrey. He left £53 5s to his wife.

Alfred Taylor

After his release from prison in May 1897, Wilde's co-defendant moved to America, eventually settling in Chicago. He worked as a waiter there in the 1920s; this is known because he reportedly, and coincidentally, served Lord Alfred Douglas (Bosie), who was visiting there.

George Veck

Veck disappeared from view after serving his nine-month sentence in 1889–90, and in later years he remained in London, living in poverty. In 1908, he was an inmate at the St Pancras Workhouse in King's Road and worked as a medical assistant at the Rowton House charitable hostel for poor working men. By 1911, he was an inmate at the St Marylebone Workhouse in Northumberland Street. Veck died in January 1937, at the very old age of 96.

Hugh Weguelin

The stockbroker client of No. 19 Cleveland Street, who donated a considerable sum to Somerset's defence fund, was living at No. 17 Old Burlington Street in the mid-1890s and by 1909 not far away at No. 18 Clifford Street in central London. What happened to Weguelin later is unknown.

Oscar Wilde

After his release from prison, Wilde remained in France, aside from a short time living with Bosie in Naples, Italy. He eventually settled in Paris. Impoverished and in weak health, he still suffered from bouts of depression. Except for some close friends who stood by him, Wilde was a social pariah, but still managed to write *The Ballad of Reading Gaol*, dedicated to and inspired by a soldier who had been executed in the prison for murdering his wife when Wilde was incarcerated there. Wilde died, aged 46, of meningitis at the insalubrious Hôtel D'Alsace in the Saint-Germain-des-Prés district of Paris on 30 November 1900. He is famously buried in Père Lachaise Cemetery in the city.

Notes

Full archival details and how to access them can be found in the Bibliography.

Chapter One

1 DPP 1/95/3/3.
2 DPP 1/95/3/3.
3 Mark Bills, 'The General Post Office: One Minute to Six', *Burlington Magazine* (September 2002).
4 DPP 1/95/3/5.

Chapter Two

1 DPP 1/95/3/4.
2 DPP 1/95/6 (DPP letter to Augustus Stephenson, 12 August 1889).
3 HO 144/477/X24427.

Chapter Three

1 Peter Thurgood, *Abberline: The Man Who Hunted Jack the Ripper* (The History Press, 2013).

Chapter Four

1 Colin Simpson, Lewis Chester and David Leitch, *The Cleveland Street Affair* (Little Brown, London, 1976).
2 DPP 1/95/3.
3 DPP 1/95/6.
4 DPP 1/95/6.
5 DPP 1/95/6.
6 DPP 1/95/6.
7 DPP 1/95/6.

Chapter Five

1 Edward Albert Bell, *These Meddlesome Attorneys* (London: M. Secker, 1939).
2 Laura Lee, 'Strange Bedfellows: The Solicitors and Blackmailers of the Oscar Wilde Case', *The Wildean*, No. 53 (July 2018).
3 HO 144/477/X24427A.
4 HO 144/477/X24427A.

Chapter Six

1 H. Montgomery Hyde, *The Cleveland Street Scandal* (London: W.H. Allen, 1976).
2 Hyde, *The Cleveland Street Scandal*.
3 Hyde, *The Cleveland Street Scandal*.

Chapter Seven

1 GBR/0014/ESHR 12/3.
2 Hyde, *The Cleveland Street Scandal*.
3 Peter Jordaan, *A Secret Between Gentlemen: Suspects, Strays, and Guests* (Alchemie Books, 2023).
4 Barry Anthony, *Murder, Mayhem and Music Hall: The Dark Side of Victorian London* (London: I.B. Tauris, 2015).
5 George Ripley in the Kensington and Chelsea, London, England, Electoral Registers, 1889-1970, courtesy of Ancestry Records, www.ancestry.co.uk/search/collections/62285.
6 Michael Meyer, *A Dirty, Filthy Book: Sex, Scandal, and One Woman's Fight in the Victorian Trial of the Century* (London: W.H. Allen, 2024).
7 Neil McKenna, *Fanny and Stella: The Young Men Who Shocked Victorian England* (London: Faber & Faber, 2014).
8 Donald Thomas, The *Victorian Underworld* (New York University Press, 1998).
9 Leon Radzinowicz, *A History of English Criminal Law and its Administration from 1750, Volume 4: Grappling for Control* (London: Stevens & Sons Ltd, 1968).
10 Matthew David Cook, *The Inverted City London and the Constitution of Homosexuality, 1885–1914*, PhD thesis Queen Mary and Westfield College (University of London, 2000).

Chapter Eight

1 Denis Judd, *Edward the Seventh* (London: Futura, 1975).
2 Anthony J. Camp, *Royal Mistresses and Bastards: Fact and Fiction 1714–1936* (Anthony Camp, 2007).
3 Hyde, *The Cleveland Street Scandal*.
4 Andrew Roberts, *Salisbury: Victorian Titan* (London: Weidenfeld & Nicolson, 1999).

Chapter Nine

1 DPP 1/95/6.
2 Jane Ridley, *Bertie: A Life of Edward VII* (London: Chatto & Windus, 2012).

3 Hyde, *The Cleveland Street Scandal*.
4 Andrew Cook, *Prince Eddy: The King Britain Never Had* (Stroud: The History Press, 2009).
5 Hyde, *The Cleveland Street Scandal*.

Chapter Ten

1 Algar Thorold, The *Life of Henry Labouchère* (New York & London: G.P. Putnam's Sons, 1913).
2 Claire Hirshfield, 'Labouchere, Truth and the Uses of Antisemitism', *Victorian Periodicals Review*, The Johns Hopkins University Press, United States, Autumn 1993.
3 William Fize, 'The Homosexual Exception? The Case of the Labouchère Amendment', *Open Edition Journals*, 8–9 February 2019.
4 W. Sydney Robinson, *Muckraker: The Scandalous Life and Times of W.T. Stead: Britain's First Investigative Journalist* (London: Robson Press, 2013).
5 Robinson, *Muckraker*.
6 Hyde, *The Cleveland Street Scandal*.

Chapter Eleven

1 Although not named in Perkins' statement, the pub was undoubtedly the Coach & Horses, which still exists. It was built in 1711 and was under the licence of Simeon Turner in 1889. The original Georgian building was demolished and rebuilt eight years later in 1897.
2 Nicole Anae, 'Poses Plastiques: The Art and Style of "Statuary" in Victorian Visual Theatre', *Australasian Drama Studies*, St Lucia Issue 52 (University of Queensland, April 2008).
3 John Saul's testimony is reproduced from various contemporary newspaper reports, which covered the trial to different degrees of depth.
4 Theo Aronson, *Prince Eddy and the Homosexual Underworld* (London: John Murray, 1994).

Chapter Fourteen

1 Richard Ellmann, *Oscar Wilde* (New York: Alfred A. Knopf, 1988).
2 Ellmann, *Oscar Wilde*.
3 Patrick Kelleher, 'On this day, 125 years ago, Oscar Wilde was convicted of "gross indecency" and slapped with the "maximum sentence allowed"', *Pink News*, 25 May 2020.

Coda

1 *Cardiff Times*, 12 July 1902.
2 Simon Heffer, *The Age of Decadence* (London: Random House, 2017).

Bibliography

Files

NATIONAL ARCHIVES
The following files were accessed at The National Archives in Kew, London:

DPP 1/95/1–7 (Lord Arthur Somerset and others, the Cleveland Street scandal).
DPP 1/95/3/1 (Opinions of H.E. Avory, Sir Richard Webster and Lord Halsbury).
DPP 1/95/3/2 (Opinion of Lord Halsbury).
DPP 1/95/3/3 (Police report and police statements, 1/7/1889–30/9/1889).
DPP 1/95/3/4 (Transcript of Veck and Newlove's trial).
DPP 1/95/3/5 (Sworn statements of George Alma Wright, Charles Ernest Thickbroom and Charles Thomas Swinscow, 6 July 1889).
DPP 1/95/3/6 (Indictments of Charles Hammond and George Veck, September 1889).
DPP 1/95/4/1 (*Regina vs Ernest Parke*, correspondence, 28/11/1889–18/12/1889).
DPP 1/95/4/2 (John Saul, original statement and correspondence, 10/8/1889–5/2/1890).
DPP 1/95/5/1 (*Regina vs Arthur Newton & Frederick Taylerson*, chronological summary, 4/7/1889–3/2/1890).
DPP 1/95/5/2 (*Regina vs Arthur Newton & others*, correspondence, 4/11/1889–30/1/1890).
DPP 1/95/5/3 (Note of Charles Gill's defence of Arthur Newton, 23/1/1890).
DPP 1/95/5/4 (Algernon Allies police report by Inspector Abberline, 26/9/1889).
DPP 1/95/5/5 (Statements of Algernon Allies, 25/9/1889–1/10/1889).
DPP 1/95/5/6 (Algernon Allies, correspondence, 1/9/1889–31/3/1890).
DPP 1/95/6 (Lord Arthur Somerset and others. Offence: Buggery; gross indecency and procurement; conspiracy to incite; criminal libel; conspiracy to defeat course of justice; perjury: Labouchère papers).
DPP 1/95/7/1 (Lord Arthur Somerset and others, miscellaneous correspondence, 1889).
DPP 1/95/7/3 (Various newspapers and gazettes, September 1889–January 1890).

HO 144/477/X24427 (George Veck & Henry Newlove, 1889–91).
HO 144/477/X24427A (Arthur Newton, Cleveland Street scandal, 1889–91).
J 55/6/134 (*The Midland Railway Company vs George Veck*, 1877).
PCOM 8/432; PCOM 8/433; PCOM 8/434; PCOM 8/435 (Oscar Wilde, conviction at Old Bailey, 20/5/1890).
WO 76/519 (Army service record of Robert Jervoise).

Cambridge University Library
GBR/0012/MS Add.9248/4513 (The papers of Sir Frederick Ripley).
GBR/0014/STED 1/45 (The papers of W.T. Stead).

Churchill Archives Centre
GBR/0014/ESHR 12/3 (The Esher Papers: The Case of Lord Arthur Somerset).

Other Primary Sources

Abberline's Scrapbook 1891–92, Accessed at the Metropolitan Police Museum, Sidcup, Kent.

Newspapers, Magazines & Journals
The dates and issues of all the newspapers, magazine articles and journals below are given in the main body of this book's text as they appear:

Auckland Star
The Barking & East Ham Advertiser
The Boston Globe
The Cardiff Times
The Cork Examiner
Chicago Tribune
Daily Chronicle
The Daily Telegraph
Evening Chronicle
Evening Express (Wales)
The Evening Mail (Stockton, California)
The Evening Sentinel (Stoke-on-Trent)
Flintshire Observer Mining Journal and General Advertiser for the Counties of Flint and Denbigh
The Illustrated Police News
John Bull
Lippincott's (Philadelphia, and British edition)
The London Gazette
Los Angeles Herald

The Man of the World
The New York Herald
The New York Times
The North London Press
The North Star (Darlington)
Northern Whig
The Nottingham Journal
The Observer
The Pall Mall Gazette
The Plain Speaker (Hazleton, Pennsylvania)
Police Gazette
Reynolds's News
San Francisco Chronicle
Seattle Post-Intelligencer
The Scots Observer
The Sketch
The South Australian Chronicle (Adelaide)
The Staffordshire Sentinel
The Standard (London)
Sunday Dispatch
The Times
Truth

Articles

Anae, Nicole, 'Poses Plastiques: The Art and Style of "Statuary" in Victorian Visual Theatre', *Australasian Drama Studies*, St Lucia Issue 52 (University of Queensland, April 2008).

Cook, Matthew David, *The Inverted City London and the Constitution of Homosexuality, 1885–1914*, PhD thesis, Queen Mary and Westfield College (University of London, 2000).

Elfenbein, Andrew, 'On the Trials of Oscar Wilde: Myths and Realities', online at BRANCH: Britain, Representation and Nineteenth-Century History, edited by Dino Franco Felluga. Extension of Romanticism and Victorianism on the Net (accessed 2024).

Field, Marcus, 'Is Oscar Wilde's reputation due for another reassessment?', *The Independent*, 4 October 2014.

Fize, William, 'The Homosexual Exception? The Case of the Labouchère Amendment', *Open Edition Journals*, 8–9 February 2019.

Hirshfield, Claire, 'Labouchere, Truth and the Uses of Antisemitism', *Victorian Periodicals Review*, The Johns Hopkins University Press, United States, Autumn 1993.

Kelleher, Patrick, 'On this day, 125 years ago, Oscar Wilde was convicted of "gross indecency" and slapped with the "maximum sentence allowed"', *Pink News*, 25 May 2020.

Lee, Laura, 'Strange Bedfellows: The Solicitors and Blackmailers of the Oscar Wilde Case', *The Wildean*, No. 53 (July 2018).Ross, Alex, 'How Oscar Wilde Painted Over "Dorian Gray"', *The New Yorker*, 1 August 2011.

Savage, George, 'A Case of Sexual Perversion in a Man', *Journal of Mental Science*, Vol. 30, Issue 131 (1884).

Books

Anonymous (Saul, John/Jack), *The Sins of the Cities of the Plain; or, The Recollections of a Mary-Ann, with Short Essays on Sodomy and Tribadism* (Valancourt Books, 2012).

Anthony, Barry, *Murder, Mayhem and Music Hall: The Dark Side of Victorian London* (London: I.B. Tauris, 2015).

Aronson, Theo, *Prince Eddy and the Homosexual Underworld* (London: John Murray, 1994).

Bell, Edward Albert, *These Meddlesome Attorneys* (London: M. Secker, 1939).

Bloch, Ivan (translated by William H. Forstern), *Sexual Life in England* (London: Corgi Books, 1967).

Bradford, Sarah, *King George VI* (London: Weidenfeld & Nicolson, 1989).

Camp, Anthony J., *Royal Mistresses and Bastards: Fact and Fiction 1714–1936* (Anthony Camp, 2007).

Cook, Andrew, *Prince Eddy: The King Britain Never Had* (Stroud: The History Press, 2009).

Ellmann, Richard, *Oscar Wilde* (New York: Alfred A. Knopf, 1988).

Fulford, Roger, *The Prince Consort* (London: Macmillan, 1949).

Glinert, Ed, *West End Chronicles* (London: Allen Lane, 2007).

Heffer, Simon, *The Age of Decadence* (London: Random House, 2017).

Hindmarch-Watson, Katie, *Serving a Wired World: London's Telecommunications Workers and the Making of an Information Capital* (University of California Press, 2020).

Hudson, Roger, *The Jubilee Years 1887–1897* (London: The Folio Society, 1996).

Hunter, Andrew Alexander (ed.), *The Cheltenham College Register* (London: George Bell & Sons, 1890).

Hyde, H. Montgomery, *The Trials of Oscar Wilde* (London: William Hodge & Co. Ltd, 1948).

Hyde, H. Montgomery, *A History of Pornography* (London: Heinemann, 1964).

Hyde, H. Montgomery, *The Cleveland Street Scandal* (London: W.H. Allen, 1976).

Jordaan, Peter, *A Secret Between Gentlemen: Suspects, Strays, and Guests* (Alchemie Books, 2023).

Judd, Denis, *Edward the Seventh* (London: Futura, 1975).

McKenna, Neil, *The Secret Life of Oscar Wilde* (London: Arrow, 2002).

McKenna, Neil, *Fanny and Stella: The Young Men Who Shocked Victorian England* (London: Faber & Faber, 2014).

Meyer, Michael, *A Dirty, Filthy Book: Sex, Scandal, and One Woman's Fight in the Victorian Trial of the Century* (London: W.H. Allen, 2024).

Middlemass, Keith, & Antonia Fraser, *The Life and Times of Edward VII* (London: Weidenfeld & Nicolson, 1972).

O'Connor, T.P., *Memoirs of an Old Parliamentarian* (London: Ernest Benn, 1929).

Plowden, Alison, *The Case of Eliza Armstrong* (London: BBC, 1974).
Radzinowicz, Leon, *A History of English Criminal Law and its Administration from 1750, Volume 4: Grappling for Control* (London: Stevens & Sons Ltd, 1968).
Ridley, Jane, *Bertie: A Life of Edward VII* (London: Chatto & Windus, 2012).
Roberts, Andrew, *Salisbury: Victorian Titan* (London: Weidenfeld & Nicolson, 1999).
Robinson, W. Sydney, *Muckraker: The Scandalous Life and Times of W.T. Stead: Britain's First Investigative Journalist* (London: Robson Press, 2013).
Simpson, Colin, Chester, Lewis, & David Leitch, *The Cleveland Street Affair* (Little Brown, London, 1976).
Spencer, Colin, *Homosexuality: A History* (London: Fourth Estate, 1995).
Stead, W.T., *Portraits and Photographs: An Album for the People* (London: Mowbray House, 1891).
Thomas, Donald, *The Victorian Underworld* (New York University Press, 1998).
Thorold, Algar, *The Life of Henry Labouchère* (New York & London: G.P. Putnam's Sons, 1913).
Thurgood, Peter, *Abberline: The Man Who Hunted Jack the Ripper* (Stroud: The History Press, 2013).
Walkowitz, Judith R., *City of Dreadful Delight: Narratives of Sexual Danger in Late-Victorian London* (University of Chicago Press, 1992).

Maps

Booth, Charles, *Booth's Maps of London Poverty East & West 1889* (Old House Books, 2013).

Caricature Collections

Ward, Sir Leslie, *Vanity Fair*, various caricatures by 'Spy'.
Pellegrini, Carlo, various caricatures 1872–73, The Royal Collection Trust, London.

Websites

www.casebook.org (Jack the Ripper and related materials).
www.famous-trials.com/wilde (testimonies of Oscar Wilde and Alfred Taylor, 1895).
rictornorton.co.uk (many essays on LGBT history, including of the late-Victorian period, by the leading cultural historian Rictor Norton).
scoop-database.com (compendium of the lives of journalists).
www.twickenham-museum.org.uk (a history of the area, including theatre anecdotes about the actress Henrietta Hodson).

Acknowledgements

Many thanks to the staff at The National Archives, Kew, and the Churchill Archives, Cambridge. Also, to Edward Smith and Clare Smith (no relation to each other) at the Metropolitan Police Museum, Sidcup, Kent.

Thank you to Clive Goddard, an excellent genealogist, whose expertise saved me many hours when delving into the backgrounds of some of the people in this story.

To Trevor Dolby, my friend and agent at Aevitas Creative Management, for his encouragement and guidance in preparing the proposal for this book.

At The History Press, thanks to Mark Beynon for commissioning this book, and to Claire Hartley, Jezz Palmer and the team there for working so creatively and productively on it.

To my mum, Len and Mr Ripley for all their long-term championing of my writing.

To my late brother Math, who was always so supportive and encouraging of my writing: 'Let's get this done …'

And finally, as always, to my wife, Tracy Medlicott, for all her love and support.

Index

Illustrations are entered in *italics*

No. 19 Cleveland Street
  description 23
  illustration *121*

Abberline, Frederick George 7–10, 23–37, 46–8, 53–6, 101–8, 149–51, 155–8, 172–4, 179–80, 206–9
  313 Clapham Road 7
  appearance 8, 31
  Jack the Ripper 8–10, 34–7, 208–9
  Judge Hawkins criticises 172–3
  knowledge of East End 36, 37
  marriages 33, 34
  Monro appoints 22
  Newton's counsel attacks 179
    gives evidence at Newton's trial 190
  parents and siblings 31
  police career 32–4
    promoted to chief inspector 206
    retires 207–8
  Scrapbook 208
  still searching for Hammond 47–8
  warrants and attempted arrests 23–5
  working on Newton's prosecution 149
Abrahams, Bernard 52
Abu Klea, Battle of 41
Albert, Prince 87, 88
Albert Victor, Prince 92–4
  American Press articles 137–40
  father's protection 212
  Hammond's supposed papers 198
  illustration *122*
  Knollys responsible for 111
  Newton connects with Cleveland Street 117
  Somerset uses as shield 156
Allies, Algernon Edward 54–6, 101–7, 180, 189
Ames, Herbert 60–1, 71, 78, 95, 199–202
Angel, Miriam 46
Asquith, Herbert 159, 162, 216
Avory, Horace 47–8, 68, 70, 192, 222

Barber, Charles Montague 78–80
'Barber, George' 48, 53, 60, 68–9, 80
Battersea, Lord 74
Bayham Street 26
Besant, Annie 83
Bills, Mark 18
Blandford Forum 31, 32
Bloody Sunday (1887) 45
Bolton and Park 84–5
Booth, Charles 7, 35
Bosie (Lord Alfred Douglas) 215–17, 221
Bradlaugh, Charles 83–4
Brett, Reginald 40, 57–8, 71–5

see also General Post Office (GPO)
London Gazette 79

Mahdists 41
'Maiden Tribute of Modern Babylon, The' (Henry Thompson) 66, 115
Map of London Poverty (Charles Booth) 7
Marlborough Club 42, 54, 91, 114
Marlborough Street Police Court 25, 65
Mary-Anns 82
Matchgirls' Strike 45
Mathews, Charles 68
Matthews, Sir Henry 43–8, 97–8, *124*, 178, 194, 207
Metropolitan Police 19–21
  Abberline's time 32
  Confidential Enquiry Branch 20
  interview procedures 13
  Police Bill, 1890 207
  rulebook 37
  shortest tenure as commissioner 207
Middlesex Hospital 13, 15, 23
Monro, Commissioner James 112–15
  appoints Abberline 22
  background 43
  complains of lack of action over Somerset and Newton 112
  DPP finally involved 47
  frustrated in efforts on Newton case 180
  Hammond in France 29
  and Somerset 43
  on John Saul 48
  points of action drafted re Somerset situation 118–19
  praised by Parke 145–6
  press infuriate 95, 112
  professionalism 109
  pushing for Somerset's arrest 108
  resigns 206–7
  Sladden's case 154
  Taylerson 104
Montagu, Colonel Oliver 108–9

New York Times 137–8
Newlove, Henry
  arrested 26
  committed for trial 65, 67–70
  Hammond and 47
  names aristocrats 26
  recruiter for Hammond 25, 39
  Somerset's concern about 53
  Swinscow first meets 14–15, 16
  Swinscow names 17
newspaper articles 129–30, 137–41
Newton, Arthur 51–3
  Abberline works on prosecution of 149
  Algernon Allies 56
  appears at Bow Street Magistrates 154–61, 179, 189
  attempts to pay rent boys to go to Australia 150–3
  Brett in contact re Somerset 73
  case moved from Old Bailey 191
  gets Hammond to America 106, 200–1
  indignant letter to DPP 104–6
  insinuations against Albert Victor 92–3
  involvement in Oscar Wilde prosecution 222
  Labouchère defends 181–2
  preliminary criminal proceedings against 148
  Somerset advised to get new lawyer 114
  trial begins 192
    judge addresses 193–4
    sentenced 194
    time in prison 194–5
Nichols, Mary Ann 34, 36, 37
Nile, River 41
North London Press 94, 141, 143

Obscene Publications Act (1857) 83
O'Connor, Thomas Power 142–3, 186
Oliver Twist (Charles Dickens) 23

Pagani's Restaurant, London 211–12
Pall Mall Gazette
  Charles Dilke 44
  General Gordon 40–1
  John Philip Collins at 8
  potential cover-up by powers that be 65
  Stead leaves 65–6, 137
Parke, Ernest 141–8, 158–75
  addresses court at his trial 173–5
  background and career history 142–3

first appearance of scandal in press 94, 144–5
found guilty of libel and sentenced 173–5
illustration *123*
time in prison and subsequent career 178
trial 158–75
  defence 162–70
    John Saul 165–70
  Judge Hawkins 158–9
    summing up 172–3
  prosecution 160–2, 170–1
  reflections on 175–7
  writ issued against 146–8
People of the Abyss, The (Jack London) 36
Perkins, William Meech 149–50, 189
Phillips, 'Chief Constable' John 14, 21, 22
Picture of Dorian Gray, The (Oscar Wilde) 211, 212–15, 217, 222
plea bargaining 70
Poland, Henry Bodkin 68
Port of London 45
poses plastiques 160
poverty maps 35
Probyn, General Sir Dighton 110–20, 139, 144, 157, 186
prostitution 36, 59, 66, 84, 227
psychopathology 85
Pygmalion (George Bernard Shaw) 66

Queensberry, Marquis of 52, *128*, 215–20

Review of Reviews 66
Ripley family 80–2
Rosebery, Lord 216
Royal Courts of Justice 191
Rubenhold, Hallie 36
Russell, Sir Charles *128*, 160–4, 168–71, 192–3

Salisbury, Lord 98–100
  beaten by Gladstone (1892) 216
  blocks putting pressure on French re Hammond 47, 59
  closing the door 201
  illustration *126*
  Labouchère, the threat from 131, 134, 137–9, 181–2, 185–7, 191

accuses Salisbury of criminal conspiracy 185–6
  nature of 119
  position at head of Conservative Party 29
  Prince of Wales writes to 120
  Prince of Wales's influence on 88
  Probyn meets re Somerset 116–17
  Truth article a warning 131
Saul, John 165–70
  Abberline interviews 48
  Charles Montague Barber 80
  Dublin Castle 137
  Labouchère indignant 181
  Parke's trial 165–75, 177
  publication 83–4
  trial judge concerned at Abberline's lack of action against 172
Secret Life of Oscar Wilde, The (Neil McKenna) 177
Shaw, George Bernard 66, 142
Sins of the Cities of the Plain, The (Charles Saul) 83, 84, 148, 165
Sladden, PC Richard 24, 39, 41–2, 149–56
Slater, Minton 147
Smith, James 21–2
sodomy 17
Somerset, Lord Arthur 39–43, 156–8
  Algernon Allies 54–5
  arrest warrant 130–1
  concern over Veck's arrest 58
  Euston's evidence at libel trial 171
  government top brass continue to discuss 96–8
  in Hanover 67
  illustration *121*
  interviewed by police 48–9
  long way to fall 87
  Newlove mentions 26
  Pall Mall Gazette warns of 65
  permission given (and then withdrawn) to prosecute 48–9
  Prince of Wales letter to Salisbury 120
  returns to England 72
    leaves again 101
    returns once more 108
  solicitor for 51–3

still has confidence of Prince of Wales 51, 72–3
loses that confidence 90
meets on return to England before escape to France 100–1
Prince refuses to give reference 156
Prince sends seemingly friendly telegram 107
travels to Germany to 57
tipped off by unknown source 186–7
veiled threat to name names 58
South Australian Chronicle 160, 162, 174–6
Star, The 142–3, 146–7
Stead, W. T. 8, 40–1, 44, 46, 65–7, *127*, 135–7
Stephenson, Sir Augustus
evades answering Monro's letter 119
on Newton corrupting Sladden
politically sensitive decisions 42, 65
required to take charge as DPP 47, 96
Truth magazine concerns 134
Straight, Sir Douglas 8
Sudan 40
Swinscow, Charles
appearance 13
background 21
gives evidence in Newton trial 190
illustration *126*
Marlborough Street Police Court 25
questioned by PC Hanks 13–17, 20
Sladden meets 41–2

Taiping Rebellion 40
Taylerson, Frederick 52, 101–5, 148, 156, 179, 189
Taylor, Alfred 217, 221–5
telegrams 17–18
Thickbroom, Ernest 17, 25, 42, 150–2, 155, 189, 192
Thompson, Henry 66–7, 137
Thurgood, Peter 33

Tichborne Claimant 159
Todhunter, Alexander 196–9, 204, 205–6
Tottenham Court Road 15, 23
Truth 131–5, 137
Two Loves (Lord Alfred Douglas) 217, 222

Vanity Fair 41, 52
Veck, George
admits to knowing in Euston 175–6
Avory's advice on 48–9
committed for trial 65, 67–70
Hanks overhears 27–8
sentence inadequate 183
warrant issued 53
Victoria, Queen 44, 45, 83, 87–90, 92, 99

W.H. Smith 214
Walker, PC John 150–6
Webb, Captain 163–4, 168–9, 172, 176
Webster, Sir Richard 48–9, 96–7, *125*, 186, 192–3
Weguelin, Hugh 71–5, 166, 196, 202
West End (London) 86
Wilde, Oscar 212–28
bankruptcy 225
book on 177
criminal arrest and trial 220–5
explanation and defence of male-male love 223
illustration *128*
libel writ 216–18
Pagani's Restaurant 212
Picture of Dorian Gray, The 212–15, 217
prison life 225–7
reader of *Sins of the Cities of the Plain* 84
references to Cleveland Street 214
telegraph messenger boys 215
Wolfenden Report 217
Wright, George 22
Wright, George Alma 17, 23, 25, 190